The Golden Fleece

The Golden Fleece

Why the Stock Market Costs You Money

by
Walter Stewart

Canadian Cataloguing in Publication Data

Stewart, Walter, 1931-
The golden fleece: why the stock market costs you money

Includes bibliographical references and index.

ISBN 0-7710-8303-3

1. Stock-exchange – Canada.   2. Stocks – Canada.
3. Investments – Canada.   4. Finance, Personal – Canada.
I. Title.

HG5152.S83 1992   332.64'271   C92-094391-8

Printed and bound in Canada on acid-free paper.

McClelland & Stewart Inc.
The Canadian Publishers
481 University Avenue
Toronto, Ontario
M5G 2E9

For Eric Kierans, after thirty years of friendship, help, and sage advice, some of which I followed.

Contents

Customers are like the grass; they come up every spring, and we mow them.
– Vice-president of a New York investment firm, in Lewis Lapham's *Money and Class in America*, 1988.

Don't Call Me a Gambler, or I'll Hit You with my Roulette Wheel

Think of it. Tens of thousands of people getting up every morning, reacting to the morning's news, interpreting the complex signals from within their own businesses and their own stomachs, weighing their fears for the future against their own ever-welling optimism; and somehow, every instant of every trading day, it all comes together in a set of numbers that float across those electronic screens in the brokers' offices. There's something so adorably *human* about it, a great thrumming dance of shifting emotions and self-interested calculation. In the face of a phenomenon so infinitely complex, so very much like life itself, one can only gape in delight.

– Alexander Ross, *The Traders*, 1985.

$

My dictionary defines "stock exchange" this way:

> A highly organized market facilitating the purchase and sale of securities and operated by professional stock brokers and stockjobbers according to fixed rules.

All very true, no doubt, but it doesn't explain Ivan Boesky milking a couple of hundred million dollars out of insider trading, or Canadian Tire shareholders staring at their non-voting stock and wondering why some shareholders got to collect $30 million, and they got nothing, or the fines levied the other day on three traders at the Chicago Mercantile Exchange for "pushing and spitting," or Ernest Saunders, chairman of Guiness PLC, getting tossed into the hoosegow in London for fraud, theft, and false accounting in a little scheme he and a gang of high-toned pals worked out to jack up the price of Guiness shares, does it? (Nor does it explain why Saunders will be paid about $150,000 a year in jail.)

The standard texts – *How the Stock Market Works* and others of that ilk – contain lucid explanations of what constitutes the "primary" and what the "secondary" market, and how "the Curb market" got its name (from the curb outside the original exchange on Wall Street, in New York). But they are strangely silent on how, in this place of fixed rules, it came about that a Toronto broker managed to blow away $272,295 from the account of a widow who had asked him to invest her savings only in "conservative" stocks. In eleven months the broker picked up $125,220 in commissions on these money-devouring transactions. "No need to thank me, Ma'am; just part of the service." This, of course, is hardly a patch on the Florida broker who ran down his great-uncle's investment fund from $17 million to $8.2 million, while collecting $5.2 million in commissions.

The standard texts do not even contain the word "churning," which is what these rascals were doing, just as they leave out much of the really interesting stuff that happens on the world's markets. The worshipful, wide-eyed approach doesn't explain bucket shops, or boiler rooms, or such novel phenomena as "greenmail" and "shark repellent." The former is the technique by which someone suitably unsuitable grabs enough of the stock of a target company to threaten control, and has to be bought off by the current management, who repurchase the stock from the raider at a premium price. "Give me your wallet, or I'll buy your house." The latter – also known as "the poison pill," or "saving the Crown jewels" – describes the techniques by which one company, about to be gathered in by another, will deliberately do itself harm, to make itself less attractive. Some tribes in Africa used to follow a similar practice; a bride, once purchased, was mutilated in order to render her less seductive to lustful strangers. However, there is no record of a bride volunteering for the practice, as happens quite often these days in the stock market, every time one firm, about to be gobbled up by another, goes out and buys a third firm that is loaded down with debt, thus making itself less attractive to the takeover artist.

If you look at the standard texts and look at the way stock exchanges work, you are inclined to quote King David when he first clapped eyes on the Queen of Sheba and remarked, "The half was not told unto me." Nor will it be, if the bright lads who actually run the stock exchanges have their way.

It is hard to find instances where stubborn reality is so successfully bypassed as in conventional descriptions of the stock exchange. Perhaps at the annual meeting of the Flat Earth Society; no other example springs to mind. Here, for instance, is the way Paul Samuelson and Anthony Scott, authors of that seminal text, *Economics*, explain the role of the stock exchange's key ingredient, the common stockholder: "The common stockholder is providing equity capital. He shares in the profits and in control of the business decisions."

No, he doesn't. Indeed, it is the very uncommon stockholder who shares in either the profits – except to the minimal degree unavoidable – or in the control of business decisions. It is fair to say that, in more than 99 per cent of all cases, the common stockholder has diddley-squat to do with business decisions. Nor is he or she intended to have such control; indeed, the whole notion of the untamed masses actually deciding what a company should do on the spurious grounds that they own it is anathema to any well-regulated management.

Rather, the stockholder is supposed to *think* he or she has decision-making powers, quite a different matter.

To get a grip on how the markets actually function (we will come to the technical explanations later in this book; here, we are dealing with the broad sweep of the thing), it is best to forget about dictionaries, textbook explanations, and the reassuring claptrap contained in the business pages of our daily newspapers and to picture, instead, an institution formed by combining a church with a crap game.

Like a church, the stock market is sustained by faith, not reason, with the theology laid out by bankers and the mechanics carried out by brokers. The investment houses furnish altar boys, and the press provides the choir. Collections are taken regularly.

Like a crap game, this institution offers the opportunity for great gain and stupendous loss in the act of gambling; much of the money is ventured on side-bets and, as with every established, permanent floating crap game, the fix is in. Certainly, the little guy – beloved in song, story, and stock-market press release – can actually win, just as five sevens in a row have been known to emerge from carelessly cast dice, but it is not the usual occurrence. Far more usually, the small investor provides not the venture capital that keeps our great enterprises going, but the fleece, the golden fleece, that lines the pockets of the insiders.

I do not mean, here, that the small investor is discriminated against because he lacks the sophisticated computer programs necessary to trace the twisted path of modern commerce – that is true, but it is by far the least of it – I mean that a sizeable share of the people who benefit from the operations of the exchange cheat. Cheat regularly, cheat massively, cheat without compunction or remorse. They always have; they probably always will. Nor is it the case that they can't help themselves; they can, and do, to the contents of ordinary market-players' pockets, on every possible occasion.

In March 1987, the Securities and Exchange Commission in

Washington released a study of 172 cases in which offers had been tendered to take over stocks of various companies. In every single instance, abnormal rises in the price of the target stocks were recorded three weeks before the bid was announced and the great unwashed were let in on the action. The gains thus skimmed off ran between 39 and 50 per cent. These gains, which were either obviously illegal or wonderfully opportune, did not take place occasionally, but every loving time. The insiders were cashing in; the outsiders, such is the remorseless logic of the market, were paying for these gains. It is like buying tickets for the lottery without realizing that most of the winning numbers have been given out in advance to a select few. Otherwise, everything is above board. (Incidentally, I have not seen the exercise repeated by the SEC or any other stock-watching commission; probably, in this time of severe restraint, it was felt to be an unwise expenditure of funds.)

If you reject the notion of the stock exchange as crap game, I ask you to consider two recent instruments created, for the benefit of the worthy, by the New York Stock Exchange and the Toronto Stock Exchange. In New York, you can buy something called an Exchange Stock Portfolio (the initials work out, happily, to ESP) at the starting price of $5 million a pop, and gamble on whether a whole basket of 500 stocks on the exchange will go up or down. If you think it will go up, you hold on, and sell to someone else when the price rises, pocketing your gain. If you think it will fall, you "short" the purchase; that is, you gamble that the price will go down, and collect the difference between the current price and the new, lower price. Of course, if the price does go up, you lose.

The TSE has a more modest version, called TIPs (for Toronto Index Participation Units), which started with an $800 million issue. Each TIPs unit represents an interest in a trust that holds baskets of shares in the Toronto 35 Index, a cross-section of the largest corporations traded on the TSE. The value of the units tracks the value of the whole parcel on the exchange, moving up or down with the index. As with the ESP unit, you can hold on for a gain or short the unit and hope the market goes to hell in a hand-basket. Or, you can dance with Lady Luck and bet on the Toronto 35 Index itself, which doesn't even have any stocks behind it; you just lay down your money on whichever way you think the index will go.

None of these dice-rolling instruments has anything to do with bankrolling enterprise or participating in decision-making or, indeed, anything to do with anything but shouting, "Baby needs a new pair of shoes!" and praying not to roll craps.

Shorting a stock (the opposite is "going long" – you buy the shares and hold them, selling only when the price rises) has no connection with helping a worthy company along its way; indeed, the whole idea is to gamble that the targetted firm will fall on its face. The faster, the better. The standard way to short a stock is to borrow it from a broker, with a contract to replace it later; usually, you put up only part of the purchase price. If you short 1,000 shares of Amalgamated Kumquats at a time when they are trading for $10, and they go down to $5 a share, the broker, who has in the meantime sold them on your behalf, will pay you the difference. You will make $5 a share, less his commission and any financing charges involved; you could double your money in a few days. On the other hand, if the stock went to $20 – which it might very well do – you would have to put up another $10 a share to replace those borrowed shares. You would lose your stake and as much again, besides.

A key difference between shorting a share and going long is that, if you buy a stock and hold it, you can only lose the amount you invested; if you short it, there is no limit to how much you could lose if the price of the stock continued to shoot up before you got it covered (i.e., bought it back).

Daniel Drew, one of the great stock manipulators of all time, put the crucial rule about shorting in the form of a couplet:

He who sells what isn't his'n
Must buy it back, or go to pris'n.

Well, if not to prison, at least to the poorhouse. The whole idea in shorting a stock is to sell something you don't own, then buy the replacement at a lower price. You earnestly hope for the worst. What has that to do with Samuelson and Scott's definition of "providing equity capital"? What the gambler is in fact providing is simply the stock-player's curse, helped along, if he is in a position to work the trick, by a shrewdly planted story in the newspapers that the chief executive of the relevant firm was last seen lugging a bulging briefcase to the international counter of an airline, and booking a ticket for Uruguay. It does not matter – here is the crucial point – whether the planted story is true or not. Its publication will produce the desired effect of dropping the price of the stock.

During the Gulf War, a rumour circulated that a U.S. jet aircraft had been shot down over Iraq. It hadn't. The stock market plunged, and stayed down until the rumour was finally squelched. Bettors who believed the rumour, and shorted stocks, were rewarded for being wrong. Those who discounted it lost money. You don't need brains to win in this atmosphere, just a finely tuned panic button.

One of Wall Street's many characters over the years was Short Eddie, a tipster who made it his practice to short a stock, then go to the Securities and Exchange Commission and complain about the company involved. Then he would inform the newspapers that the company was "under investigation by the SEC," wait for the stock to drop, and cash in.

I guess I was first captured by the romance of the stock exchange a couple of decades ago, when, as a reporter, I was investigating the operations of a large real-estate firm (it has since changed its name slightly and mended its ways importantly, which is why I do not name it). A provincial dignitary, formerly a widely respected judge (he has since gone to the great boardroom in the sky), sat on its board of directors, and the firm gave him an option to purchase thousands of its shares at $5 each, exercisable at any time within the next year. (The shares were then selling for about $7.) Then, they trotted out the dignitary to cut ribbons and announce wonderful new projects for the firm, upon which its shares shot up to about $14. The dignitary exercised his option, bought shares for $5, sold them for $14, and kept the change.

The wonderful projects did not come about, but they had served their purpose. A lot of money was made for insiders sitting on options; a lot of money was lost for people not so advantageously positioned, when the stocks drooped on their stems as time passed and the projects remained unfulfilled. All part of the market's fearful symmetry.

The thought flitted through my mind then that perhaps the people who bought the dignitary's shares at $14 were working under something of a handicap. It was only later, when I came to study the market thoroughly, that I realized that this handicap was not accidental or occasional; it is, by and large, the way the system works. By and large, the money that is gained on the markets drains into the pockets of a happy few with access to special information; by and large, it flows out of the pockets of the suckers who think they are going to beat the system. It is not just a gamble, it is a gamble played with a fixed deck. And it has not changed since I covered that story.

On September 29, 1989, the *Globe and Mail's Report on Business* published two telling little items side by side. The first noted that the managers of the Toronto Stock Exchange were miffed because they had been "snookered" into allowing a six-day halt in trading of the shares of Campeau Corporation, a public company then going through one of its periodic fainting fits. The time when trading is halted is, of course, the very moment when the hand is lifting one of the shells to reveal where the pea is hiding. When the trading halt was called, Campeau shares were going for $13.50;

when it resumed six days later, the price was $9.50. The shell was back on top of the pea. In the meantime, effective control of the firm was taken by Olympia & York Developments, the giant conglomerate owned by the Reichmann brothers. The item went on to note, "As for management and directors of the stock exchange, they are diligent in protecting the reputation of the exchange as a fair and open marketplace." Except, of course, when it is not fair and not even open. This ritual sentence about the fair and open marketplace is an incantation, counted over and over again on the rosary of the *Report on Business.*

The second item reported that the TSE had sicced its lawyer onto the Ontario Lottery Corporation over a newspaper advertisement that used the former TSE building on Bay Street in downtown Toronto as a backdrop. The ad pictured a shirtless man standing in front of the building with a caption that read "Who couldn't use some instant luck?" The idea, see, is that this shirtless gent had come to that condition in a building that had formerly been, but no longer was, inhabited by the TSE. "Several brokers from member firms," the *Globe* explained, for those too dim to get the point, "were not amused by having the TSE tied to gambling ads." So, they hauled out their legal guns and threatened nameless reprisals. The Ontario Lottery Corporation withdrew the ad, of course, and mumbled an apology that "there may have been a negative interpretation of the ad."

Well, I should think so. The ad, you understand, attacked the theology of the exchange: the notion that this place, where you can gamble millions on TIPs, among other things, has anything to do with gambling (even in a building with which it now had no connection). The joint had been desecrated, and only the burned incense of a formal apology could help to right the wrong.

In one of the many books I consulted while preparing this volume, called *Mugged on Wall Street,* written by C. David Chase, vice-president of the brokerage firm E. F. Hutton, we meet a market-player who rejoices in the name of Blackie Sherrode, and who explains why it is so unfair to think of the stock market as gambling: "If you bet on a horse, that's gambling. If you bet you can make three spades, that's entertainment. If you bet cotton will go up three points, that's business. See the difference?"

Chase also makes note of something mobster Lucky Luciano is reported to have said after his first visit to the floor of the New York Stock Exchange. "A terrible thing happened. I realized I had joined the wrong mob."

It is the purpose of this volume to examine the way the stock markets actually work, as opposed to received theory and orthodox theology. And the way they ought to work. And how we might make the former into the latter.

The stock markets ought to occupy an important, but limited, role in the economy. Their key function is to provide a place for people to buy and sell shares that are already in existence. When companies issue shares, they are sold into the "primary market" – so called if the proceeds of the sales go to the issuer of the security. Let us say ABC Lightbulbs issues shares; they are bought by a group of investment houses and the money goes into the company treasury. That is a primary market. The investment houses sell the shares to other institutions and the general public; then these folks buy and sell them back and forth. That is the secondary market. The ability to buy and sell stocks easily and quickly, a function captured in the phrase "liquidity," helps investors. It can be vastly overdone, and vastly overrated, but it is the main legitimate occupation of the exchanges.

It may help to remember that the primary function of the stock exchanges is to provide a secondary market.

Stock markets also play a much smaller role, over which they make an inordinate fuss, as a place where, just as the textbooks stipulate, capital can be raised for various ventures. They are not, by any means, the only venue for such ventures, but they are and always have been a player in the system. However, when the markets become "the driving engine of capitalism," one of the favoured clichés, or a bearpit for the operations of pitchmen and pirates, one of the avoided descriptions, then something has gone wrong. We will not know what has gone wrong, or how to correct it, without two things. The first is an understanding of the history and development of the markets; the second is a quick course in the mechanics of the exchanges at the heart of the system.

Touching the first, we will discover that skullduggery, scandal, cheating, and the use of insider information to empty the pockets of the unwary have been part of stock markets since the days of the infamous South Sea Bubble three centuries ago. The ranygazoo is not quite as ripe as it was in the heyday of John Law (of whom more later), but it is still there. In the middle of the seventeenth century, yearning investors were persuaded to buy shares in a company that was formed for the express purpose of recovering items from the bottom of the Red Sea during that biblical occasion when, as the song puts it, "Pharaoh's Army got drownded." Money poured down on the founders of this company too, like manna from heaven, and the investors were some ticked-off when the venture came to nothing. "No sound is sweeter to the gambler's ear," my father used to say, "than to hear the suckers squeal." It has always been thus.

Touching the second, the quick course in the mechanics of the market, we will discover that, despite the proliferation of complications, what the exchanges do is essentially simple in nature; indeed, much of the complication may be attributed to the invention of new and snakier ways to carry out stale frauds, once they are discovered, by relaunching them tarted up in fresh disguises. Or, when positive fraud is not involved, the complications are introduced to make it easier to gamble more and faster by betting on which way stock indices are going to go, or on what the rumour of a presidential heart murmur will do to the shares of a golf-club manufacturer.

When Eric Kierans became president of the Montreal and

Canadian stock exchanges, he was given a tour of his new splendours. He remarked to the accompanying group of officials that his understanding was that the operation was "very complicated, but very simple, like Bonsecours Market." Well, no, not quite, an official explained, we were dealing here with a complex bit of machinery, sophisticated and subtle and . . . "Yeah," interrupted Kierans. "Buying and selling, like Bonsecours Market."

It is the Bonsecours rather than the sophisticated approach that marks the following pages. The intelligent reader will learn, if he or she doesn't already know, something of the terms used and the tricks employed; he or she will learn the difference between a put and a call, and how a convertible bond differs from a debenture and what it is that makes a preferred share preferable. But these explanations, which grow out of the day-to-day operations of finance, may differ somewhat from the worshipful definitions available in the plethora of *How To Make Millions Without Risking a Dime* books – books for which so many trees have already been condemned to die in our time.

I like these books; I admire them tremendously; but I do not intend to venture any of my poor share of capital on their advice. I particularly like the pamphlet I get in the mail from time to time, written by somebody who obviously knows a great deal more about stocks and bonds than I do, who invites me to join him in scooping cash out of the market only if I give the right answer to one question: "Do You Sincerely Want To Be Rich?" Apparently, there are a gang of imposters out there, investing away, who don't sincerely want to be rich; who yearn, if the ugly truth is to be known, for honest poverty. Actually, if that is the case, investing in the stock market may do the trick. (I can't help wondering if the authors of this pamphlet realize that their catch-phrase, "Do You Want, etc." was the slogan of Bernie Cornfeld's 1960s Fund of Funds, which managed to make so many investors sincerely poor, and landed Bernie in jail.) I do not attempt to emulate the author of this forthright pamphlet. I belong to the cynical circle who reckon that the only people who make money out of how-to-make-money books are the authors thereof.

It is not my thesis that the purchaser of this book will be able, thus armed, to stride out into the markets and clean up. Indeed, it is my thesis that the reader who pays careful attention will do well to stay the hell out of the markets until that happy, unlikely day when someone else cleans *them* up. This is a cautionary volume; it attempts to describe the world of the markets as they exist, for the purposes of providing information and provoking reform. The clean, thrustful, unquenchable greed that marks the truly significant tipster book is not, alas, contained within these pages, and if I make any money at this, it will go into the timid bank account, under the virtuous mattress, or be wasted on food and shelter; none will go to purchase stock.

That is because what really bothers me about the way the stock markets work is that they are so bloody unfair. It is unfair that the world's economy should be held in thrall to a gang of gamblers, and it is unfair that those gamblers who do best are so often cheaters. The theology tells us that the shrewd investor, by studying hard and keeping in close touch with the markets, will be rewarded by gaining money in his stock speculations, while the indolent, the ignorant, and the out-of-touch will lose. The facts tell us that winners and losers are far more likely to be determined either by blind luck or insider information to which the ordinary investor can never have access, than by any merit of the stock-player.

When the *Wall Street Journal* held a stock-picking contest in January 1990, it invited four of the shrewdest and most experienced analysts on Wall Street to pick a group of stocks destined to go up. At the same time, a reporter threw darts randomly at a listing of the New York Stock Exchange companies. The dart-selected stocks did far better than those chosen by pros; bear that in mind the next time you hear someone boasting about how his shrewdness was made manifest by winnings on the market.

Dumb luck or insider knowledge are the keys to success for the small trader in managing a portfolio, and the ordinary stock-player today faces not merely the operations of the smart cookies and inside tipsters, but the huge machinations of the pension funds, mutual funds, market managers, and stock manipulators, all armed with computer programs designed to react to market trends. In fact, the program-driven computers make the trends, they don't react to them, and it turns out that computers are twice as hysterical as even the ordinary panic-driven small investor.

The fix is in, folks. Play the markets if you will, and God bless you, but play them as you would any other gambling game, with full knowledge that only a large lashing of luck or a temporary suspension of skullduggery, or both, will ever give you a chance to win.

I would not trouble you with all this if the stock markets simply stuck to what they do best – vacuuming the suckers. But they affect every one of us. Even if you don't use the markets, the markets use you. They set the tone for the economy, as you can see every day on TV when the newsreader burbles while he tells us that the market has gained, and scowls when reporting a tumble. The newsreader knows, as we all know, that today's particular results don't matter a tinker's dam; but if the market keeps going down, businessmen, the world's spookiest set, stop investing. Money dries up. Factories close. It may not make economic sense, but reports of the market's decline become a self-fulfilling prophecy.

Then, there is the waste, the appalling waste. We are told, by the best and brightest among us, that we must become competitive. This turns out to mean that everybody ought to work for Mexican wages, while the corporation presidents draw down millions, but let's not be cynical. We must be competitive, productive, and efficient – these are the buzzwords of our time, the litany of unemployment lineups. "Tough about having to fire you, folks, but the firm must stay competitive."

How competitive is it when, as we will see in detail in Chapter Five, about half a cent of every dollar thrown onto the table in our stock exchanges actually goes to provide new equity for firms? The rest is just gambling money, chasing bets around the wheel. Our competitors, the Japanese, are too smart for that; their giant corporations raise their capital internally, by re-investing their profits, or they borrow from the bank.

How productive is it when most of the money actually raised on the exchanges goes, not to build factories and hire workers, but to pay off the brokers, investment houses, advertising firms, accountants, lawyers, and other bystanders whose collective efforts make it so expensive to sell shares?

How efficient is it when, as happened in October 1987, one trillion dollars disappear, overnight, from the collective value of the companies traded on the world's exchanges? "What happened to that trillion bucks, Bill?" "Dunno, Harry. It was around here someplace, but it's gone."

That trillion dollars of vanished money represents an amount equal to the annual budget of the United States, a nation that can no longer afford to take care of its sick, its poor, its undereducated. How can it be efficient to throw teachers out of work to save a few millions while blowing away a trillion dollars in the burp of a stock market "readjustment"?

We all paid for that vanished money, so, send not to ask for whom the stock market tolls; even if you don't play the game, it tolls for thee. Its disasters are financed by all of us, even if they are precipitated by the greed of a handful. Is that fair?

When you have asked yourself these questions, ask one final one: Is this any way to run an economy?

PART I

The Way We Were

To be absent from Change . . . at the time when the merchants go about to buy is quite simply to court disaster.

– Daniel Defoe, *The Villainy of Stock-jobbers Detected*, 1701.

CHAPTER ONE

The Pernicious Art of Stock-Jobbing

Beginnings

The pernicious art of stock-jobbing has so perverted the end and design of companies and corporations – erected for the introducing and carrying on of manufacturing – to the private profit of the first projectors, that the privileges granted to them have commonly been made no other use of by the first procurers and subscribers, but to sell again with advantage to ignorant men drawn in by the reputation, falsely raised and artfully spread, touching the thriving state of the stock.

– Report of the Commissioners for Trade and Plantations, London, 1841.

$

We are so used, these days, to the concept that stocks – share certificates, securities, call them what you will – embody the ownership of companies, that we forget what a clever, and revolutionary, idea it was originally. What P. G. Wodehouse calls "oompus boompus" has always been a part of the business, but that ought not to blind us to the fact that modern capitalism, a singularly efficient mechanism, owes a good deal of its evident success to this simple idea. In the mercantile age, roughly between 1500 and 1800, it was hazardous to form any sort of business enterprise, and impossible to create any really large enterprise except by and through the agency of the state. The really big profits went to the Crown, for, if the monarch was not in on the swag, there was none.

The king or queen alone handed out the monopolies that determined who could trade, and where, and with whom, and even, to some extent, for how much. The mercantile system was based on the notion that everybody should export goods to other countries in return for precious metals, which could be turned into arms and armies for the religious wars thought necessary for the greater glory of God, Allah, whomever, as well as to pay the rising costs of civil government. Land, which had been at the heart of the feudal system, was being replaced by metal as wealth and capital.

Foreign trade was better than domestic trade and manufacturing was superior to agriculture as a source of bullion. It followed that you had to export more than you imported, in order to accumulate wealth. Therefore, to reduce the amount coming in and to protect your own markets, duties were imposed on foreign goods. This had the additional advantage of producing revenue for the Crown.

The instruments for all this trading activity were the trading corporations, whose charters flowed from the monarch. These charters, like modern television-broadcast permits, were licences to print money, but the catch was that the corporation was utterly dependent upon the whim of the monarch who granted its charter and who could, and often did, withdraw it. The company and the country were one and the same thing in many ways.

Thus, India was ruled for nearly two centuries by, and on behalf of, the East India Company, and Robert Clive, the soldier-hero of Britain's Indian empire, wasn't even in the British army. He was a clerk, and later a soldier, in the East India Company, which had its own army, and it was to protect that same company's monopoly on tea that George III had imposed the tax that led to all the unpleasantness in Boston harbour in 1773.

The state and the trading companies were joined together in a national crusade; in theory on behalf of the nation, and in fact on behalf of the king and his gang. The difficulty was that the system didn't work; it had the built-in flaw that, if every nation tried to export more than it imported, somebody was bound to lose the contest. Worse, even if this imbalance somehow balanced, the end result of importing huge amounts of bullion was to produce an oversupply of money at home, and thus, serious inflation. Moreover, the concentration of all the risks of enterprise in a few hands made it difficult to raise anything close to the amount of capital required for really enterprising ventures.

The honest merchant who set out to do a bit of business overseas, for example, was expected to pony up the money for the expedition himself, wave the boys goodbye from the quayside, and sit at home biting his nails until, literally, "his ship came in." Or not. Hard to work up anything really impressive this way; there was no continuity, nor could there be when the entire operation could be cancelled on the whim of a single person, even if the ship survived pirates, typhoons, and rascality at sea.

To spread out the risk a little, a form of association sprang up in Europe known as the *societas,* a partnership in which the contributors put up money for one of their number who conducted the enterprise and shared out the profits in proportion to the amount invested by each of the partners, the division taking place at the end of the voyage, or the year, or whatever period had been agreed upon. This grew, in England, into two forms of corporation – the regulated company and the joint-stock company.

Partners in the regulated company traded on their own accounts, but within regulations as to divisions of territory and terms of trade, laid down in the partnership agreement. They joined together to insure the voyage, and each withdrew his own profits from the venture on the end of the agreed-upon period.

When the East India Company was first established, in 1600, it was a regulated company, with the partners all withdrawing their own profits. However, it was becoming clear that for more ambitious ventures and greater profits, some of the take would have to be left in the till, as working capital and for investment in long-term projects (to wit, the subjugation and exploitation of the Indian subcontinent). A joint fund was set up to finance new ventures, and the partners were invited to contribute – or not – to this fund. Those who contributed more received more of the joint profits. In 1653, a permanent joint fund was set up within the company and, in 1692, trading on a partner's own account was forbidden. Now the partners were paid a dividend (from the Latin, *dividendum,* literally, "the thing to be divided"), representing part of the profits of the enterprise each year, and the balance was left to reinvest within the firm.

The partnership arrangements in a regulated company were described in the Deed of Settlement drawn up when the company was originally founded and amended from time to time as the members saw fit. The joint-stock company was an advance on this form of association. In this arrangement, a certificate representing ownership of a specific share of the company was made out in the owner's name, and he paid in the necessary capital before he got the share certificate. His subscription was listed in a book – it still is – along with the date of purchase and other pertinent information. Keep your eye on that share certificate; it was the key to much of what happened later, and its fundamental nature hasn't changed much from that day to this. The share certificate still represents a portion of the ownership of the firm (there is a move afoot to abandon the paper, and store the certificate as a blip in a computer; the principle will be the same). Dividends are paid out to the shares, and the dividends must be paid in proportion to the shares owned.

The first significant Canadian joint-stock company was *La Compagnie de la Nouvelle France,* which was formed in 1627 and given, by Louis XIII, the exclusive right to trade, colonize, govern, and promote religious teaching in all of New France, from Florida northward. It didn't work out; the directors (does this sound familiar?) scooped out too much of the proceeds for themselves in the form of salaries and indemnities, and the company was dissolved in 1663, with control of the colony passing back to the king.

Seven years later the world witnessed the launching, again by royal charter, of the Governor and Company of Adventurers of England Trading into Hudson's Bay. Now, just another limb of the corporate Thomson empire, the Hudson's Bay Company was a joint-stock firm. Individuals put up capital, for which they received stock certificates from the company treasury, which gave them the right to elect or appoint officers to manage their joint investment. Usually, the profits were withdrawn after a single voyage, but, as with the East India Company, the managers soon saw the advantage of leaving capital in the company, and expanding into lines of business other than trading. The Governor and Company, etc., went into the insurance game, among other things.

By the end of the seventeenth century, there was not much practical difference between a regulated company and a joint-stock company, except for the share certificate. Both kinds of firm operated on monopoly charters granted by the Crown to cover trading and other rights in a specific area. Each kind came to enjoy the advantages of incorporation; that is, the company became more or less permanent and did not, like a partnership or proprietary firm, dissolve with the death of its owners. It was itself a legal person, and the acts of the corporation (*Corporatus* – Latin for "made into a body") were separate from the acts of its members. The East India Company, not the governor, had the right to rule India; the governor was simply appointed as the corporation's agent for the work.

The corporation, whether joint-stock or regulated, was a much better instrument for raising and employing capital, but it was still operating within the constraints of a mercantile system, it was still dependent on the Crown for its charter, and it was still, in all policy matters, the servant of the state.

If the corporation ran into money problems, however, the state was not expected to pay up. Instead, the company charter usually contained a clause allowing the managers to call on individual members to make up the shortfall, in proportion to their owner-ship of the firm. To put it another way, there was no limit to the liability of the shareholders. In some charters, however, wording began to appear that excluded or limited the company's right to make levies on the members, except under conditions which they themselves approved.

There was only one element missing to make capital com-pletely mobile, and that was the transferability of shares. When mercantile corporations were first formed, their membership was confined to "those who had been bred to the trade of merchan-dize," as William Scott, an early historian of the joint-stock com-panies, put it. You could be fined for trying to sell your shares to a stranger, and the company would refuse to record the transfer. The advantage of this was that the members of the company were all in the business; the disadvantage was that it left out many of the people who had money to invest.

Shares were usually referred to as "adventures" during the seventeenth century, and with good reason; the profits could be staggering, and so could the losses. The more investors who could be drawn into the firm, the better it could withstand the ravages of fate, the king, and the weather.

It was the transferable share that tapped this market. There had always been exceptions to the rules about selling shares to strangers, and as the seventeenth century wore on, the fines were lowered, and finally dropped. Actions in shares became so com-mon that most joint-stock companies began to print lists, from time to time, of the holders of their stock.

Now, instead of the certificate being issued directly from the treasury to a named subscriber, the share itself was sold from hand to hand and the transfer recorded. Now the dividends payable to John Brown, as owner of the share certificate, became payable to Joe Black, who had bought the certificate from John Brown. It was the blink of an eye, historically speaking, from that first stock transaction to the modern world of stock markets, where billions of shares change ownership every year.

A marketplace to buy and sell stock certificates was ready-made in the exchanges that had existed here and there even in Roman times for money-changing, buying and selling commodities in bulk, and organizing maritime insurance, where the risk was spread among several guarantors. As early as the year 1111, in Lucca, a city in northern Tuscany, money-changers met regularly near St. Martin's Church, and merchants and notaries began to congregate around them to form an open-air exchange where spices, pepper, and barrels of herring were bought and sold much as they are today at the Chicago Mercantile Exchange. Buildings to house this activity appeared in the fourteenth century, and historian Charles Carrière, in a book on the merchants of Marseilles, describes a scene in the year 1400 in the great Gothic hall called the *Longa*, which served Barcelona as an exchange:

> A whole squadron of brokers [could be seen] moving in and out of its pillars, and the people standing in little groups were *corredors d'orella*, the brokers by ear, whose job it was to listen, report and put interested parties in touch.

Because the important businessmen and intermediaries – brokers, jobbers, and tipsters – met for a few hours every day in these exchanges, it was inevitable that they would become the locus for the selling of stock certificates, and also inevitable that, as the business grew, the exchanges would become specialized.

Amsterdam had a separate corn exchange at the beginning of the seventeenth century, and, not long after, a separate stock-market building. This is usually referred to as "the world's first stock market" although, in fact, state loan stocks had been bought and sold in the Casa di San Giorgio in Genoa during the fourteenth century. In any event, the Amsterdam Exchange, completed in 1631, was the first large, permanent exchange and, like its modern counterparts, quickly moved from investment to speculation to the wildest sort of gambling. Every day, between 12:00 and 2:00 p.m., somewhere around four thousand people would crowd into this building, and about one thousand brokers, assigned numbered places according to their branch of trading, would shout buy-and-sell quotes, creating a fearful din.

At first, the only shares were government stocks and the certificates of the Dutch East India Company, but, as the share certificates of other companies became transferable, a huge and frenetic business emerged.

Amsterdam was, after all, the centre of the tulip mania (the seventeenth-century frenzy that saw the Dutch burghers winning and losing fortunes on tulip bulbs, and paying, sometimes, thousands of dollars for one bulb), and gambling on commodities soon gave way to gambling, not only on shares, but on futures – buying and selling at set prices on future dates. The Dutch were able to work out ways to speculate without having any shares or money at all. The brokers, who took a commission whichever way the gambling went, as well as plunging into the action themselves, formed gangs to try to push stocks up or down. The gangs were called *rotteries,* and they were fiercely competitive. If one gang pushed up the price, another, known as "underminers" – these would soon become the "bulls and bears" of modern markets – would try to push it down. Unlike modern brokers, these ones specialized; you were either a pusher or an underminer, and to change camps was tantamount to treason.

A technique called "blank buying" developed, in which the speculator would contract to sell shares he didn't own, for a price that was higher or lower than the current market. When the time for settlement came, money would change hands, even though the share certificate that was the object of the exercise never appeared. That is, if you contracted to sell a share of the Dutch East India Company for 2,000 guilders on May 1, and its value on May 1 was 2,500 guilders, you paid across 500 guilders to the other party. If the price was 1,500 guilders, he paid you the difference. The speculator was buying or selling something he didn't possess and never would; the pay-off was on the gamble, pure and simple. Today, we call this stock index trading, and deny that it is gambling.

Any rumour could send shares soaring, or reeling, and, since there was no official listing of share prices, the market could be jerked back and forth with very little reference to reality. An account by Joseph de la Vega, in Fernand Braudel's *Civilization and Capitalism,* describes a scene in a Dutch coffeehouse in 1688 this way:

> There then comes into one of these houses during the opening hours of the Exchange one of the "bulls," or bidders-up. People ask him the price of shares, he adds on one or two per cent to the price of the moment, takes out his little notebook and pretends to write in it what he has only done in his mind, letting everyone believe that he has really done it, and in order to encourage in every heart the desire of buying some shares, for fear they should go up again.

The broker's victims in this little game were those who did not have the right to go into the exchange to find out the true price of the shares. That, at least, has changed.

As Amsterdam blossomed on the gambling trade, the English grew envious and copied the idea. The Royal Exchange, where commodities and currency were traded, saw the trading of shares in the Bank of England and a few other companies as early as 1695, although there was no formal and separated stock exchange building until 1773. Instead, as the space inside the Royal Exchange became more and more cramped, the business spilled out into the coffeehouses of 'Change Alley nearby. Share brokers worked out of Garraway's and Jonathan's, while specialists in maritime insurance congregated at Edward Lloyd's, two blocks away, on Cornhill. As in Amsterdam, speculation provided much more of the action than anything we would recognize as investment, and the insiders cleaned up.

In 1701, a clever merchant named Medina paid an army captain £6,000 a year to get himself attached to the entourage of the Duke of Marlborough, during the War of the Spanish Succession. His contact kept him in touch with the campaign by express courier. Medina was thus among the first in England to learn of the outcome of Marlborough's various battles – and cleaned up by buying and selling according to his advance bulletins.

Until 1767, every stock that was sold had to go through the hands of a broker, although the commissions were usually one-eighth of 1 per cent of the value of the stock. Beneath the brokers were stock-jobbers, who did the same job but were not registered and sworn as brokers were. The distinction between them didn't really disappear in England until the so-called Big Bang of deregulation in 1986.

Stock-jobbers were not highly regarded. A contemporary author, George White, referred to "this strange species of insect known as the stock-jobber," and Daniel Defoe, the author of *Robinson Crusoe*, wrote a pamphlet in 1701, a quote from which begins this section of the book, called, straightforwardly, *The Villany of Stock-jobbers Detected*. Not so straightforwardly, he published the pamphlet anonymously. It is hard to see, from our vantage point, that there was much difference in the activities complained of. Both brokers and jobbers manipulated the market as best they could, for their own advantage.

During the first two decades of the eighteenth century, speculation on stocks in London was confined to gambling on the future value of Exchequer bills, Navy bills, and the shares of about sixty companies, led by the East India Company and the Bank of England. Fortunes were being made and lost – but mostly, in an opening market, being made – and it seemed as if the ever-rising spiral of stock prices would continue forever. But two abrupt setbacks, one in England and one on the continent, both came to a climax in 1720. They were the collapse of John Law's Mississippi Company, in France, and the bursting of the South Sea Bubble, in England.

John Law was a Scotsman, the son of a jeweller, who left his native land after he killed a man in a duel and was accused of murder. He went to live in Amsterdam, where he gambled, whored, and studied finance. His gambling led to a meeting with the Duc d'Orléans, himself an inveterate gambler, and his study to the writing of an essay, *Money and Trade Considered.* (Nothing much came of his whoring.) In *Money and Trade Considered,* Law proposed the founding of a national bank, whose notes would be secured by the value of land, most of which belonged to the Crown. This notion was rejected as far too radical by both the Dutch and the Scots, but it appealed greatly to Law's old pal, the Duc d'Orléans, who became, in 1715, Louis XV, the king of France. Louis XIV, his father, had left his nation on the verge of bankruptcy, and Law persuaded his friend that an expansion of credit would restore prosperity. He turned out to be quite correct.

In 1716, Law was given a charter to form the Banque General, with a capital of six million livres and the right to issue notes as currency, based on the state's land holdings. Most of these notes were issued to the government, which used them to pay off its debts, and in turn accepted them as legal tender for the payment of taxes. This hocus-pocus produced an infusion of credit; trade prospered, prices rose, and employment increased. In 1718, the bank became a royal institution, and was renamed the Banque Royale. So far, so good.

The next year, John Law had another bright idea. He would form a company to exploit the riches of the French colonies overseas, and finance it through the Banque Royale; he would give the king some of the money from the stock sales, keeping only a fortune or two for himself. The king gave him a monopoly on trade into the Mississippi region of North America – much of what is today the central United States. With that in hand, Law launched a furious campaign to flog stock in his Mississippi Company. Prices shot through the ceiling as bright-eyed Frenchmen counted the worth of the untold supplies of gold along the Mississippi Valley. That is, until they realized that the reason the supplies of gold were untold was that there weren't any, and that the money they had put into shares was not developing colonial trade, but paying government expenses. Law was named Comptroller General of France and the Duc d'Arkansas, but that didn't put any money in the tills of the Banque Royale, or profits in the coffers of the Mississippi Company. Stock prices plummeted as fast as they had shot up and, since the company was backed by the bank, a run on the bank ensued in 1720. Fifteen people were crushed to death trying to get into the bank's premises to withdraw their funds, the bank collapsed, and John Law fled to Venice, where he lived as a gambler for another ten years.

Meanwhile, back in London, the English, determined never to be bettered by their foes across the Channel, were blowing up and then bursting the South Sea Bubble. In England during the first part of the century, Parliament began to assert itself more vigorously against the prerogatives of the Crown, and one way it did this was to issue company charters on its own behalf. Most business was still conducted on personal lines by individual proprietors or partnerships, but the obvious advantages of the joint-stock corporation overseas were beginning to be applied to the growing number of manufacturing concerns in the home market, and, before long, a busy trade sprang up in the charters of companies which had, for one reason or another, vanished, leaving nothing behind but the formative scrap of paper. (As long as you had a charter, you could sell shares, even if the original purpose of the company had disappeared.) A banking company emerged, prospered, and sold shares on the basis of a charter from a defunct sword-blade company, and shares were even issued in a company whose prospectus described it as being formed "For an undertaking which shall in due time be revealed."

The climax was reached when a group of MPs was bribed to issue a charter to a company formed to acquire part of the national debt, in particular, the war debt, in imitation of John Law's gimmick. Why would anyone be crazy enough to want to buy a piece of the national debt? Because it pays interest, and stands a good chance of being repaid. It's what we do, at least in theory, when we buy a Canada Savings Bond. The government had issued £9 million worth of bonds to finance the War of the Spanish Succession, and holders of these bonds were allowed to exchange their bonds for shares in the new company. (These were not quite the same as convertible bonds, which we will meet later.) This corporation, called the South Sea Company, was given a monopoly of British trade with the islands of the South Seas and South America. The idea was that the Spanish would grant generous trading concessions to the British in return for peace. The company would then clean up, discharge the government bonds out of its huge profits, and keep the rest for its shareholders. This sounded so good that a brisk trade in shares of the South Sea Company began, and prices were soon soaring.

In 1720, the company was doing so well, on paper, that it proposed to take over, not merely the debt from the war, but the entire national debt, by exchanging its stock for government bonds. Jolly good, said the boys over in the coffeehouses of 'Change Alley. The shares went from £128.5 in January 1720 to £1,000 in August. The customers fought to lay out their money at ever-increasing rates, and those who had bought at £150 and sold a month later for a 100 per cent profit cursed themselves for not having had the nerve to hold on.

Dozens of imitators leapt into the fray, some with charters, some without, some with a monopoly on trade, or something, somewhere, some with nothing to sell but stocks themselves, and they all did well, and prospered, and multiplied.

Came the dawn. The Spanish did not, as it turned out, offer huge trading concessions to end the war, and the British were unable to wring any substantial concessions in trade out of them. Money did not come flowing in, and the entire stock market tottered and then toppled. Most of the stock purchases, in the South Sea Company and its imitators, had been bought with bank loans, and when the banks tried to collect, and forced the sale of the stock certificates that had served as collateral for the loans, shares came onto the market for which there were no buyers at any price. (In theory, this can't happen, but it does; nothing that occurred in the Great Crash of 1929 was much different from what happened in 1720.) Thousands of investors, including the MPs who had hatched the original scheme, were wiped out.

The government then passed the Bubble Act, closing the barn door just as the tail end of the horse disappeared over a neighbouring hill. This act made it illegal to sell stock without a charter, and illegal to manipulate the market. But there was only one prosecution, ever, under the new law, which contained one lovely clause permitting existing companies, with or without charters, to continue "behaving in such a manner as hath hitherto usually and may lawfully be done." The problem was that what had hitherto and lawfully been done was to skin investors, so this was not entirely reassuring.

However, the dreadful lessons of the Mississippi Company and the South Sea Bubble produced what might be called a shortfall of suckers for quite some time to come, and things were comparatively quiet along 'Change Alley until 1748. On March 25 of that year, the whole district burned down. The brokers made a number of abortive attempts to put up a new building, but were unable to raise the necessary funds until 1773, when the Stock Exchange went up, right behind the Royal Exchange.

As the eminent French historian Fernand Braudel remarks in *The Wheels of Commerce,* "The surroundings might change and become more official, but needless to say the game went on much as before."

In 1776, three years after the Stock Exchange went up, Adam Smith, a moral philosopher, wrote *An Inquiry into the Nature and Causes of the Wealth of Nations* as a scathing attack on the mercantilist system. Real wealth was not produced by fooling about with bags of bullion, Smith argued, but by creating and exploiting productive power and productive capacity. The real wealth of nations was the sum total of all the exchange values that any nation possessed, and the way to produce more of it was to take advantage of the efficiencies produced by a rational division of labour. Although it was not immediately apparent, Smith's study marked the end of the age of mercantilism and the onset of capitalism. Capital had been made central to the economy, replacing the land that had been central to feudalism, but mercantilism had no way to organize its use effectively.

Mercantilism was coming apart; the issuing of charters by Parliament saw to that in England, by removing much of the royal prerogative over commerce. In any event, the world had become too small to be parcelled off into royal monopolies; nor could the privy purse begin to provide the capital required to finance the Industrial Revolution, which had already begun. The new machines, and the factories to house them, demanded vast pools of capital, as did the expanding transportation system.

The corporation was a far more efficient way to mobilize capital than having the king pass around his hat and hope for the best. The corporation could be financed and expanded by issuing bonds, which are, in effect, promissory notes, which bear interest at a declared rate and are redeemed on a set date, but it is rather hard to persuade people to buy bonds on a company that has not yet begun. Stocks were the answer; let the great unwashed in on the action by sharing the ownership.

To make this work effectively, it was first necessary to remove the aspect of share-ownership that made it most onerous – unlimited liability – and to make incorporation a right, not a privilege to be handed out or withdrawn by the Crown. This second goal was accomplished in 1844, when William Ewart Gladstone bulldozed a new Companies Act through Parliament. It spelled out the difference between partnerships and incorporated companies – the essential difference being that in corporations the shares could be transferred freely. Any company with more than twenty-five members sharing ownership, or any company in which the shares could be transferred freely, had to be registered. That was the act of incorporation, but it was a right, which any group of investors who met the test could invoke. Mercantilism was dead, because the monarch no longer controlled who could trade.

The 1844 Act did not provide limited liability; even if you sold your shares in a company, a creditor could come after you for part of what was due to him at any time up to three years after you sold. In the market slump of 1845-48, a number of the newly incorporated companies went bankrupt, destroying the fortunes of investors who had played, in fact, only a minor role in their activities.

The argument for limited liability soon became an argument on behalf of the middle classes and against the rich, curiously enough. Only the rich could afford to speculate, under the then-rules, and it is not hard to see why, if we take a modern parallel: would you buy shares in the Toronto-Dominion bank if you were in danger of losing, not just the money you put into the shares, but the roof over your head, because the bank made a bum investment in Iran? There were a number of committees to investigate limited liability, and John Stuart Mill, a witness before one of these, put the argument this way:

> There is no way in which the working classes can make so beneficial a use of their savings, both to themselves and to

society, as by the formation of associations to carry on the businesses with which they are acquainted.

It was a good point and, in due course, the Select Committee on Investments for the Savings of the Middle and Working Classes reported in 1850 that:

> Any measures for the removal of these difficulties would be particularly acceptable to the Middle and Working Classes and would tend to satisfy them that they are not excluded from fair competition by laws throwing obstacles in the way of men with small capitals.

Men (and women) with small capitals have provided stock-market fodder since 1855, when the law was changed to provide for limited liability – that is, if the company became insolvent, the investors could lose the money they had put up to buy shares, but nothing more; the creditors could not come after them to make good their debts.

The way had now been cleared for the emergence of the modern corporation, the triumph of the stock market, and the multiplication of opportunities for worth-while enterprise, nefarious gambling, and blatant rascality.

All of which would reach their finest flower in North America.

CHAPTER TWO

I Have Ways Of Making Money
That You Know Not Of

The Robber Barons

Who is it that supports every one of the ruddy-faced and round-bellied brokers, furnishes their brown-stone houses in velvet and ebony, their tables with wine and silver, their wives and daughters – aye, and mistresses, too – in silks and diamonds and laces? It is the lamb, the meek-eyed, confiding and innocent little lamb."
  – A successful operator, in *How To Win in Wall Street*, 1881.

$

Securities were exchanged in the United States long before there was an official building for the purpose. In the mid-1700s, most of the action moved through London, naturally, and it was attended by the same generous lashings of rascality that have always accompanied the operations of high finance. One of the ripest stock scams of colonial America involved no less a person than Benjamin Franklin, and turned on an attempt to establish a fourteenth American colony, to be called Vandalia, in the western wilderness.

Ben Franklin, while in London as agent for Massachusetts,

the province of was approached by his illegitimate son, William, the colonial governor of the province of New Jersey. William presented him with an offer which, we would now say, he could not refuse. A group of white traders had laid claim to a huge tract of land west of the Ohio River, as compensation for wrongs they had suffered, they said, during Pontiac's Uprising in 1763. A company, called the Indiana Company, was formed to pursue the interests of these "suffering traders," and William wrote to his father to offer him shares in the company in return for his support of the land claim. Ben agreed at once, and quickly got the approval of the Earl of Shelburne, who was in charge of colonial matters. Alas, Shelburne fell out of favour with King George III, and was replaced by Lord Hillsborough, who was opposed to colonial expansion. There was, as Claude-Anne Lopez and Eugenia W. Herbert, authors of *The Private Franklin*, note, "panic among the investors."

However, they pulled themselves together and, led by Philadelphia merchant Samuel Wharton, they decided to forget Britain for the time being, and approach the matter from the Indian end. In 1768, Sir William Johnson, who was both the British government's Superintendent of Indian Affairs and a shareholder in the Indiana Company, arranged the purchase of 2.5-million acres of land – most of what would later be the state of West Virginia – for £10,460, from chiefs of the Six Nations, at Fort Stanwix. This deal was embodied in the Treaty of Fort Stanwix, which had then to be ratified by the British government. Because of the competing claims of other gangs of speculators, speedy ratification was of the essence. It was not, however, forthcoming.

Samuel Wharton sailed to England in 1769, and Ben Franklin took him around the coffeehouses and salons of London to meet members of "the Bloomsbury gang," a group of politicians and speculators clustered around Thomas Walpole, an MP and nephew of Sir Robert Walpole. Shares were dealt out to the Bloomsbury gang. The way thus prepared, Franklin escorted

Wharton on a visit to Lord Hillsborough, and Hillsborough astounded his callers by telling them that they weren't asking for enough land. They should put in a claim for 25-million acres, enough to form another American province, Hillsborough told them. Say, that sounds nice.

By late 1769, a new corporation had sprung from the loins of the Indiana Company, and shares were handed out to all the necessary politicians, financiers, and speculators. This was the Grand Ohio Company, dedicated to erecting a new colony which would embrace parts of Pennsylvania, Indiana, Kentucky, Virginia, and North Carolina, as well as the entire area of the present-day states of Ohio and West Virginia. It only remained to give the province-to-be a name. Queen Charlotte believed that she was descended from the royal line of the Vandals (she came from Mecklenberg, in Germany, an area known as Vandalia; in the eighteenth century, the Vandals were held in a higher regard than was the case later). So, one night at the Crown and Anchor Tavern, one of new company's shareholders proposed that they call the new province Vandalia, which might persuade King George III to sign on the dotted line. That sounded nice, too, and it was done.

The prospectus and supporting pamphlets, which were pushed out as fast as eighteenth-century presses could handle them, made Vandalia sound like an earthly paradise, just waiting to be occupied, and the Grand Ohio Company's shareholders like charitable benefactors, rather than speculators. There was no need to mention the tedious business about the land being occupied already by thousands of Indians who might not take kindly to the scheme. The British Crown had given its solemn word, in the Proclamation of 1763, that no settlement would be allowed west of the Ohio River. Breaking that solemn word presented no difficulty – it was done all the time – but the Indians might not see it in the same, broad-minded way that the settlers and speculators did. Better to play that part down in the company prospectus. The shares did very well.

Then came an abrupt snag. Lord Hillsborough, when he encouraged this massive land-grab, was actually playing a devious game of his own. He was opposed to land speculation in America, knowing that it would lead to problems with the Indians. He had encouraged the Ohio Company to ask for such a huge tract in the belief that their greed would arouse the ire of every other claimant; he calculated, correctly, that the result would be a balance of competing interests in Parliament, and a stalemate, with no land grants being made at all. In the meantime, he began the process of drawing up the necessary petition to the Privy Council with marvellous slowness. Franklin wrote to Joseph Galloway, an old friend in Pennsylvania, that the whole business was so slow that it reminded him of a sailor's story: "They were handing a Cable out of a store into a ship, and one of 'em said, ' 'Tis a long, heavy Cable. I wish we could see the End of it.' 'D—n me,' says another, 'if I believe it has any End; somebody has cut it off.'"

In this case, the cutting off had been done by Hillsborough, and Ben Franklin was in a rage when he worked out how he had been duped. By this time, because of his increasing involvement with the colonial resistance to the Crown, Franklin had ceased to be an effective lobbyist for the Grand Ohio Company, and withdrew to the sidelines. However, Samuel Wharton, the Philadelphia speculator, was still in London, and was not to be put off. He persuaded the "suffering traders" to ladle more money into the till, and dispensed it liberally in the form of bribes, aimed at getting the attention of the king. He got it, too, when William Strahan, one of the English financiers to whom shares had been dispersed, and the publisher of David Hume, the philosopher, enlisted Hume's aid. Hume had been secretary to the Lord Chamberlain, Lord Hertford. Hume wrote to Hertford, Hertford talked to the king, and the king sent for Lord Hillsborough and said – in a kingly way, of course – What the hell?

Accordingly, in March 1772, Hillsborough forwarded the company's petition to the Privy Council, with a recommendation against it. The Grand Ohio Company weighed in with bogus petitions from landholders eager to settle in Vandalia and letters from such "disinterested" colonials as William Franklin, in support of the scheme. Still stalling, Hillsborough got the matter put back for further study, and it was not until he was replaced in office in 1773 by the Earl of Dartmouth that the matter was revived. The Grand Ohio Company petition worked its weary, bribe-greased way back to the Privy Council. The Council gave its approval, conditional upon ratification of the Treaty of Fort Stanwix, and passed the paper along to King George. He finally signed it in early December, 1773.

Bad timing. On December 13, 1773, the Boston Tea Party darkened the waters of Boston harbour and drowned the hopes of Vandalia. The Treaty of Fort Stanwix was never ratified, and the share certificates in the Grand Ohio Company, like so many to follow, became scrap paper. Many of the speculators went bankrupt, and William had to borrow from his father to keep himself afloat. One of those who was stuck with worthless shares was George Washington.

The Vandalia adventure contained most of the elements of future stock scams: bribery, corruption, false claims and, in the end, worthless stock. However, in contrast to later practice, no one really made much money out of the shares while they could still be pedalled. That was because the market lacked "liquidity," which is the wonderful term for the capacity of the exchange to allow customers to buy and sell shares almost instantly, without overly affecting their prices. This process was to be aided, as we saw in the last chapter, by the invention of limited liability, but it also required a centralized stock exchange.

The exchange was provided almost as soon as the din died from the American Revolutionary War. Even before and during the war, merchants met on the piers of Manhattan's East River, to trade in bills of lading for the cargoes off ships. The unit of exchange was silver – there was no paper money exchanged, for the very good reason that it was not a reliable medium, and gold was hard to come by. Bars of silver were cut into eight pieces to purchase shares in a cargo, which is why North American stocks are traded in eighths to this very day (although, led by the New York Stock Exchange, we are moving to the more manageable decimal system). In 1789, Congress authorized the issue of $80 million in government bonds, and these were soon trading in most American cities along with stocks in the Bank of North America, which had been established in Philadelphia in 1781, and the paper of a number of insurance companies that had sprung up, mainly to underwrite maritime trade.

The market for the emerging securities blossomed where most of the business was being done, above the docks in Lower Manhattan. The dirt path leading up from the waterfront was called, rather grandly, Wall Street. It rambled uphill to the front of Trinity Church, a few hundreds yards away. Beneath a buttonwood tree along this path, on May 17, 1792, twenty-four brokers met to regularize their transactions. The "Buttonwood Tree Agreement" bound each of the brokers "that we will not buy or sell from this date for any person whatever, any kind of public stocks at less rate than one quarter of one percent commission." They also agreed "that we will give preference to each other in our negotiations." This group, which called itself the New York Stock and Exchange Board, moved into permanent quarters at what is now 40 Wall Street, early in the nineteenth century. Today's NYSE actually sprawls around the corner onto Broad Street, in the building into which it moved in 1863.

The NYSE, in all its various guises, has seen many strange sights, much skullduggery, and many scandals. As stocks became more plentiful, more readily exchanged, and less dangerous to own with the advent of limited liability, the natural American bent for speculation asserted itself. And, when the Industrial Revolution came along, with its proliferation of manufacturing companies and its insatiable appetite for capital, business boomed.

Stocks were soon flying from hand to hand almost as swiftly as in London and, when new issues were considered to be too speculative for board members to trade, they were traded anyway, by non-members. These men could not usually afford office space, and did their deals right in the street. They became known as "curbstone brokers," and their market was called The Curb. A number of the hand signals still used on the floors of exchanges around the world were developed by traders leaning out of the windows along Wall Street to make deals with the curbstone brokers below.

The tremendous energies released by the Revolutionary War, and the monumental confidence it engendered in the newly independent Americans, were reflected during the next sixty years in a restless surge westward, and to hell with the niceties of Indian land ownership. The newly developed corporation, floated on stocks and bonds, free of all but limited liability, and aided by the transferable share, came along just in time to lend muscle to this westward thrust. The process was enormously aided towards the end of the nineteenth century by the development of a new philosophy, in which individualism replaced any sort of concern for the community, or, indeed, any sense of responsibility to anyone except the owners of the corporation. These were the shareholders, bless 'em, in whose name forests could be flattened, rivers poisoned, widows fleeced, workers robbed, and the law flouted. The new philosophy was "The survival of the fittest," a businessman's adaptation of the ideas of Herbert Spencer, a sociologist, to the theories of Charles Darwin.

When Darwin's ideas first began to spread across the world after 1859, Spencer set out to give a pseudo-scientific twist to the business application of Darwinism. Just as nature worked automatically in selecting her highest form – mankind – so society would approach perfection to the degree that it allowed its best and finest members to express themselves. Screw the poor. Or, as Spencer put it: "There cannot be more good done than that of letting social progress go unhindered; an immensity of mischief may be done in the artificial preservation of those least able to care for themselves."

Cupidity was part of the universal struggle for existence, and the piling up of wealth was the only legitimate sign of success in the struggle. John D. Rockefeller told his Sunday School class that the fact that he was so rich, and others so poor, reflected "The working out of a law of Nature and a law of God."

No sympathy was to be wasted on those who fell by the wayside, or who were not clever enough to detect that they were about to be swindled by those with whom they dealt. After all, it was Rockefeller's own father who had said, "I cheat my boys every chance I get, I want to make 'em sharp. I trade with the boys and skin 'em and I just beat 'em every time I can. I want to make 'em sharp."

Thus were born the robber barons who bestrode the stock markets, first of America and then of the world. Such men as Rockefeller, J. Pierpont Morgan, "Wizard" Jim Keene, J. W. "Bet-a-Million" Gates, Daniel "Great Bear" Drew, Edward Harriman, "Diamond Jim" Fisk, Andrew Carnegie, "Commodore" Cornelius Vanderbilt, and Jay Gould, the richest of them all. Mark Twain said of Gould, "The people had *desired* money before his day, but he taught them to fall down and worship it."

The robber barons began to emerge shortly before the Civil War, when the beginnings of the railway boom led to the creation of a number of companies of singularly virulent rascality, whose stock was unloaded on the unsuspecting public in both Canada and the United States. But this activity was as nothing compared to the fervour unleashed after the war, when the American nation was being rebuilt, expanded westward, and filled up with immigrants. Capital was needed, and companies to organize it, and stocks to finance the companies. The floaters of these issues would become rich, but that was all part of God's marvellous plan.

To interfere with the stock-market machinations of these men was probably wicked, certainly inefficient, perhaps even blasphemous. They ought to be allowed to go about their business, and the nation's business, free of restraint. Edwin P. Hoyt, the official biographer of the Vanderbilt family, in his book *The Vanderbilts and Their Fortune* set down six rules about how to "improve" a railroad through the manipulation of its stock – rules that reflected this untrammelled approach:

1. buy your railroad;
2. stop the stealing that went on under the other man;
3. improve it in every practicable way within a reasonable expenditure;
4. consolidate it with any other road that can be run with it economically;
5. water its stock;
6. make it pay a large dividend.

Number 5 in this list brought a new phrase to the fore. Stock watering was the invention of Daniel Drew, who began his business career as a cattle drover in Putnam County, New York. He gathered up cattle from his neighbours and hustled them to New York City, without allowing them to drink anywhere along the way until just before they reached the drovers' market. Then the thirsty beasts were allowed to drink their fill, and, since they were sold by the hundredweight, the unwitting purchasers ended up buying water on the hoof. Drew became the owner of the Bull's Head Tavern on Third Avenue near the drovers' market, then a money-lender, and finally a stockbroker. He founded his own firm, Drew, Robinson & Company, which dealt in bank stocks, steamship shares, and the paper of the burgeoning railway companies. Drew learned to water all this stock, too.

In 1854, he loaned $1,500,000 to the Erie Railroad, a trunk line from New York to the Great Lakes, in return for a chattel mortgage on its trains and equipment. The line had been built, with the usual attendant corruption, mainly through government subsidies, at a cost of $15 million, but the company had issued stock worth far more than this. It had been watered all the way up to $26 million. In fact, the railroad was worth very little, because its tracks and bridges were in a ruinous state when Drew, by virtue of his loan, got himself made treasurer. He promptly looted the till and used the company's own money to short-sell its stock, driving the price down to the point where he was able to buy up control for a fraction of the stock's former value.

He then needed to jack up the prices again, which he did by what came to be known as "the handkerchief trick." One day when Drew was said to be in difficulties in his heavy market speculations, he visited a club near the Stock Exchange that was frequented by his fellow brokers. He pulled out an old red handkerchief to mop his brow when he sat down, and a slip of paper fluttered out of the handkerchief to the floor. One of the brokers swiftly put his foot over the piece of paper, which Drew had apparently not noticed. When he left, the broker snatched it up and read what was obviously a copy of a large buy order on the shares of the Erie Railway. That was enough for the roomful of brokers; they all streamed back to the exchange to buy railroad stock, and Drew cashed in.

He met his comeuppance, however, when he tangled with Cornelius Vanderbilt, a roughneck who had begun as a coastal barge-owner, and liked to be known as Commodore. His stock-market philosophy was summed up in a single phrase. "What do I care about the law?" he thundered. "Hain't I got the power?"

Vanderbilt made his first fortune, about $11 million, during the Civil War, and, despite a little fuss over one of the ships he provided for troop transport, which turned out to be riddled with rot, he was awarded a medal by Congress for his services.

With his winnings, he jumped into the railway business, buying control of the New York and Harlem Railroad at $9 a share and, by buying and selling his own shares, ballooned the price up to $50. He used some of his gains to pay off members of the

New York Common Council, then operating under the aegis of William M. "Boss" Tweed, and quite accurately referred to as "The Forty Thieves."

In return for cash and stock, The Forty Thieves gave Vanderbilt a franchise to operate his railway along Broadway; New York and Harlem shares, as a result, were soon trading at $120. This attracted the envy of others, and Daniel Drew began to short the stock on the NYSE, contracting to sell blocks of shares at lower and lower prices, but Vanderbilt just kept buying, at higher and higher prices. Drew and his partners were trapped; they ended up having to "cover" their short sales – by buying and delivering the contracted stock – at $179, far more than they had earlier sold it for.

Richer than ever, Vanderbilt bought up the Hudson River Railway and ballooned that stock from $25 to $150. Once again, Drew and others began to short the shares in both the Harlem and Hudson railways, although, this time, they took the precaution of bribing the New York State legislature to pass a series of laws interfering with the operation of the lines. This, they were sure, would cause the stock to plummet and make them rich. But it didn't. Vanderbilt had enough accumulated capital by now to keep on buying, and eventually forced Harlem shares to $265. Members of the state legislature, who had joined the fun by shorting stocks, had to slink home from Albany without paying their boarding-house bills.

Next, Vanderbilt made a grab for the New York Central, running between Albany and Buffalo, which connected to his own lines at Albany for the trip to New York. When the Central's main shareholders, among them William Astor and Edward Cunard, resisted his advances, Vanderbilt cut his own service at the Albany Bridge. He did this suddenly, in mid-winter, forcing passengers to stumble across the frozen Hudson River, dragging their own baggage, to get from the Central to the Hudson line. When a storm of protests arose, Vanderbilt asked innocently, "Can't I do what I want with my own?" He refused to restore the connection until the Central shareholders caved in and turned over their lines to him. He then merged ten railways into one, and raised ticket prices. Then he recapitalized the new corporation and paid out a stock dividend of $44 million, most of which went to him, as principal shareholder. One night, according to W. A. Croffut, another Vanderbilt biographer, he left the downtown New York office of his son-in-law carrying a suitcase which turned out to contain $6 million in cash, just part of his loot. "There was," wrote Croffut, "another $20 million besides."

To complete his railway system, Vanderbilt began buying into the Erie Railway, and again ran up against Drew, who now had two new and younger partners, Jay Gould and Diamond Jim Fisk. The result was a five-year contest, called "The Erie War," in which each side bought judges, bribed legislators, and manipulated stock. Drew, Fisk, and Gould authorized the issuance of $10 million worth of Erie bonds, which were "convertible," that is, they could be exchanged for stock in the company. These are now a conventional market vehicle, but they were not so common in the 1860s. The bonds were ordinary debt instruments, loans to the company, with a fixed interest rate. To get control of the railway, Vanderbilt would not only have to buy up more than half the shares, but all the convertible bonds as well. He was pouring out real dollars and getting back paper, and he didn't like it much.

The Commodore bought a judge to bring injunctions against his rivals to stop issuing shares; Gould went out and bought another judge to issue counter-injunctions. The more shares Vanderbilt bought, the more the Erie Ring, as they came to be called, printed. Jim Fisk told a reporter, "If this printing press don't break down, I'll be damned if I don't give the old hog all he wants of Erie!"

Vanderbilt got his tame judge to order the arrest of Drew, Gould, and Fisk for contempt of his injunction, but, forewarned, they fled across the river to New Jersey, holed up in a hotel, and continued their war. Gould came into his own at this time, running the railroad, dictating the ring's strategy, and booming the stock, all at the same time. In the end, it was Vanderbilt who sued for peace, sending a handwritten note to Drew that read: "Drew: I'm sick of the whole damn business. Come and see me. Van Derbilt."

The Erie Ring agreed to pay the Commodore about $4.5 million, a portion of the money he reckoned had been stolen from him via the ring's printing press, and he left the railroad alone after that.

These stock-players had made it clear that the real money was to be made, not in running companies, but in gambling with the stock and, as William Vanderbilt, the Commodore's son and heir, was to say later, "The public be damned."

Gould, the manager behind the Erie Ring, was, in many ways, the most interesting of all the robber barons. A dour, shrewd, manipulative man, he never seemed to get the slightest pleasure out of all the millions he piled up. A country-store clerk and surveyor's assistant in Delaware County, New York, he saved up $5,000 by the time he was twenty, and went into partnership with Zadoc Pratt, a wealthy and experienced tanner in the town of Goldsborough. Pratt allowed Gould to run the business, which somehow never made money, and Pratt suspected, though he was never able to prove, that Gould was looting the till. He finally sold out to Gould for half the amount he had invested. Gould got another partner, Charles Leupp, and tried to corner the market in hides, but he ended by losing all the firm's capital. Leupp shot himself, and Gould moved on to New York to try again, investing in railroad stocks. He was one of the first takeover artists, although the phrase did not exist in his day. He would buy enough stock in a company to gain a directorship and, from that vantage point, do all he could to wreck the business. In the case of railway companies in which he was interested, this included spreading false rumours about the dangerous state of the line's equipment.

Stock prices would plunge and, when they hit rock bottom, Gould would buy up control. Then he would either fix the line up again and run it for a profit, or simply boom the stock up to the point where it could be unloaded at a huge profit.

The Public, a contemporary business journal, wrote:

> When he began to wreck railroads again – to squeeze the juice out of his oranges, and offer the empty skins to the public at an advanced price, we called attention to the fact that he was swallowing the juice, and advised investors not to buy empty skins at twice the price of good oranges.

Soon, people had other matters to occupy their minds, as the robber barons unveiled some new implements to aid in the shearing of the lambs. One of the great shearers of all time was John Davison Rockefeller. Rockefeller, like most of the robber barons, had a profitable, rather than a militant, Civil War, as a wholesaler of grain, hay, and meat. After the war, he invested his gains in the oil business but, unlike his rivals who took off as much as 100 per cent of their investment as profits each year, Rockefeller ploughed his back into the business for expansion. In 1872, he organized the South Improvement Company, to "rationalize" the oil industry. Then he forced the railway companies, who moved the oil in those days, not only to pay a rebate to himself and his fellow members of the South Improvement Company, but to charge other refiners a premium for using the same railway. The premium was then turned over to Rockefeller and his cronies. Any railway company that refused to pay the kickback was attacked, often physically, by gangs of hired goons.

With this considerable economic advantage working in his favour, Rockefeller approached his rivals and persuaded them to follow his lead on prices, profit margins, and production quotas. If they didn't like it, he would buy them out at between thirty and fifty cents on the dollar, or drop prices and hold them down long enough to drive them out of business.

God and Herbert Spencer approved. "I had our plan clear in mind. It was right. I knew it as a matter of conscience. It was right between me and my God," said Rockefeller. One of those who sold out to the combination of God and Rockefeller later recounted that when the oil millionaire came to see him, he said, "I have ways of making money that you know not of."

He did, too, and the best of these ways was the trust, invented by Samuel T. Dodd, a Rockefeller lawyer, in 1879. The Standard Oil Trust required the shareholders of a number of oil companies to assign their stock to a board of trustees. In return, they were given trust certificates that received dividends out of the pooled profits. The shareholders still owned the stocks, but couldn't vote them; all the decisions were made by the Supreme Council of the Trust, which met every day for lunch in Rockefeller's New York office to set prices and policies on crude oil, marketing, and transportation in a way that would ensure massive profits. Rockefeller owned his own OPEC. In 1879, on a pooled capital of $3.5 million, the Standard Oil Trust paid out dividends of $3.15 million. Despite a huge drop in the price of crude oil, the trust managed to keep prices to consumers up for two straight decades.

Trusts sprang up in every sector, from sugar to steel, from oil to coffins. There was a meat-packing trust, which turned diseased swine, goats, and cows into sausages and tinned meat, and a whisky trust whose only outside rivals seemed to get blown up, until, pretty soon, everyone was charging the same price for whisky.

No one could control the trusts, least of all the officials of the stock exchange, although an attempt was made in the Sherman Anti-Trust Act of 1890. (So named, another senator commented, because "Sen. John Sherman had nothing whatsoever to do with it.") The act made it illegal for a firm to "attempt to monopolize" its line of business, or to combine with others for that purpose. The trusts' lawyers only had to say in court that their boys weren't attempting to monopolize, just getting together to talk things over, and that was the end of that. The trusts were never outlawed, they simply became outmoded with the spread of a new stock gimmick invented by a "rosy little lawyer" named James Brooks Dill in 1888.

Dill had been asked by the governor of New Jersey to dream up some way to make more corporations settle in New Jersey. Sure, said Dill: simply allow corporations to buy the shares of other corporations. At that time, this was illegal, but the government of New Jersey passed a 132-word law making it legal for any corporation doing business in New Jersey to own the shares of other corporations. Without this law, you would never have heard of half the companies that rule the markets today.

J. Pierpont Morgan became the busiest user of the new law. It worked this way: if there were ten companies in competition with each other, each with capital stock worth, say, $1 million, a holding company would offer the owners collectively $2 million for their shares. The owners would sell. The holding company would then launch itself on the stock market and, based on its monopoly of the business, would either immediately begin to make large profits or – it came to the same thing – appear likely to make large profits, upon which its shares would shoot up. Frederick Lewis Allen, who wrote the most interesting biography of Morgan, *The Great Pierpont Morgan,* commented that Dill's invention was "a device for the manufacture of millionaires."

Morgan, using holding companies, put together a steel conglomerate that grew large enough to challenge Andrew Carnegie's Carnegie Company, the nation's largest by far. To avoid competition – always saluted in stock-market myth, always avoided if possible – Carnegie, who owned 58 per cent of his own firm, was offered more and more for his shares, until he finally accepted. In 1901, in return for $500 million in stocks and bonds of the new United States Steel Corporation, Carnegie sold out. His share of the takeover came to $225,639,000 in paper, which an eager stock market would soon double. The American Wire and Steel

Company, owned by "Bet-a-Million" Gates, and Lake Superior Consolidated Iron Mines, owned by Rockefeller, were folded into the mix, again in return for stocks in U.S. Steel. The total capitalization of the new company was $1,402,846,817. That was the amount of paper issued to the companies taken over. U.S. Steel wasn't worth anything like that. The company later wrote off $768 million of this watered stock, added the cost to its customers' prices, and went on its merry way.

Morgan then hired "Wizard Jim" Keene, one of the great stock boomers of the era, to create a market for all the stock he had to issue to pay for his conglomerate, and Keene began churning the market. Common shares, issued at a value of $38 each, were soon selling for $55. Morgan and his allies awarded themselves 1.3 million shares for their work in putting together U.S. Steel, and walked off with a profit of $57,515,000.

Like many of the deals worked by our much-touted "risk takers," this involved no risk whatever. Carnegie was paid off in paper – stocks and bonds issued from the company treasury – and this was commuted into money when the customers rolled up to buy it. Because the new company now had a lock on the market, and could charge exorbitant prices for its products, the money to pay the interest on the bonds and dividends on the stocks would be wrung out of the withers of ordinary consumers. So when the gang issued themselves shares, they were simply manufacturing millions out of thin air, which would be paid by everyone who bought anything made of steel.

It was now clear that more money could be made out of stocks than steel, that money could be made to shoal out of the market in almost unimaginable quantities, that stocks themselves could be used as instruments to control, not merely other companies, but entire markets, and that the essential nature of the stock-market game was not to produce and create goods for consumers, but to gamble.

As for the exchange itself, where all this activity took place, it was self-regulating. Better not to meddle. God and the brokers would look after matters, operating under the one rule that Diamond Jim Fisk gave to a congressional committee that had investigated one of the recurrent stock-market scandals: "Let everyone carry out his own corpse."

It would remain that way, pretty much, until the whole wild and untrammelled affair came thundering down in the Great Crash of 1929.

CHAPTER THREE

The Great, Thrumming Dance: Maple Leaf Division.

Canadian Stock Markets

Resolved: That Toronto being the most central point of attraction to capitalists seeking investment in Canada, this city is deemed in every respect the most convenient locality in which to establish an Association of Brokers. In doing so we consider we are discharging an important duty to Canada by the establishment of this Association and are helping to promote and extend the general business of the country through the greater circulation of credit.

    – from the Resolution to establish a Toronto Stock Exchange, July 26, 1852.

$

Canadians are unduly modest about their own history, which they see, by and large, as dull and boring and lacking in the dash, flair, and rascality that marks American history. Not true. While we have never had anyone quite match Jay Gould's lifelong practice of shearing the lambs, we did have the nation's highest elected official, Prime Minister Sir John A. Macdonald, up to his hips in the Canadian Pacific Railway Scandal, one of the great stock scams of all time, and in general, on the rapscallion front, we have no need to hang our heads in shame. I would put our scoundrels up against their scoundrels every time. And here, as elsewhere, they have found their freest expression in what Alexander Ross refers to as "the great, thrumming dance" of the stock exchange.

We had securities markets before we had a country. Brokers trading in securities on the London markets began to emerge in a number of cities in the 1830s, at a time when Canadian industry scarcely existed. They dealt in the paper of the formative banks, railways, land developers, and the bonds of a number of provinces and municipalities, as well as a handful of utilities. There was really no need for an active native market in equity securities – stocks – for two reasons. One was that so much of our economy was owned or directed from England and capital was provided there; another was that the few large firms that did exist were tightly held, in private hands, and the Family Compact in Upper Canada and the Château Clique in Lower Canada meant to keep it that way. When the Bank of Upper Canada, which was securely in the hands of Family Compact members, became the mortgagee in 1836 of the first machinery works in the nation, it foreclosed on the mortgage, broke up the foundry, and disposed of the pieces at a sheriff's sale. People went back to buying their machinery in England as the lord and the British intended.

Lacking a formal stock exchange, our forefathers were forced to run their stock swindles on their own, at least at first, and considering the handicap they worked under, they did it remarkably well.

Take Francis Hincks. Born in County Cork, in Ireland, he emigrated to the town of York in 1830, and became the cashier, later the manager, of the Bank of the People. With the backing of his business friends, he plunged into politics, and became prime minister of the united Province of Canada in 1851. In that post he helped with the stock manipulation of the railway companies whose major financing was government subsidies. He was a land speculator, swindler – he once helped push through a swindle on City of Toronto bonds with the help of the mayor – and the cheerful recipient of bribes. For helping to sell the charter of the scandal-ridden Grand Trunk Railway to an English firm, he received a pay-off of £50,400 in Grand Trunk stock. However, he was exposed by George Brown, a Reform Liberal MP. He said the stock wasn't really his; he was just holding it for anyone who might be interested in buying shares in such a wonderful new venture. When the Grand Trunk scandal, which featured pay-offs to almost every elected politician in the land, got too ripe, Hincks was forced to resign. However, the Governor General, Lord Elgin – who had also pocketed Grand Trunk stock – got him a job as governor general of Barbados and the Windward Islands, and he left the country for a few judicious years. When he came back in 1869, Confederation had taken place, and Hincks went to Ottawa as Sir John A. Macdonald's minister of finance. He was soon back at the trough, selling off the Canadian fishing industry to raise money for more railway speculation. He also steered Canada's first Bank Act through Parliament, which was only right, since he held a lot of bank stocks on the side. He capped his career by arranging the Canadian Pacific Railway contract that led to the Pacific Scandal.

Ousted again by that scandal, he put together the merger of two shaky banks into the Consolidated Bank, which forthwith went belly up – but not before Hincks had managed to sell out at a profit. When the bankruptcy occurred, it was revealed that Hincks didn't even own enough stock to qualify as a director of the bank, although he was. It was also revealed that he had falsified company returns to the federal government during the struggle to keep the bank afloat, and he was charged with fraud, and convicted. He appealed, and the conviction was reversed on a technicality. The most influential financial paper of the period, the *Monetary Times*, while unable to deny that Hincks had done what he was convicted of doing, opined editorially that he must have been temporarily insane when he did it. He died full of riches and honour, with a knighthood.

Hincks's story suggests that about the only real difference

between our early stock manipulators and the American ones was that they didn't knight theirs.

I do not intend to retell here the oft-told tale of the Pacific Scandal that temporaily incommoded Hincks, except to note that the men behind the CPR managed, in their manipulation of its stock, to achieve feats of legerdemain and outright theft worthy of an Ivan Boesky. More than eight hundred thousand shares were spread around as bribes, and very little of the money raised from investors was actually wasted on the railway; it went back to the investors, with dividends, while the taxpayers picked up the bills. In 1885, Edward Blake, the Liberal leader in Parliament, pointed out that, before the road was open for traffic, every cent of cash put in by the initial shareholders had either been repaid to them or set aside as guaranteed dividends.

Another of our rapscallions did even better than Hincks: he became a lord. This was George Stephen, president of the Bank of Montreal, who siphoned $8 million out of the bank, without the knowledge or consent of its directors or shareholders, to gamble in the stocks of the St. Paul and Minneapolis Railway. Actually, this wasn't as much of a gamble as most stock investments, because Stephen took the precaution of having a fabricated report prepared for the line's major shareholders in Holland, which indicated that the railway was on the verge of financial ruin. They sold out, cheaply, and Stephen got himself a pretty good railway for very little money, all of which had been provided, interest free, by others – even if they didn't know about it. However, the American accountant who had written the fake report brought a lawsuit against Stephen, because he said he had been cheated on his share of the proceeds. The first judge to hear the case threw it out, on the grounds that it was not his job to decide "how plunder should be divided among different members of a gang," but an appeal court allowed the suit to go forward. By the time it had worked its way through the courts, and the plaintiff's claim had been dismissed, the railway was doing so well that Stephen was able to put the money he had stolen back in the bank, and no harm was done. Stephen went on to greater wonders in the bank, Parliament, and the C P R, and finally became Lord Mount Stephen.

For really effective plundering, however, we needed a stock exchange. It was founded in 1852 because, according to Robert E. Forbes and David L. Johnston, authors of *Canadian Companies and the Stock Exchanges,* "By this time the need for central, specialized and efficient market places to facilitate corporate financing requirements in the increasingly complex economy was apparent."

The men behind the Association of Brokers, whose founding resolution is quoted at the top of this chapter, were, in the main, merchants, grain dealers, and what was called "bill brokers" – buyers and sellers of commercial paper. The major concern of these men was wheat and flour in the export market. At the same time, a good deal of speculation swirled around the stock of the Grand Trunk Railway, which, like so many construction projects of the time, was far more efficient at extracting and dispersing the funds of investors than it was at building a railway. All this stock activity was taking place almost entirely through the London market, which did not seem right. It was felt, correctly, that until there was a place for local investors to tap into the markets, there would be no significant capital accumulation in Canada. This first 1852 attempt to found an exchange in Toronto didn't come to much, since very few meetings of the brokers ever took place, so the exchange was relaunched in 1854, and moved into its own building on Wellington Street. This didn't work, either, despite the fact that the exchange building had a barber shop, a refreshment salon, thirty-one offices, and a trading hall. What it didn't have was much business, since Canada was still operated mainly as a producer of staples for the British market, so the exchange withered away. The Imperial Bank of Canada took over the building.

In 1861, there was yet another attempt, as the old exchange

was reorganized into a loose assemblage of brokers. A second exchange, called the Toronto Stock and Mining Exchange (TSME), was formed in 1867 around the increasing trade in mining stocks, but the early gold boom that gave rise to it collapsed, and, after a series of bank failures – the banks, by and large, were looted into insolvency by their own directors – both exchanges failed. That was in 1869. It seems possible, though I have nowhere seen the theory put forward by a reputable historian, that one reason these exchanges had a problem getting customers was that they were attended by so much fraud and manipulation, but it is also true that there was very little Canadian money available for investment at anything like a reasonable rate until after 1870, when Confederation brought an economic boom to Ontario.

In the meantime, in Montreal, a Board of Brokers had been established in 1863. It became the Montreal Stock Exchange in 1872, and was officially incorporated two years later. It grew very slowly, but did not keel over like its Toronto counterpart and, as money became more available in the 1870s, even Toronto revived. The exchange there was restarted for a third time in 1871, given a provincial charter in 1878, and incorporated in 1879. Henry Pellatt, later Sir Henry, was one of the driving forces behind the new group, and if he was a little strange – he built a monstrous "medieval" castle called Casa Loma on a cliff overlooking downtown Toronto – he certainly had energy. The new exchange leased office space in 1881 and established a stock ticker there, on which the broker-members could receive quotations from the New York market. Five years later, when the first trans-Atlantic cable was in place, they could buy and sell on European markets as well, and handle orders in Canadian stocks.

Not that there were many. For many years, these exchanges dealt mainly in banks and transportation companies because, as Tom Naylor notes in *The History of Canadian Business, 1867-1914,* "the corporate form in industry remained rare until near the turn of the century." If you wanted to start up a manufacturing concern, you got a bank loan, if you could. Alexander Galt's Sherbrooke Cotton Mill was established in 1844 as a joint-stock company, but it was a rare exception.

The fact that they were dealing in bank stocks, transportation issues, and, beginning in the early 1880s, insurance firms, should have ensured that the markets were run with modest decorum, but this was not the case. Almost from the beginning, brokers hit on the happy practice of shorting bank stocks as a quick way to make money. The trouble with shorting, as we have already seen, is that, if the shorted stock goes up rather than down, the gamble backfires. This happened to one Montreal brokerage, C. Dorwin and Company, causing its owner to flee the country, lugging with him what remained of the firm's cash.

To show that they were up on all the latest fads, some of the Canadian brokers used a technique called "kiting," which had been developed in the United States. Two brokers would exchange cheques and pass them back and forth without cashing them, using the credit thus created to buy up the stocks of a target company on margin (we will come to a detailed explanation of "margin" later). The new company would then be looted to provide the cash that would allow the cheques to be covered.

This system went badly awry when, in 1876, a deal was made between Louis Forget and Strathy and Strathy and Messrs. Bond Brothers, two of Montreal's top firms, to take control of the Montreal Telegraph Company. If there was one rule to this business, it was "don't cash the damn cheque," but somebody at Bond Brothers forgot this, and very foolishly presented a cheque for $54,000 from Louis Forget to the Exchange Bank, when there wasn't a dime in the till to meet it. This happened right in the middle of the takeover, and the end result was the failure of Bond Brothers.

The exchanges no sooner got going than competition sprang up in the form of "bucket shops," which were soon doing a roaring business. A bucket shop was a brokerage house operated on even more broad-minded and less inhibited terms than the ordinary brokerage house. Sometimes the brokers would execute trades for clients in the normal way, and sometimes they wouldn't. It all depended. Quite often they would take orders for a purchase of stocks or commodities and simply sit on them, waiting to see which way the market went. A judge in Napanee, Ontario, dealing with the case of a local bucket shop that specialized in pork futures, referred to it as "dealing in pork without any pigs."

Suppose a customer put in an order for 100 shares of Company A, when the price was sitting at $10 a share. The customer would pay over $1,000, and the bucket shop would say thank you very much. If the shares went down to, say, $5, the broker would explain to the customer that they had sold him out at a loss of $5 a share, give him back $500, less commissions on buying and selling, and pocket the rest. But if the price went up, and the contract he thought he had purchased was worth more, the operator would simply throw the order in the trash, "the bucket." Let 'em sue. If the customer shorted a stock and turned out to be wrong, the same thing could work in reverse. The borrowed stocks were sold – in theory, anyway – for $10 on the day the deal was made, and now had to be replaced – again, only in theory – for $15. The customer owed the broker an additional $500 on a trade that had never taken place. This was a variation of the "blank buying" game used earlier in Amsterdam. The difference between this and ordinary short-selling was that no shares were ever exchanged; the entire arrangement was a fiction.

The regular brokers began to press for legislation to have the bucket shops classified as ordinary gaming houses, but there was a snag. As economic historian Tom Naylor points out,

> It proved exceedingly difficult to define the bucket shop operation in such a way as not to include the activities of virtually every established broker in the country. Their business was, after all, precisely the same, and the sole

objective of the bill was to open up the business formerly done by the bucket shops for takeover by the established brokers.

However, when the Bucket Shop Act was passed in 1888, it got around this difficulty, by making it illegal to perform a share sale without transferring real shares. In the bucket-shop transaction, there was no assurance that there would ever be a delivery of merchandise or stock certificate or futures option. It was a gamble, pure and simple, while in the case of the orthodox broker, there was at least a piece of paper at the end of it all. In court, it proved difficult to get convictions under the new law, in part because in some cases the same brokers ran bucket shops and ordinary brokerage operations.

In one of the more intriguing cases, William Weir, the president of the Banque Ville Marie in Montreal, ran a regular brokerage house alongside the bank, and sometimes got the funds confused. He also invested money lifted from the bank in a bucket shop, through another broker. At the same time, the bank's accountant was using bank funds to gamble in stocks in the same bucket shop. When the constant drain on its resources began to put the bank in trouble, Weir and his business colleagues started to manipulate the stock to raise money. Then a bank teller, getting into the swing of things, made off with $58,000, and when word of that leaked out, there was a run on the bank, which promptly collapsed. Hard to know whom to blame.

With the completion of the CPR in 1885, the rich resources of western Canada were opened to an eager, and speculating, public. New exchanges sprang up to handle the mining business. In 1897, the nation's first mining exchange was formed around the new mines in Rossland, B.C., but it didn't last long, since most of the money for investment was elsewhere. That same year, fifteen brokers in Toronto were charged with misrepresenting the capital of the mining companies they represented to attract subscribers, but nothing came of the charges. However, when another boom started around gold mines near Cobalt, Ontario, the government issued certificates to attest that there was, indeed, ore in the claim, and the stock promoters used these to con British investors into believing that the stocks they were flogging had the backing of the Canadian government. Stock promoters would also buy up mining claims from prospectors and float companies and issue stocks for these companies. Then they would manipulate their prices upward by planted rumours and outright lies. The same thing happened in Rossland, where a local newspaper cried out that, "It is high time that some warning was given to investors of the futility of supplying money to dig holes in the ground in the hope that Canada may at some time produce a few odd pieces of precious metals."

This editorial writer had missed the point; it wasn't the holes in the ground that produced the money, but the hype behind the holes.

In 1898, the Mining Stock Exchange was opened in Toronto, with a membership of fifteen brokers. It passed a resolution saying that no others need apply, and that led to the creation of the Toronto Mining and Industrial Exchange. The two were merged in 1900 and were folded into the TSE in 1934. In 1903, the Winnipeg Stock Exchange was incorporated by an act of the Manitoba legislature, but it didn't open for business until 1909, and didn't even have a trading floor. The brokers chatted with each other or, later, called each other on the telephone. They still do. The real trading in town is done in commodities, over at the Winnipeg Commodity Exchange.

The Vancouver Stock Exchange, taking up where the Rossland Exchange had left off, opened in 1907, and immediately began to give off a stench of corruption and speculation that extended, with very little interruption, until very recently.

The British Canadian Wood Pulp and Paper Company, one of the VSE's early listings, was run by a promoter named J. C. W.

Stanley, but he came under fire when another of his ventures, the euphoniously named Fish Oil and Guano Company, Ltd., was petitioned into bankruptcy in Ireland, and an English newspaper reporter noted that,

> Mr. Stanley is now turning from fish to paper, and he has submitted to the board a process of his own, by which he not only extracts soda, but also gas and turpentine from wood. Some years ago Mr. Stanley had an invention by which he was to convert the refuse of the dustbin into paper. The only thing this company did in this line was to issue shares, and I venture to think that the only gas which this new process is likely to emit is that which emanates from Mr. Stanley himself.

David Cruise and Alison Griffiths, whose instructive and delightful book on the VSE, *Fleecing the Lambs*, contains this quote, add, "Stanley's schemes sound remarkably similar to many of the industrial ventures launched on the VSE in later years."

The Calgary Stock Exchange was formed in 1913 to trade in petroleum and gas stocks, in response to the first oil boom in Alberta's Turner Valley. Edmonton, its rival city, got an exchange in 1953, but it was unable to attract enough business to survive, and disappeared again in 1958. The Calgary Exchange very decently renamed itself the Alberta Exchange in 1974.

A second exchange for the city of Montreal was added in 1926. This was the Montreal Curb Market, and it grouped together brokers who had formerly met on the sidewalk in front of the Montreal Stock Exchange to deal in securities not listed there (sometimes, for every good reason). "It met the need," write Robert E. Forbes and David L. Johnston, "for a market in less mature and more speculative stocks, the issuers of which might not have been able to comply with the listing requirements of the MSE." High flyers and low scramblers, most of them, with a few worthy and indigent unknowns thrown in. The Curb changed its name to the Canadian Stock Exchange in 1953, and was merged with the MSE on January 1, 1974.

We had all the major exchanges in place in Canada quite early in this century. We had also, by then, established what I think can be called the flavour of our exchanges. They were lively places, where the incautious investor could be stripped down to the skivvies in short order, but where those in authority could always be counted on to look upon the transgressor with a forgiving eye. I find instructive the tale of Sir Rodolphe Forget, as told by Tom Naylor.

Forget was frustrated by the fact that most of the action seemed to be taking place elsewhere, that Canadian stock exchanges, in the late 1800s and early 1900s, dealt far more in American stocks than they did in our own, and that it was very difficult indeed to raise equity for Canadian ventures. In 1907, Forget began to put together a venture, La Banque Internationale, with French financing. The bank would have, as its major purpose, the provision of loans to Canadian stockbrokers, equity underwriters, and promoters, notably himself. In his search for capital in France, Forget was forced, as so many promoters are, to edit the facts a trifle, and indeed, led the French investors to believe they were in one of those no-lose situations you read about but seldom meet. When the Ministry of Finance found out about this, it refused to issue the necessary approval for the bank.

That was corrected in 1911, when there was an election, and Forget ran for the Tories against the mayor of Quebec, a close friend of Liberal Prime Minister Sir Wilfrid Laurier. The Tories won, and Forget got his bank certificate, along with a seat in Parliament. This did not turn out to be good news for the French investors, who had put up 80 per cent of the capital for the fledgling bank, because the Canadian directors immediately began to deal themselves stocks and engage in the other little bits of chicanery that so often accompany this kind of operation.

When a group of alarmed French directors arrived to investigate, they were barred from a Canadian directors' meeting. They then persuaded the French government to launch an investigation, which caused the near collapse of the bank stocks, and in 1912 Henry Pellatt stepped in and merged La Banque Internationale with the Home Bank, a merger that was effectively bankrupt by 1914. More wallpaper for the shareholders.

As punishment for his illicit activities, Sir Rodolphe was appointed to the the Banking and Commerce Committee of the House of Commons, which, Naylor notes, "was responsible for shaping legislation regulating the operation of financial institutions and otherwise standing on guard for the monetary morality of Canada."

By the time activities on the stock exchanges were suspended at the outbreak of the First World War in 1914, Canadians had shown that they were as adept as Americans at the various ways of milking money out of the markets, although it was still, for the most part, a game played by the rich (or, all too often, the erstwhile rich). It was only after that war that a wide sector of the population was exposed to the possibility of investing in the stock markets, in a boom that ended, as it was bound to end, with the Great Crash of 1929. We will turn our attention to these developments in the next chapter.

CHAPTER FOUR

Pardon Me, but Are You Using This Ledge?

The Depression and Its Aftermath

The consensus of the judgment of the millions whose valuations function on that admirable market, the Stock Exchange, is that stocks are not at present over-valued. Where is that group of men with the all-embracing wisdom which will entitle them to veto the judgment of this intelligent multitude?
   – Joseph Stagg Lawrence, *Economist,* June 1929.

$

During the first quarter of this century, playing the stock markets was, by and large, an occupation of the well-to-do – the only ones who had money for the game – or of outright gamblers and speculators, who used other people's money or substituted gall for cash. It was not, at least not yet, the widow and the orphan who got fleeced. All that changed, however, with the burst of prosperity that followed the post-war depression of 1920-21. Not only did national incomes increase in Canada and the United States, they shifted. In Canada, income from agriculture rose 36 per cent between 1926 and 1929, while in mining, it shot up 171 per cent, in manufacturing, 96 per cent, in trade, 193 per cent, and in commercial services, which included finance, 137 per cent. (The figures are from A. E. Safarian's monumental study, *The Canadian Economy in the Great Depression.*) We were in the process of moving from an agrarian, rural society – great gamblers, of course, but on the weather and wheat futures, not stocks – to an industrial and urban society.

There was a lot more money sloshing about, and more people had some of it, and invested. Thus, when the Crash came, it flattened more than the rich (indeed, some of the richer scoundrels not only survived, but prospered, as they went short in the collapsing markets – although they were the exceptions). An inevitable result of the wider distribution of wealth was contained in one of the nuggets dug out of these events by Douglas Fetherling in *Gold Diggers of 1929: Canada and the Great Stock Market Crash:* "According to the *Daily Star,* the events of October and November were estimated to have cost $12 million to a total of 35,000 Torontonians in various walks of life, about 6,000 of them women."

Toronto, I hasten to add, was not Canada's main financial centre at the time; the numbers in Montreal must have been at least double. Everybody played the market: bootblacks exchanged tips with the brokers whose shoes they polished; hotel maids borrowed and bought stock on rumours disturbed while they dusted; everybody who could lay his or her hands on the wherewithal with which to gamble did so, because, as everybody knew, in this wonderful new world anyone could be a millionaire.

Is there a familiar ring in all this? Doug Fetherling, in trying to account for the Crash – once he finishes dealing with contributing causes, such as a credit system that was much too loose – writes that, "The real scoundrel was greed, avarice, the get-rich-quick psychosis which overtook a remarkably wide spectrum of the North American population."

I have not noticed any diminution of greed of late and, as we will see, modern gamblers can actually spin more money over faster than ever they could in 1929. It may therefore be illuminating to look back to the Crash with two narrow issues in mind. The first is to examine some of the wondrous ways that were used then, first to bloat and then to sink the market; the second is to try to guess whether we should expect the same thing to happen again. Alas, the only lesson to be learned is that we apparently learned nothing.

In what follows, I am going to spend much more time explaining the tricks and dodges used than in detailing how we have not learned anything. How can ignorance be detailed? It should not therefore be assumed that the second point is less important. The two are joined. All the old dodges are being repeated today, with a few new variations. Nobody seems to care. The stock markets lost more, far more, and far faster, in October 1987 than in October 1929, but because the economy was not so profoundly affected, we went merrily along as if there was no need to account for the loss of a trillion dollars in investment money, much less to do anything substantive about it. There is more opportunity to gamble in more ways today, with greater risk, than in 1929. It isn't a question of whether another financial catastrophe will strike – only when.

The market boom of the 1920s, as everyone now knows, was built on a series of expansions in the underlying economy, which were translated into stock prices that quickly outran reality. Corporate profits were good and growing in a wide variety of firms and economic sectors, and yields were favourable on bond issues. But there was a sea-change in the air. In 1924, an important study in the United States concluded that, for the first time, common stocks were a better way to invest money than bonds, which, until then, made up the major part of every prudent portfolio. With the emergence of scores of new companies eager for capital that could be translated into factories and machinery and inventories to be sold at a profit, people began to be willing to incur the greater risk of share-buying, rather than the staid, steady, and less profitable bond.

After all, a bond is simply a debt instrument. It pays a set rate of interest for a set period of time, and then returns the principal;

there is not the same opportunity to make a real capital gain that there is with the common share. To help things along, some companies with stock issues to plug began to give away shares to persuade customers to invest in their bonds, and that may have created clients for other stock sales too. But the crucial factor was that there was a growing managerial and professional class with money to invest, and an increasing number of firms of solid reputation and proven worth in which to invest. Finally, there was the overlay of nonsense, tricked out as economic wisdom, which then, as now, persuaded the intelligent investor, i.e., anyone with money or credit, that he or she could reap riches while playing a key role in the wondrous saga of the free-enterprise system. Gambling is not gambling, it is "investing in Canada" – or America.

The market began to move. At first, it moved modestly. The *New York Times* Industrial Index, which tracked 25 stock prices, went from 106 to 137 between late May and the end of 1924, and to 181 by the end of 1925. After drooping in early 1926, the market recovered and rose steadily through 1927 and, with some lurching, took off through 1928 and the first eight months of 1929. The Dow Jones Industrial Average, created in 1884 by *Wall Street Journal* Publisher Charles Dow to track 30 stocks, beginning with Allied Corporation and ending with Woolworth's, marched steadily forward from 90 in mid-1924, with brief hiccups in early 1926 and early 1928, to 381 in September 1929.

This upsurge did not reflect a parallel increase in earnings; it was the pressure of speculation. Between 1923 and 1929, the dividends on National Biscuit stock rose from $35.42 per share to $57.20, a nice gain of $22.22; but the stock went from $319 to $1,316 – a jump of $997 that had only the most tenuous connection with earnings. This pattern was repeated time and again in stock after stock. A bull market was under way, and the sheep, as they had done before and will do again, were persuaded to believe that this one would never end. It was this belief, more than anything else, that turned investors into crap-shooters.

An investor seeking to place his or her funds with the best advantage will look at the underlying value of any corporation whose stocks appear to have appeal. The easiest and quickest measure of this value is to examine the firm's price-earnings ratio, always referred to as the "P/E." If a company whose stock is currently selling for $10 earns profits at the rate of $1 per share annually, then the P/E is 10 (it's actually 10/1, but the 1 is dropped), and not bad, either. (We will look at the P/E again, since it can be manipulated, but for the moment, this simple guide will do.) A P/E of 10/1 represents a 10 per cent return on your money, and if it keeps on being paid, this is a sound investment. It will likely return a capital gain when the time comes to sell, because the price of the share will have risen; you get your 10 per cent per annum and a bonus besides. The P/E on National Biscuit in the example above was 35.42/319, or a P/E of 9 in 1923, a good buy, and 57.20/1316, or a P/E of 23, which should have been a goodbye, in 1929.

A speculator, wishing to fling his or her money on the table, doesn't really give a hoot about the P/E ratio of stock to be acquired – except to the extent that others, potentially purchasers, may be influenced by it. What concerns the speculator is the stock price shown in the morning paper or on the afternoon stock-ticker; nothing else. The speculator buys a stock because it has become "hot" or is about to become hot, according to someone, anyone, with an interest in the market, claimed expertise, or even a good grip on a rumour; the speculator holds the stock until it is judged that the maximum price has been attained, and then sells. Simple, eh? The trick is, and always has been, to pick that hallowed moment for unloading. Move too soon, and you have lost a profit; you sit weeping on the sidelines while the Wild River Oil you bought for $2 and sold for $5 goes to $10, $15, $20. Hold too long, and your $5 stock is back down to fifty cents. Instead of winning $3, you lose $1.50. Curses.

No one has ever made the point better than John Maynard Keynes did in *The General Theory of Employment, Interest and Money* in 1936:

The actual, private object of most skilled investment today is to "beat the gun," as the Americans so well express it, to outwit the crowd, and to pass the bad, or depreciating, half-crown to the other fellow.

The battle of wits to anticipate the basis of conventional valuation a few months hence, rather than the prospective yield of an investment over a long term of years, does not even require gulls amongst the public to feed the maws of the professional – it can be played by professionals among themselves. Nor is it necessary that anyone should keep his simple faith in the conventional basis of valuation having any genuine long-term validity. For it is, so to speak, a game of Snap, of Old Maid, of musical chairs – a pastime in which he is victor who says *Snap* neither too soon nor too late, who passes the Old Maid to his neighbour before the game is over, who secures a chair for himself before the music stops.

In 1929, everybody was playing Snap, or, as it turned out, strip poker; investment was swallowed by speculation. The process was aided by the increasing use of five instruments that had been around for some time: trusts, margins, wash-trading, bucket shops, and boiler rooms.

This time the trusts were investment trusts; that is, they held shares in other trusts, which held shares in still others, unto the seventh generation. Doug Fetherling calls these, rather neatly, "capitalist co-operatives"; they were the precursors of our modern mutual funds (in Britain, investment trust is still the preferred term for mutual funds) and they were everywhere. To fill the gaping maw of public credulity, and in response to the law of supply and demand, companies began the wholesale manufacture of stocks whose only apparent purpose was to be sold. Thus, the ordinary stock-player, instead of having to guess which stocks were going to do well, could invest his tiny mite with an investment trust by buying its shares, and then allow the all-knowing managers of the trust to make the decisions for him. This meant that he had less and less control of or participation in the companies involved, but that was, if anything, a blessing. One less thing to worry about. John Kenneth Galbraith, in *The Great Crash 1929*, says, "The machinery by which Wall Street separates the opportunity to speculate from the unwanted returns and burdens of ownership is ingenious, precise, and almost beautiful."

One of the most monumental of the manufacturers of stock was the House of Morgan, revered since its first successful stock-watering operation with United States Steel, as the finest and most conservative financial operator in America. Morgan floated three companies to hold utility shares, in a market that had an insatiable appetite for them. Between 1924 and 1929, Morgan raised $5 billion on U.S. markets to buy utilities shares, but the money didn't go to buy plant and equipment; most of it went to buy up other companies and layer them together in a growing pile, spinning out still more shares. This way the holding company could parlay a small amount of equity into a huge quantity of shares. United Light and Power transformed $4 million of its own stock into voting control over $430 million worth of investments in seventy-five other companies simply by swapping with its subsidiaries. The effect, wrote William Z. Ripley, a contemporary chronicler, in *Main Street and Wall Street,* was "something like the nozzle on a hose-pipe, in speeding up the flow."

These huge holding companies were not manufacturing widgets or selling electricity, they were selling stocks, and selling stocks was far more profitable than the mundane business of business. That way madness lay, as Keynes noted:

> Speculators may do no harm as bubbles on a steady stream of enterprise. But the position is serious when enterprise becomes the bubble on a whirlpool of speculation. When the capital development of a country becomes a by-product of the activities of a casino, the job is likely to be ill-done.

In 1929 alone, 265 investment trusts were established in the United States and began churning out shares (there were about forty extant in Canada, three of which had no other purpose than to hold shares in Canadian banks). Canadians bought into the trusts in their own country, as well as across the border. Our stock markets sold more U.S. shares than Canadian; the border has never been a barrier for securities speculation.

The trusts were defended at the time as stalwart bastions against decline. If the stock market began to slide, the trusts would step in with more money to prop it up, in defence of their own interests. Then, as now, there were few voices on the sidelines to mutter, "Oh, yeah?"

Margins had been in existence almost as long as stocks had been sold. The margin is one of the many ways by which an intermediary – the broker, usually – establishes a credit account for the stock-player. You want to buy ten shares of the very prestigious and expensive Let Her Rip Enterprises at $500 a share, so you contact a broker, who will, if your credit is sound, allow you to establish a margin account with him. Instead of putting up the entire $5,000 necessary, you put up $2,500 and borrow the other $2,500 from the broker, who borrows it from the bank. Of course, you have to pay interest on the borrowed money, but that will all come out of your earnings. Why worry?

Margins declined from a normal 50 per cent down to 20 per cent and, in some cases, 10 per cent. At 20 per cent, you needed only $1,000 in cash to buy $5,000 worth of stock. But, hold on a minute, the stock you bought yesterday for $1,000 in cash and $4,000 in credit has gone up. Let Her Rip is now fetching $700 a share; your stock is worth $7,000, not $5,000. You have gained $2,000 overnight. Are you going to be fool enough to take the money and run? Of course not. Re-invest it in more stocks. Now, with the margin working for you, you can buy another $10,000 worth of stock on the basis of your $2,000 of paper earnings, on a 20 per cent margin. You own stock worth $17,000, on $1,000 down. You can march on the margins all the way to the bank; you will be a millionaire.

Hundreds and then thousands of Canadians and Americans rolled into the market with margin accounts, and, with the leverage of investment trusts multiplied by the leverage of margins, built the finest bubble the world had seen since the good old days of the South Sea Company. By late summer of 1929, the New York market was supported by, or about to buckle under the weight of, $7 billion in debt. All over the world, financial companies poured out loans to brokers for margin financing – the usual interest rate was a healthy 12 per cent – confident that they would always get it back, because the stocks backed the loans, didn't they?

We have already met wash-trading, which is the process of a group of conspirators, or a brokerage house, or a company itself, buying and selling shares over and over to manipulate the price. Sometimes, it was done through other brokerage houses in other cities, but quite often – so loose was the regulatory framework of the time – no subterfuge was necessary. As mounds of Snake River stocks crossed over at increasing prices on the ticker, outsiders, and even some insiders, would soon see the opportunity for profits. Pretty soon the wash-trading would lead to real trading, and the original holders of Snake River would unload.

All these games added to the volatility, which the stock-market officials would prefer us to call the liquidity, of the exchanges. The process was aided by the bucket shops, which blossomed and took on new devices. In one variation, the crooked broker would use part of the customer's money to provide the margin for the requested stock purchase, and the rest to short the same stock; they would use the sucker's own funds to bet against him. Sometimes the broker was in a position to influence the movement of the stock, in which case, this wasn't even a bet, it was a sure thing. Then, as now, the customer could not demand delivery of the share certificates until full payment had been made into a brokerage account, and since this was all done on margin, the suckers didn't even know what had happened to them until they were down to their socks and underwear.

Boiler-rooms had been around since the early days, but were greatly aided by the continuing spread of the telephone, the boiler-room operator's best friend. The boiler-room – which got its name from some early examples that literally operated out of the boiler-rooms of brokerage houses – is a collection of stock salesmen, investment counsellors, and con men gathered in one place, with banks of telephones, to sell stocks, not always or even usually by telling the truth. They were high-pressure salesmen, with tales of fortunes to be made only if you moved quickly. Boiler-rooms still exist, although they are somewhat less conspicuous now; in the 1920s, they reeled in customers by the thousands. And why not? The best and brightest and most experienced brains all agreed that, in the phrase of the time, "the economy was fundamentally sound," that stock speculation was a win-win situation, and that only idiots or political zealots could harbour misgivings about the process.

The preoccupation with making money was no longer frowned upon. Indeed, it was hailed as a virtue in a way that Ivan "It-is-okay-to-be-greedy" Boesky would recognize. In June 1929, the National Waterworks Corporation sprang into being, its goal to buy into the water companies in major cities. The corporation announced its presence with newspaper ads that held out the money to be made: "If by some cataclysm only one small well should remain for the great city of New York – $1.00 a bucket, $100, $1,000, $1,000,000. The man who owned the well would own the wealth of the city." Of course, he might have to dynamite all the pipelines to keep the price up.

While it was good to acquire wealth, the process was to be seen as part of the wonderful economic system, working to manufacture millionaires with their own skills, and not merely as the operation of blind chance. Not for the first time, the experts were careful to distinguish between a gambler and an investor; the gambler, they pointed out, can only win when someone else loses, whereas the investor is part of a system in which everybody gains. One magazine article of the time showed how it worked: a man buys General Motors stock for $100, sells it to another investor for $150, and the second sells to a third for $200. Everybody wins, nobody loses. That was exactly what Carlo Ponzi, the nineteenth-century Italian swindler who invented the pyramid scheme, used to say in selling his scam, and it contained the same flaw: it only worked as long as the supply of suckers kept expanding; as soon as someone went short on suckers, the whole pyramid would collapse.

There were a few grouses who thought the markets had ceased to reflect reality, among them, ironically enough, President Herbert Hoover, who noted in his autobiography, "There are crimes far worse than murder for which men should be reviled and punished." He meant speculation. But these qualms were seldom voiced aloud, and if they were, no one paid any attention.

In October 1929, when the whole quivering structure was emitting small eruptions of distress, the *Financial Post* in Canada noted, "The long term outlook for shareholders in sound Canadian companies remains good," which turned out not to be the case. In the United States Professor Irving Fisher, then a guru but shortly to become a laughing-stock, told the *New York Times*, "I expect to see the stock market a good deal higher than it is today in a few months."

If it was okay with Professor Fisher, it was certainly okay with the men and women who saw their meagre savings suddenly begin to blossom into real wealth, with the promise of prosperity and independence and security forever. Why wouldn't they buy?

To spur them on and whet their appetites, there were the con men, who printed shares for companies that did not exist or, if they did exist, did not do whatever it was they were supposed to do, whether it was mining gold or extracting the stuff from seawater. There was even, Doug Fetherling tells us, a scam especially for widows. One con man would spot the obituary of a company director in the newspaper, and quickly take out an option on shares in the company. That is, for a small share of the cost, he would gain an option certificate that gave him the right to buy a number of shares at the current price within a short period of time. Options in hand, he would call on the widow and offer to buy her late husband's shares to, you know, help tidy up the estate. Leaving the offer with her, he would depart, promising to return for her answer the next day. Then, a confederate would telegraph the widow with the glad news that developments in her late husband's company were about to break, and his shares would be worth a good deal more. Don't sell any shares, the confederate would warn; if anything, buy them. When the first con man turned up the next day, he would be persuaded by the grieving widow to sell her his options, at a nice profit. Only a greedy grievor could be reeled in by this stunt, but whether that makes it better is a moot point.

The tale of how the soaring markets came apart is now familiar; a few nervous speculators began to grumble, a few greedy operators began to collect their profits, and, as with every Carlo Ponzi scheme, the underlying fragility of the markets became apparent, and the point of the pyramid emerged. Now, the reverse side of margin buying (margin = a down payment) went to work, with a vengeance. If you have bought, as in our margin-buying example above, ten Let Her Rip stocks with a face value of $5,000 on a deposit of $1,000, you put up the shares as collateral for the remainder, then borrowed on the paper profits to buy more stocks. In the example on page 78, you parlayed your original $1,000 investment to support $17,000 worth of stock. But if the shares drop in value, you will have to put up more money to maintain the 20 per cent margin. Twenty per cent of $17,000 is $3,400. You put down $1,000 and borrowed $16,000 to buy shares now worth, say, $4,000. Because the value of your collateral has dropped, the broker now issues a margin call to you for $2,400, plus his fees and interest, and if you can't come up with the money, he has the right to sell your stock to cover the loan. But now, since everyone else is caught in the same boat, you can't sell the stock, and it plunges into free fall. It slumps to $500, but you owe $16,000, plus interest and commissions. You are wiped out. Not only you, but everybody else, even Goldman, Sachs, the investment house. It had formed one of these lovely trusts, the Goldman, Sachs Trading Corporation, with a paper value of $100 million, represented by $10 million from the company and $90 million from the public. Shares went from $104 each to $1.75.

It was this reverse leverage that burst the bubble so rapidly, and, just as thousands had plunged in without prudence, they now jammed the exits. There was Black Thursday on Wall Street, followed by Black Tuesday, the biggest Black of them all, when, on Tuesday, October 29, 1929, shares were repeatedly offered on the floor of the New York Stock Exchange for which there were no takers at any price. The stock ticker couldn't keep up with transactions that did take place in New York, Toronto, or Montreal; the trading floors were in chaos, orders were lost, brokers wept, suckers bled. Crowds formed outside newspaper offices in cities all across the continent, as people begged for news that turned out to be even worse than they feared.

The boom was over, the Crash with a capital "C" had begun, and all the posturing of all the wise men, who kept issuing statements that all was well, could do nothing to right the situation. John D. Rockefeller, making his first public pronouncement in decades, announced that, "Believing that fundamental conditions of the country are sound . . . my son and I have for some days been purchasing sound common stocks." Comedian Eddie Cantor cracked, "Sure. Who else had any money left?"

As stock prices plummeted, a new factor was added to the mix. There are two main categories of stock (with many variations), namely, common and preferred. The common stocks are usually the voting stocks; those that control the company.

Preferred stocks very often do not carry a vote, but they do carry something else, a preference; if there are dividends to be paid, these must go first to the preferreds, and only afterwards to common stocks. If money is tight, it is the preferreds that get paid, even if that means nothing is left for the common-stock investor. More importantly in the situation then developing, preferreds come ahead of common stocks in the event of the break-up or bankruptcy of a company.

When you want to know whether the value of the shares you own, or those you might want to buy, has any relation to reality, you can look at the balance sheet of the company in its annual report. It will contain an item called "assets" and another called "liabilities." Subtract the liabilities from the assets, and you arrive at something called "net worth." Assuming that the accountants haven't cooked the books – not always a safe assumption – you can calculate the "book value per share" by dividing the number of shares outstanding, which will also be shown, into the net worth. If there are, for simplicity's sake, 100,000 shares outstanding and the net worth works out to $1 million, it is a reasonable guess that the book value of each share is $10. If the shares are then trading for $20, watch it; if for $2, buy, because, in the worst case, if the company goes under, you will receive the book value of each share you own, if all the other claims are met.

What is left in the till goes first to secured creditors – banks and bonds – then what is left is distributed among the preferred shareholders, and only if there is anything left do the common stocks get their portion. Thus preferreds usually cost more, are more of an investment vehicle, and do not usually provide the same risk or reward by way of capital gain or loss as common stocks. In the chaos of the market in the 1920s, this didn't matter much; stock prices were constantly rising. However, when prices fell, the preferreds still exercised their claim on the profits, if any, of the firm, and the assets, if any. It didn't take much mathematics to work out that, in the event of a bankruptcy, the claims of the first two classes would wipe out those of the third in most companies. The common shares would have no book value because, by the time the claims of the secured creditors and the preferred shares had been met, there would be nothing in the till for them to share. They were literally worth nothing. This did not make them easier to sell.

Between 1920 and 1933, $50 billion worth of securities were sold on American exchanges. By the end of 1933, half of them had been turned into wallpaper, as company after company keeled over and conked out. The total value of all stocks, new and old, on the NYSE on September 1, 1929, was $89 billion; in 1932, it was $15 billion. Clearly $72 billion, or 81 per cent, of the public's investment had vanished. The small investors who had been marched into the market were taken, not to Nirvana, but to the cleaners.

The time had now come for the investment trusts to exercise their stabilizing influence, as advertised, but this did not work out either. The trusts had invested heavily in each other, and had advanced huge sums of money to finance the call market – that is, they had lent their pools of cash from the investing public to finance their own and each other's speculation. They had closed the circle; they were gambling on the gamblers. When the Crash came, they were far more concerned about protecting their own share values than they were in coming to the rescue of anyone else. They began to buy their own stocks, in a desperate attempt to demonstrate that there was a market and thus to support their prices, in vain. The money disappeared down a hole they themselves had dug. "The autumn of 1929," wrote John Kenneth Galbraith, in *The Great Crash 1929*, "was, perhaps, the first occasion when men succeeded on a large scale in swindling themselves."

There were suicides, although not so many as myth has given us; in fact, the death rate by suicide was no higher than normal in Canada and the United States at this time. But the suicides that were reported (it was not usual, and still is not usual, for newspapers to report suicide) caught the public eye. In one celebrated case, two men jumped hand-in-hand from a lofty hotel window. They had a joint stock account. A grim joke of the time had a man registering for an hotel room, and the clerk asking, "Will that be for sleeping, or jumping?"

There were investigations. There are always investigations. These turned up an impressive number of embezzlements on both sides of the border, as trusted employees who had dipped into the company till to gamble in the markets found themselves unable to repay. It was discovered that the Chase National Bank, one of the two largest in the United States, had financed the short-selling of stock as prices plunged, netting a profit of just over $4 million, which somehow wound up in the pockets of the bank's chairman, Albert H. Wiggin. The main victim of this short-selling had been the bank itself. Wiggin later told a Senate investigating committee that it was perhaps, all things considered, not such a good idea for a senior officer of a company to sell his own firm's stock short. He was, in 1933, eased from his post with a lifelong salary of $100,000 per annum, but a public outcry persuaded him to forego the salary. He kept the $4 million though.

Charles E. Mitchell, chairman of the National City, the other largest bank, was not so lucky. He had, through a complex series of transactions, swindled his own wife, among others. He was charged with tax evasion on these transactions, but was found not guilty (the *New York Times* reported that he seemed surprised at the verdict). The government sued him for back taxes, and, in 1938, after much travail, collected more than a million dollars. He had also unwisely persuaded his bank to help underwrite $90 million in Peruvian bonds, although he had information in his own files that showed the issue would almost certainly end in a default, which it did.

The investigations turned up many nuggets, including the fact that J. P. Morgan, Jr., the son of the titan, and a titan in his own right by now, had paid no income tax for three years. He had also run a little scam through the House of Morgan by which his friends and allies were dealt stocks at far below the listed prices. One of these beneficiaries made an instant profit of $229,411. The names in Morgan's "preferred list" included a number of politicians, among them Calvin Coolidge and William H. Woodin, who by this time was a member of Franklin D. Roosevelt's cabinet, in the key role of Secretary of the Treasury. Similar favours went from the House of Morgan to such national heroes as General John Pershing and Charles A. Lindbergh.

Governor Alf Landon of Kansas called the preferred list "nothing less than bribery," and added, "I confidently expect the President to demand the resignation of Secretary of the Treasury Woodin." That never happened.

The mood of the nation was probably caught by Huey Long, the governor of Louisiana, and no angel himself. He commented that the American people were making sure that the only lions they kicked out of the den were the dead ones. "First we prod them, kick them, poke them, make sure they're dead. Then, once we're sure of that, we all shout together 'Let's go after them,' and we do."

In Canada, it took three years and a vigorous public campaign by Floyd Chalmers, then editor of the *Financial Post* (well, fairly vigorous; a series of articles detailing various stock-market scams carried by the *Post* named no names), to bring any substantive action. Then the authorities pounced and arrested twenty-seven stockbrokers, including several millionaires, a few of whom went to jail for short periods.

There were many, many protestations that the worst was over. The Harvard Economic Society issued periodic bulletins to deny that the "present recession" was the precursor to a depression, and then to insist that the recession (later depression), was about to come to an end. Someday. Soon.

There was even some legislative action in the United States with the passage of the Securities Act of 1933, which was one of the first pieces of legislation passed by President Franklin D.

Roosevelt when he took office. It required full disclosure in the sale of new securities (many companies then listed on the NYSE didn't even file annual financial statements). In 1934 came the Securities Exchange Act, which regulated margin selling and set up the Securities and Exchange Commission, which has been more successful, as we will see in Chapter Eleven, in disclosing what goes on in the markets than in actually restraining rascality.

When all was said and done, there were, I think, five clear conclusions that could be drawn from the Crash with a capital "C":

1. Anyone can make money in a rising market, but in a falling market, crooks and insiders have a distinct advantage. Intelligence, judgement, even experience have little to do with success or failure, any more than in any other crap game.

2. Once the speculators take over, the price of the stock has little to do with the real value of the company. A standard stock-market story tells of the man who tries to buy a can of sardines, which has been traded back and forth until he finally has to bid $100 for it. He opens the can and exclaims, "These sardines taste terrible!" The seller tells him, "Those are not eating sardines, those are trading sardines."

As the stock market favours the speculator over the investor, it is the sardine stocks that dominate. At the height of the market, White Sewing Machine shares sold for $48; on October 29, they sold for $1.

3. Mob psychology will always exaggerate the effects of market swings. They did not have computers to egg the process on in 1929, but they did well with what they had. There is no defence against this phenomenon; when first greed and then panic drive stock prices, there is no point in rational choice. "There is nothing so disastrous," wrote Keynes, "as a rational investment policy in an irrational world."

4. For the speculative investor, who rules the market, share ownership has nothing to do with participation in the company. This is in direct defiance of the story line put out by the stock

exchanges themselves, which hold that (I am now quoting from the 1991 version of the gospel according to the TSE) "People who buy a company's shares become part owners of the firm and participate in its fortunes." Not if they can help it; rather, if all goes well, they will get in, clean up, and sell out as quickly as possible, and what happens to the company is no concern of theirs. One of the advantages of looking back to the 1929 Crash is the spectacular way that it made clear the difference between theory and actuality on the stock markets.

5. When the values placed on the shares in the market do not represent the value of the assets of the company, but rather a guess as to what value will be placed on the shares by the market, the scene is set for disaster. And that is, necessarily, the way most of the market works most of the time.

The increasing web of regulations that sprang up after the Crash did not really make much difference; when greed takes over, rules don't mean much, they simply force the crooks into more sophisticated dodges.

But crookedness is not the main concern here. The point is that well-meaning, intelligent, worthy, and honourable people ended up screwing their friends and neighbours when the gambling fever hit, and will do it again.

The Crash merely highlighted these five points, which had been demonstrated before and would be again. What is remarkable is that they were never absorbed. There was a new boomlet, in mining stocks, within three years of the Crash, and the only thing that snuffed stock speculation was the disappearance of money. The desire for speculation never dimmed. Thus we had, on October 19, 1987 – Black Monday, almost six decades after the Crash – another in a recurring series of crashes, without the capital "C." This one wiped out a trillion dollars in wealth overnight and showed us a market that was much more volatile even than that in 1929. On the infamous Black Tuesday of 1929, 500,000 shares were sold on the Montreal Stock Exchange, about five times the normal for a day; in Toronto, 330,000 shares were sold, instead of the usual 25,000. By 1987, the average trading day in Toronto saw 29,200,000 shares sold, to say nothing of millions of options, warrants, rights, futures, mutual funds, money markets, index gambles, and all the marvellous array of tricks we can play with stocks these days. Accounts of the chaos in 1929 always refer to "the staggering total" of 16 million shares that shot through the NYSE on Black Tuesday; an *average* day today sees ten times that whisked through the NYSE, and at least as many more sold Over the Counter. The Toronto stock market sold 23 billion more shares in 1987 than the 50 billion that were sold throughout the United States during the entire period between 1920 and 1933.

These huge turnovers owe far more to dice-rolling than to investing. Louis Lowenstein of Columbia University estimated in *What's Wrong with Wall Street* that, in mid-1987, stocks traded on American exchanges had a total market value of "about $3 trillion, but the total value of new common stocks offered publicly for cash averages no more than $25-30 billion annually."

To me, these are the most astounding statistics available about what the stock markets mean. Out of $3 trillion in funds washing back and forth between buyers and sellers, the amount devoted to new stocks, as opposed to merely trading in shares already on the market, comes to less than $30 billion. And less than half of that actually gets through to the companies that go to the market for funds; the rest is eaten up in fees and commissions. One half of 1 per cent goes to real investment in real firms; everything else goes to gambling. Lowenstein added, "Turnover of the already listed shares has returned to the level of 1928-29, and yet leaders in Washington assure us that this hyperactive trading is good for the country." Wash-trading has become an international pastime, and the gambling element has even taken on a certain respectability. John S. R. Shad, then chairman of the Securities and Exchange Commission, was quoted in *Fortune* magazine in October 1986, as having said that "arbitrage, and for that matter speculation, are good for the market, not bad. They increase market efficiency and tend to smooth out price fluctuations." Before long, they would smooth a trillion dollars right out of existence. What could be more efficient than that?

Margins in 1929 were occasionally 10 per cent, often 20 per cent. In 1987, they had been fixed by fierce regulation: 50 per cent on stocks worth between $2 and $5; 30 per cent above $5; full payment on penny stocks. And, of course, stock-players were not confined to one or two markets; they could roam the world in a nano-second.

The gambling had been speeded up and licensed, that's all, and it led to the same spot it had led to in 1929. The 1987 crash did not bring about a depression with a capital "D," and that adds weight to a long-held theory that the Depression would have happened anyway, and was merely speeded up and exacerbated by the Crash. Just the same, the 1987 debacle did provide a rude awakening for thousands of people who had been cruising along, as in days of yore, on dreams of an ever-rising market, and who were no more able than their foreparents had been to distinguish between investment and gambling.

The next crash will no doubt occasion the same hurt surprise as the one in 1987, because the theology of the market has never really been challenged, much less shaken. It is still the deep conviction of the wisest and most respected among us that this crap game is not a crap game, but, as the TSE has it in their promotional pamphlets, "The opportunity to own a piece of Canada's most exciting companies – and potentially earn a profit as well."

In short, neither the Crash of 1929 nor the Slump of 1987, nor all the fun in between, has taught Canadians very much. We still believe that the markets are about capital formation, that justice triumphs, that intelligent investment pays off, and that anyone can make a million.

Faith is a wonderful thing.

PART II

The Way We Are

Securities markets are extensively regulated to protect the public.

– *How To Invest in Canadian Securities,* The Canadian Securities Institute, 1988.

CHAPTER FIVE

The Terrific Adventure of Locket, Socket, and Trunk

Launching a Public Company

Wall Street, in these matters, is like a lovely and accomplished woman who must wear black cotton stockings, heavy woollen underwear and parade her knowledge as a cook because, unhappily, her supreme accomplishment is as a harlot.
  – J. K. Galbraith, *The Great Crash 1929.*

$

I have read enough stock-market tipster books now to know that one thing I absolutely must include here is the formation and public launching of a corporation, a process that will explain a good deal of the mechanics of the business along the way. In by far the most successful of these books, *How To Buy Stocks,* the 1987 classic by Louis Engel and Brendan Boyd, the necessary firm is called the Pocket Pole Company, Inc. It makes and distributes collapsible fishing poles.

In John M. Dalton's *How the Stock Market Works,* the handbook of the New York Institute of Finance, the company is Maxwell Manufacturing, and it makes and sells "candle figurines," although it is considering a plan of diversification, to sell plastic chess pieces. My company is called Locket, Socket, and Trunk, and it manufactures, among other things, lockets, sockets, and trunks. It began life as a private corporation, Bosky Dell Enterprises. The original certificate of incorporation, necessary to breathe life into the clay of my creation, contained one general clause under "Purposes of the Company," which said "and such other purposes as the Board of Directors may from time to time determine." Short of piracy on the high seas, anything goes.

My corporation will differ from Pocket Pole, Inc. and Maxwell Manufacturing mainly in that, rather than dealing with airy abstractions in which all goes well, rules are obeyed, and prosperity reigns – if fictitiously – my corporation will touch base with reality from time to time. I will use real models in the real world to underline the difference between stock-market theory and what actually happens.

The initial formation of a private corporation is not difficult, these days; you simply call a lawyer and an accountant, they talk to each other, and in due course send you, along with a bill for a few thousand dollars, all the necessary papers. Bosky Dell Enterprises was established this way, and registered in Ontario fourteen years ago. As a private corporation, it was in the same category as the T. Eaton Company, Ltd., or Olympia & York Developments, if somewhat smaller. There were two shares, each with a "par" value – a meaningless term in this case – of $1. I owned one, my wife the other. Like Eaton's and Olympia & York, this was a closely held corporation. However, the business has grown slowly but surely to the point where I now believe it is ready to go public. There are two reasons pushing me in this direction. The first is that I really need money to expand and, as Boyd and Engel put it, "You could get your business under way for $20,000, but you haven't got $20,000. The bank won't lend it to you on the strength of your patents, and you can't find an 'angel' with that kind of cash to put in your business. So you decide to . . . sell shares in the venture."

We decide to let in strangers. The good part is that they will bring money into the business; the bad part is that I will have to share information, even some control, with them. Not much, though. <u>Martin Weiss</u>, an American who has been through the process many times, writes in *Going Public,*

> Generally speaking, going public does not mean the loss of *control* of the company, even though that concern may be one of the first which goes through an owner's mind. For practical purposes, only a relatively small proportion of the stock ownership and/or voting authority needs to remain in the hands of the original founders/owners/managers for them to retain effective operating control of the company.

Shareholder democracy is a fiction limited to economic texts.

When I launch myself, I will certainly hire a public-relations firm to tell folks why I am doing so, and the initial press release prepared for the occasion will lay great emphasis on the wonderful opportunities that await. It will say nothing about my second reason for going public, which is that I have just worked out how to make a killing from it, with very little risk to myself (though rather more to those who buy my shares).

Take Wedtech Corporation, one of the better-known firms of our day, whose internal structure has been laid revealingly naked through a number of court cases, as well as in the fascinating volume *Feeding Frenzy,* by <u>William Sternberg</u>, a New York journalist, and by <u>Matthew C. Harrison, Jr.</u>, once a Wedtech vice-president.

The corporation began life as Welbilt Electronic Die, Corp., a partnership launched in the Bronx between John Mariotta, who had worked in machine shops long enough to know he didn't want to do that any more, and Fred Neuberger, the Romanian-born owner of a failing sheet-metal concern called Fleetwood Products. Welbilt, when it was a private corporation, was funded by a loan of $2,400, floated on Neuberger's old Buick. It did not do well until, one day in 1974, Neuberger ran across an open bid from the U.S. government's Defense Contract Administration to manufacture filters for Bell Helicopters. Welbilt knew nothing about this business, had never made a filter in its life and could not possibly win the bid in open competition unless it could qualify as a "minority" contractor. In that case, the contract could be awarded without any bidding. Mariotta's grandparents had come from Puerto Rico, but that didn't really help, because to qualify as a minority firm, Welbilt had to be at least 51 per cent owned by minority shareholders, and the Neuberger–Mariotta deal was a fifty-fifty split. No problem; the two men manufactured an agreement that showed that Mariotta owned two-thirds of the firm, and pre-dated it three years. There was another, private, agreement which showed that he didn't.

Thus armed, Welbilt began to apply for, and win, defence contracts that it had absolutely no competence to carry out. Again, no problem. The company put Mario Biaggi, whose House of Representatives district included part of the Bronx, on the payroll as a consultant, and string-pulling replaced performance. In 1980, Ronald Reagan, then running for the presidency, was taken on a tour of a new plant Welbilt was refurbishing with defence-contract money, and in front of the television news cameras, he pledged that, if he got elected, his administration would provide incentives for companies like Welbilt – about which he knew next to nothing – to work their miracles of entrepreneurship. He did get elected, and his office made sure Welbilt was solidly positioned to crawl up into Uncle Sam's lap and help itself to the contents of his pockets. They call it free enterprise.

The company staggered through a number of rocky years. The Defense Department, for some reason, seemed to think Welbilt ought to complete its contracts on time and with some faint adherence to the specifications. Meddlesome bureaucrats kept turning down the company's bids, or refusing to pay the outrageous prices Welbilt wanted, so it was necessary to line up Lyn Nofziger, then head of President Reagan's Office of Political Affairs, and Edwin Meese, his senior aide, to crush the opposition. They did. In fact, the bothersome bureaucrat in the Economic Development Administration who gave the company the most trouble was fired the hell out of office. Welbilt kept getting contracts and screwing them up until the happy day, in July 1983, when the company went public. It had to. Among other money problems, the two chief officers had borrowed quite heavily from a loan shark, had stolen money out of progress payments from the Defense Department, and had siphoned off company funds into personal accounts out of sight of the tax-collector – and then got caught doing it, by the first auditor who went over the books. He ceased to be an auditor and was taken on staff at Welbilt instead.

So far, so good. But it all cost money, to say nothing of the amounts required to keep a number of politicians, lawyers, and hangers-on sweet. Since a bank loan was out of the question – it was actually a banker who, after one shuddering look at Welbilt's books, sent them to a loan shark – they were pretty well left with the need to sell shares to the public.

This presented a small difficulty. The stock analysts and others whose opinions are crucial to such a venture would not be impressed unless a major accounting firm had looked over the books and attested to their solid worth. One of the Big Eight accounting houses was hired, which was good, prestige-wise, but not so good, looking-at-the-books-wise. The two men directly connected with the audit soon turned up the fact that, in addition to everything else, Welbilt had forged a number of invoices – had simply copied off the letterheads of government stationery and written in figures – which had been duly paid. This amounted to a direct theft of $4 million. What to do? The two men were paid off in stock in the public-company-to-be, one was taken on staff, and that was that. Oh, yes, and when they found the money that was being siphoned off into a private bank account, a promissory note, predated, appeared to turn this into a loan, which was never repaid. We like to think of these things as challenges, rather than difficulties. The audit was then pushed through, and everything was hotsy-totsy.

The new company was launched as Wedtech, taking the "We" from Welbilt, the "d" from Die, and adding Tech for the hell of it.

When the caterpillar Welbilt emerged as the butterfly Wedtech, it issued $100 million worth of shares. The underwriter, Moseley, Hallgarten, Estabrook & Weeden, staged a dog-and-pony show to woo investors and stock analysts, and filed the necessary prospectus setting out the company's aims, background, and financial situation for the benefit of prospective purchasers of the stock. In the prospectus, there was a certain leeway given to the facts; nothing was said about the loan shark, the thefts, or the failure to perform on contracts, or about bribes, fraud, or the fact that the company didn't even qualify for the minority status to which it had owed its income so far. Other than that, it was a fine prospectus. What the general public knew about the firm was mainly that Ronald Reagan had invited John Mariotta to lunch at the White House and praised him for his enterprise. What else was needed?

When the underwriter set the share price at $16 – the underwriter's guess as to what the public will stand for – Mariotta and Neuberger thoughtfully assigned themselves 1.56 million shares each. Their take would be about twenty-five million dollars apiece, if all went well, but they couldn't get it out at once. It was "restricted" by rules of the Securities and Exchange Commission. They couldn't cash in for two years. For walking-around money, and just in case the share price dropped, they paid themselves $2.7 million each, for the work done so far, out of the proceeds of the public offering. This was real money. This first launching – called the initial public offering, or IPO – involved 5.86 million shares; 3.76 million – 70 per cent – were dealt to Neuberger and Mariotta and their friends and cronies and bribees, and brought in nothing, but the other 2.1 million shares were sold to the great unwashed, who had to pay for them. On settlement day, September 1, the underwriter passed over about thirty million dollars to the company coffers. This could be spent, and it was.

And people think you can't make money on stocks.

What attracted me about the Wedtech example when I was considering the IPO for Locket, Socket, and Trunk was the straightforward way in which everybody involved just grabbed the money and, for a number of years, got away with it. We all know that the SEC is much tougher on American corporations than anything we have in Canada, and there are all those inquisitive investigative journalists swarming over the U.S. business scene, but the SEC didn't utter a murmuring word, and what we heard from *Forbes* magazine, the Wall Street Bible, was that Neuberger and Mariotta were "a shining example" of the system working as it should. The stock was listed, first on the American Exchange and then on the New York Exchange, neither of which saw anything wrong with the company. For all anybody knew, things were going along swell. It seemed just possible that I could work the same racket in Canada's less-restrictive clime.

On the other hand, the guys with the badges and manacles did eventually catch on and drop a number of the Wedtech operators in jail. The revelation came about in large part because of a falling-out between the principals; at one point, there was talk of hiring a hit man to dispose of Neuberger, by then the chairman of Wedtech. These things take their toll, so perhaps it is safer to stick to the more orthodox approaches, while noting for the record that there is really no way for the general investing public to tell whether its investments are going into an honest, straight firm (the vast majority), or another shining example like Wedtech. It is also a simple fact of life that, for most of the people who bought stocks, held them briefly, then sold at a profit, it didn't matter a damn that the company was riddled with corruption and built on shifting sands; they were able to pass the Old Maid before the game ended.

Maybe I can work the same trick with Locket, Socket, and Trunk. We can take the next part from *How To Buy Stocks*: "You finally decide to issue 2,000 shares at $10 apiece. Taken collectively, those shares would represent the common stock issue of the Pocket Pole Company, Inc. The $10 price you place on it would represent its *par value*. . . . By this means you raise the $20,000 capital you need. The Pocket Pole Company is in business."

No, dagnabbit, they've left something out. In the first place, I am not going to flog the whole company. I will instead create 500,000 shares to represent the common-stock issue of Locket, Socket, and Trunk, and put out 300,000 of them in the initial public offering (IPO). I will give myself 100,000 of these for the two shares of Bosky Dell Enterprises my wife and I will toss into the kitty, and lay another 50,000 on the board of directors, once I have them lined up. You can be one. If you know a former premier or two, we will shove them on the board too. A Canadian corporation without any ex-premiers has a sort of hollow sound, like a rock band without a guitar. The original charter of the company will lay down the maximum number of shares that can be issued, although the charter can always be amended, and some companies now just write "unlimited" in the relevant space. The shares named in the charter are the "authorized" shares; the authorized shares that are sold or otherwise distributed are the "issued" shares, and those left in the hands of shareholders are "outstanding." Shares not outstanding would be ones that we issued and then, for one reason or another, bought back into the company, perhaps to cut down the number of shares, which will increase the dividend per share and jack up the price again.

For our IPO, we will go to an underwriting firm, which turns out to be, guess what? An investment house. Stockbrokers. In Canada, probably stockbrokers owned by a bank. They will put together a package, probably with another stockbroker, to shove the stocks out onto the public. The underwriters literally underwrite the deal; that is, they buy the stocks and resell them, or guarantee their sale. If they buy all the stocks themselves, the arrangement is known as a "bought deal," or a "firm commitment underwriting." Anything the underwriters can't lay off on the public, they will absorb themselves. Now the salesmen in the same firm, who have given this undertaking, go out and call the Widow Brown and tell her, "Mrs. Brown, have I got a stock for you!" If she goes to the bank for advice, the bank will steer her to its investment arm, which will drop her in our lap anyway. We are very cozy in the stock business.

Setting the price of the shares is tricky. It ought to be based on the assets and past performance of the company, and here is where the dear old P/E becomes crucial. Bosky Dell Enterprises has a record of performance, so the underwriter will go over that, look at future prospects, check out the locket, socket, and trunk sales in North America over the past five years, kill a pigeon, examine its entrails, and come up with a price. This ought to be so structured that it will produce an acceptable P/E when potential customers get a look at it. That is why we can't just create all the stocks we want to. If we expect to make $1 million in our first year by our activities, and we issue 10 million shares, we'll have to set the initial price at around $1 to produce a P/E of 10 ($1 million divided by 10 million gives us earnings of ten cents a share; a share selling at ten times that, $1, will have a P/E of 10. The price, $10, is ten times the earnings, $1. Remember, the P/E is really 10/1, but the 1 is dropped.) Dollar shares are bad news; they sound too cheap. Forget it. With our present proposal to issue 300,000 shares, these will divide our potential $1 million profit. The earnings ought to be $3.33 a share, which works out to a 9 per cent return if we bring the shares out at $30. Sound okay to you?

If there are too many shares outstanding, the effect is called "earnings dilution," and if there is too much dilution, by, for example, dealing off too many shares to insiders, the prospectus will have to carry a warning to that effect, with wording such as, "The Securities Offered Hereby Involve a High Degree of Risk." The chance that many investors will actually read the prospectus that is filed when we make the share offering is remote, but the underwriters won't like it.

When all the calculations are finished, the underwriters will draw up an agreement, specifying a price. No reason why they won't go for our $30 a share. They will not collect a commission on this first offering, but will instead pay less per share for the issue and will be obliged to turn the cash agreed upon over to us on settlement day. The underwriters earn their money at this point, since, if they have guessed wrong and the shares plummet, they are going to be stuck with them, or have to sell at a loss. The other side of this coin, and one I do not find in any of the texts consulted, is that there is going to be great pressure on the salesmen to whom the underwriters assign the shares to move them, to Widow Brown or anyone else, any way they can.

Once the shares have been issued, bought, and paid for, the money goes into the company till. Let us say 150,000 shares at $30 each, since my wife and I and the other directors kept the other 150,000, making $4.5 million, minus expenses and the underwriters' cut. We have about $4 million to work with.

Then there are the options. You remember options – they are contracts to purchase the stock within a given period at a given price and, creatively used, they can do us all a bit of good.

Take the Unity Bank. This was the dream of a Toronto lawyer, Benjamin "Bunny" Levinter, a fine fellow, who wanted to build a bank to serve Canada's minority communities at a time – 1970 – when our banks seemed to be mostly for WASPs. He wasn't a banker, so he lined up as president and chief executive officer one Richard "Rich" Higgins, a man well respected in the field, who got tremendous press, despite the slight drawback that he happened to be a crook. Higgins took over, and when Unity went public, the underwriting was taken on by Gairdner & Company of Toronto as lead underwriter, with Wood Gundy in second place, and a clump of lesser firms taking smaller portions of the proferred stock. After much backing and forthing, this group undertook to distribute 3 million shares of Unity stock at $9.25 each. That would produce $27,750,000. For their role, the group would get a cut of sixty-two cents a share, or $1,860,000, and turn over the residue, $25,890,000, to Unity Bank on October 10, 1972.

However, the Unity Bank directors gave themselves the option to buy more shares directly from the company treasury, at $8.62 each, and they could "subscribe" for these, that is, order them but only pay 10 per cent down. In all, the founding directors subscribed for $3,310,105 worth of shares, for which they put up $570,000, much of it borrowed from the Toronto-Dominion

Bank. A $26 million bank was launched on, mostly, thin air. But the nice part was that the directors appeared to be fireproof. If the stocks went up, they would cash in; if not, they would just not exercise the options.

When Gairdner & Company sent out its underwriting letter to tout the stock, it valued it at $11.10 per share. Rich Higgins was sitting on options for 54,054 shares, for which he had put up $50,000. If the boys were right, his stock would soon be worth $600,000 – he would clear $100,000 on a $50,000 investment in a few weeks. (This is how it worked. He put up $50,000 in real money and borrowed the rest to subscribe for 54,054 shares at the pre-launch price of $9.25. His commitment was $50,000 on stocks worth $499,999.50. But, if the underwriters were correct, his stocks would soon be worth $11.10 per share, or $599,999.40. He would pay off the $500,000 owing, and his profit would be $100,000, even though his actual outlay was only $50,000. Beautiful.)

The great unwashed did not know about these arrangements; the only place they appeared on the record was in the office of the clerk of the House of Commons in Ottawa, as specified in the Bank Act, where I found them. The other shareholders didn't know about them either, and were ticked off when I ratted in print.

Nor did the great unwashed know, when Gairdner sent out its touting letter, that the investment house was the main underwriting firm; as far as recipients of that letter knew, they were simply being offered a wonderful opportunity to get in on the ground floor of a new bank by their friendly broker.

Alas, the issue did not go as planned. A Japanese firm that had been angling to buy much of the stock discovered that it wouldn't be able to vote most of it, and pulled back. (The law put a limit on bank shares that could be voted by non-Canadians.) The stock took a nose-dive, and the underwriters were left with what is called, beguilingly I think, "a large rump" – shares which had not been sold, but for which the money would have to be turned over to Unity anyway. It was felt best not to tell the public about the large rump, either – why upset them with the sort of details that would only drop prices still further?

Unity eventually went out of business, and Higgins was eventually cut adrift. (This occurred after I wrote an article about him in *Maclean's*, detailing a real-estate scam he had worked while employed by the Bank of Montreal in Grand Cayman.) He served a jail sentence in British Columbia for some of his Unity Bank activities, and died not long afterwards.

I think we can profit from the Unity Bank case, and give ourselves options to purchase shares of Locket, Socket, and Trunk at $28, exercisable any time in the next year. If the stock goes up, we can cash in the options, and if it doesn't, no harm done.

This first stock offering is a "primary distribution"; subsequent sales of batches of the stock from the company treasury are "secondary." All the shares issued, taken together, make up the "capital stock" – the "equity," or "shareholders' equity" – of the company. The common stocks carry one vote each; there are 300,000 issued and paid-up shares in LS & T, including the 100,000 belonging to me and my wife, so anyone who can put together 150,001 has the right to control the company, although it will be rather hard to do, when you and I and the rest of the directors already own 150,000.

Needless to say, while we get the money from the original sale of stocks, which goes into the company treasury, when the stocks are resold, the money goes to the then-owner, and we change the name on our list of shareholders. The dividends have to be paid to the owner of record at the time they are due (we will set that date at the board of directors meeting, along with the amount), which can lead to endless confusion and even lawsuits when shares whiz back and forth as rapidly as they do today. Indeed, the issuance of paper share certificates after each sale and resale is such a burden that we will probably soon see the day when all of this is kept inside the computer. (A great mistake, as I will argue later.)

I think our next step ought to be to go out and buy up one of our competitors, which will give us a greater share of the market and impress the hell out of the stock-watchers, thus giving the shares a boost. I have had my eye on a firm called Lock, Stock, and Barrel for quite some time. We will take it over, in a friendly way, by offering its shareholders stock in LS & T in a swap for their shares. Much nicer than grubby old money. We will create an issue of preferred shares, called LS & T A shares, with a par value of $40. They will be cumulative; that is, if we can't pay a dividend as called for in the share, it will accumulate, and we will have to discharge all these obligations before paying any common-stock dividends. That should reel them in. If they don't want to play, we will go out and buy some of their shares anyway, and make noises as if we are going to take them over and fire all the management team, which we will be careful to describe, off the record of course, to a newspaper reporter as "a gang of knock-kneed, goggle-eyed burglars and bums."

We may even go into the market and short their shares, while explaining to anyone who will listen that the present management of the firm has been wasting money like Billy be damned, and the only thing to do is sell Lock, Stock, and Barrel shares. To get rid of us, they will offer us twice what we paid for their stock, and we will be in the greenmail business. So we can't lose; we will either take them over or get a handsome pay-off for greenmail. (I can't find "greenmail" in any of *How To Buy Stocks, How To Invest in Canadian Securities,* or *Bulls and Bears,* which is the *Financial Times*'s contribution to this sort of literature, but dammit, we can't cover every little point.)

Should we get ourselves listed on an exchange? The advantage is an enormous boost in prestige, especially if we can break into one of the classier exchanges. Our company shares will be listed in the *Globe and Mail* every day. The disadvantage is that listing costs a lot of money and takes a lot of time and paperwork. Let's continue to trade Over the Counter for a while; we might get listed in the paper anyway, as part of the OTC market.

Because our launching was so smooth, and we make such good products, our share prices begin to move up. This is good. We don't want to be undervalued, because if there is too wide a discrepancy between the value of our shares on the market and the underlying value of the company, someone will make a grab for us, and we aren't ready for that yet. A P/E that is too low, the accumulation of too much cash within the company, or the fact that we carry assets worth a good deal of money at a low value on our books may make us a target. (Standard accounting practice has companies listing real estate at the purchase price, when it may be worth many times that.)

Should we split our stock? I mean, after the first while, when the market begins to take off and the stock soars to $70, $80, $90? Stocks that cost too much are harder to sell; if we split them two for one, the cost drops in half, but the P/E halves. (If we made our original target and hit earnings of $3.33 per share, the P/E at the end of our first year, as we have already seen, was 9. If the shares are split to $15 to make them more saleable, the P/E becomes 4.5, at least until we declare a new and lower dividend per share. The practical effect is exactly the same, since each shareholder now has two shares for one, but the psychological effect is quite different.

A great many Canadian companies took a licking in the summer of 1991, when it turned out that scandals even more odiferous than the usual were shaking the Tokyo Stock Exchange. Among other intriguing tidbits, an affiliate of one of the largest Japanese stockbroking firms had sunk money into a country club tied to the mob. Not nice. In addition, a number of firms had paid off favourite clients who lost money on the markets, which was not only illegal, but a tad unfair to the other clients, who didn't get paid. The revelations caused a lot of stock prices to nose-dive, and a lot of North American spokesmen to spout bunny poop. Henry B. W. de Vismes, head of investment for Citibank's private bank in Tokyo, was quoted in the *Globe and Mail* as noting, "The compliance offices in the U.S. and Europe would have been on this within days, if not minutes. We would have heard about it very quickly." Tell it to the boys at Wedtech.

The Tokyo scandals had absolutely nothing to do with the value of shares in other markets, but the insiders – those who knew that the scandal was about to break – guessed that share prices would drop anyway, given the well-known propensity of the market to behave like a chicken that has just met its first axe. Thus, in London, Frankfurt, New York, Paris, Toronto, Milan, Hong Kong, and Istanbul, the boys began to unload, and the computers, spotting the unloading, unloaded themselves, and we had a nice little drop in the market. This could happen to us. The president of the United States could have a pimple on the side of his nose, and the wise old market could go into one of its spasms and knock us on the head, even if we are doing our main job of making lockets, sockets, and trunks very well. When the shares drop, we will hear from our directors and shareholders.

We may even be challenged at our annual meeting, which would be too bad, since most annual meetings are dull, decorous, and as uniformative as we can possibly make them. It is at the annual meeting that our shares are actually voted, usually in great clumps by the management of the company. The shareholders will mostly send in proxies, statements giving the right to exercise their votes to someone else – us, in 99 cases out of 100.

Once we realize we are in the stock game, and not the manufacturing business, we will learn to play the press as a zither, which will turn out to be surprisingly easy; a drink and a few clichés will satisfy the vast majority of business reporters and send them back to spin out stories about a "dynamic new firm" whose "razor-sharp CEO" is fast becoming the talk of Bay Street.

Boom, Bellows, and Bragg, one of the investment houses that launched us on an unsuspecting world, can be counted on to play its role, with solemn opinions released to the press by its analysts attesting that ours is a stock worth adding to any portfolio. No one will ask the analysts if they are plugging one of their own stocks. A young analyst of my acquaintance was asked by one of his bosses to issue a report giving a glowing account of a particular stock because, "We have a customer who wants to unload 500,000 shares."

"Who's the customer?" he asked.

"We are, you asshole," he was told. Pure routine.

We will time any press releases for their maximum effect on the share price; good news in time for the media, bad news late Friday afternoon. It would be nice if we could hoke up some new breakthrough in the locket business. It wouldn't have to be real. Wedtech claimed to have developed a new coating process for metal, which it had, although there was the minor difficulty that the process was no damn good. Nonetheless, on the basis of this, Moseley Hallgarten, the original underwriter, announced in late 1983 that "the unique coating process developed by Wedtech Corp. represents an advancement of the state of the art in the coating of metals." Just kidding. Still, it helped to move the shares, and similar announcements kept the stock price at a premium right through 1986; in all, $15 million went down a rathole trying to perfect the process, but this was well worth it to the company, just for the lift it gave the stock.

Touche Ross, the giant accounting firm, was brought in to do a market-development study for Wedtech in 1985. These are always nice. Touche Ross calculated that the company would have revenues of $21 million in 1986, and make a net profit of $2.1 million; for 1987, the figures were $33.2 million and $5.4 million respectively. Who wouldn't buy the stock? Actually, the 1986 gross revenues came to a somewhat more modest $250,000, and the company lost $4 million, while the 1987 figures were never really fairly tested, because by that time the company was in bankruptcy.

"Propping up Wedtech's stock price," note Sternberg and Harrison in *Feeding Frenzy*, "meant cooking the books to show impressive quarterly increases in sales and earnings. It meant cultivating, and misleading, stock analysts and institutional investors. It meant erecting a veneer of respectability around the company. . . ." and it wasn't even very hard to pull off.

Wedtech was saluted as the "Stock of the Month" in a Wall Street newsletter in April 1983, and was given a strong "buy" recommendation in another at a time when its insiders were swiftly unloading their own shares and the company was actually about $50 million in debt to the U.S. government. In the end, shares that opened at $11.10 went to $1 and then to nothing; the stock-players lost $160 million – those who hadn't passed the Old Maid on – while the company officers stole at least $5 million, made another $15 million selling their stock, and then went to jail. In all, Wedtech took in $464 million in government contracts, none of which was completed as specified. But of course, it wasn't in the business of manufacturing, it was in the stock business.

The fixation on share prices, even in companies less adventure-some than Wedtech, can be taken to the point of self-annihilation, as witness RJR Nabisco, the U.S. food conglomerate. The long series of events that led to its dismemberment began, according to Bryan Burrough and John Helyar in *Barbarians at the Gate,* when Ross Johnson, the high-living president of the company (and a Canadian) put the company "in play," as a means of juicing up the stock price. We will look at this case again.

Maybe for Locket, Socket, and Trunk, we should do a little wash-trading, quite illegal, but quite common, using brokers in Vancouver and Montreal to buy our shares, then sell them again under "street names." In the old days, when we had to sign a form to buy a bottle of booze, a lot of us would sign Karl Marx, Sigmund Freud, or Henry Ford. That's all a street name is, a polite fiction to protect the guilty. Wash-trading is made somewhat easier when we have a series of "cross trades" going. These are transactions in which the same broker acts for both buyer and seller – although it is rather naughty if it turns out that the buyer and seller are the same person, maybe even the broker.

What we are aiming at, in the end, a year or so down the road, is the Canadian capitalist's dream. We want to be bought out by a huge American firm that will give us twice what our shares are worth and hire us back to run our own company under generous management contracts.

CHAPTER SIX

Nearer, Big Board, to Thee

At the Exchange

Only people with several loose marbles would ascribe intelligence
to the stock market.
  – Terence Corcoran, in the *Report on Business,* February 8, 1991.

$

We know enough now, I think, to stroll into the premises of a stock
exchange and have a look around. We will go armed with the
knowledge that just as many shares are bought and sold off the
exchanges as on them, and that an increasing share of the action
takes place far away, as computer calls to computer across the dismal network. Just the same, the exchanges are, well, glamorous
places to visit, and what happens here certainly sets the mood for
what happens to stock prices all over the world. Here, we will be
able to follow the process in enough detail to understand what it is
really about – selling tomatoes – and to demystify it.
    The exchange I have chosen for this exercise is the Toronto
Stock Exchange, which is accessible, well managed, and, once we
get over the first confusing blur of activity, relatively easy to

follow. The New York Stock Exchange is more exciting, especially at opening and closing, but more confusing; the London exchange has been reduced to an options market – stocks are traded over the telephone, through computers in the brokerage houses; and the other Canadian exchanges are not really a patch on Toronto in volume, reach, and interest. The Vancouver trading floor closed officially in January 1990, after eighty-three years. Now the 2,400 companies whose shares are traded there are bought and sold through an automated trading system called "the Matchmaker."

With my usual impeccable timing, I have brought you to the TSE just when they are threatening to bring it down around my ears. May already have done so. The lads in charge have decided to follow the Vancouver example and take the stock-trading part of the exchange into the innards of a computer, leaving only the futures exchange for visitors to gaze upon. A few days after this was announced, in March 1992, the computers went on one of their unscheduled holidays for several hours, and shut down the entire process. This lent force to the arguments of the old-timers who wanted to keep more of the floor open. But the computer-pushers will probably win; they usually do, so the floor may not look, in 1993, the way it does as I write this in 1992. Nevertheless, I still think the tour is worth it.

To reach the Toronto exchange, you walk through some of the world's classiest real estate, in the block that extends south and east from the corner of York and Adelaide streets in downtown Toronto. "The Exchange," as it calls itself on the sign outside, is actually an outgrowth of First Canadian Place, which runs between King and Adelaide, and houses, among others, the corporate headquarters of the Bank of Montreal and of Olympia & York. When you pass by the counters of a cigar store selling some of the world's most expensive leaves and enter the exchange premises themselves, via an escalator, you become conscious at once of the people – mostly men – buzzing around. They are mostly in

their shirtsleeves, mostly young, mostly earnest, and all self-pos-
sessed. They are floor traders, brokers and their clients, or some of
the 470 employees of the exchange itself – clerks, keyboard operators, and messengers – hurrying on their way with no indication
that they are about to get down on their knees and roll craps.
Upstairs, past a display that tells you how easy it is to "participate
in our free-enterprise system" by backing the horse of your
choice, you come to the Visitors' Gallery, a wide expanse of glass
that looks directly down onto the Trading Floor.

The floor is gigantic – 30,000 square feet – broken into a number of areas by half-walls. There are phones on the sloping wall in
front of you, just below the glass, which contain a tinned message,
in mellifluous tones, explaining in broad outline what you see
before you.

The free pamphlets in the foyer leading to the Visitors' Gallery
tell you, somewhat trickily, that The Exchange (in caps), is
operated "not for profit." In point of fact, the exchange is owned
by its seventy-four broker-members, who alone have the right to
buy and sell the securities listed here, and who collect commissions on every share they buy or sell for customers. The Bonsecours Market is operated "not for profit," too; but the money is
made here, just the same. This is the display room of your car
dealer, the model suite of a condominium operation, the gaming
floor of a casino; not some neutral, beneficent cathedral to free
enterprise, but a place where the most high-pressure salesmanship and the wildest gambling available take place. Memberships,
or seats on the TSE, went for $370,000 apiece back in 1987, but
that was before a few blips of the computer wiped a trillion dollars
off the markets; in 1990, one seat went for $75,000. Still, it is the
members who rule here, and the members want you to buy and
sell stock as often as possible, because that is how they make most
of their money.

The heart of the operation consists of eight huge trading posts,
which are long, double-sided counters surmounted by banks of

screens. From above, the tops of these counters look like dug-out canoes. The name "posts" is a hangover from the days when they were, in fact, just posts in the floor, where traders gathered to cut deals. Six of the posts are for stock trades and two are for options, while, off to your right is an area, called a trading pit, where futures (of which more in Chapter Seven) are bought and sold.

Around the walls are electronic screens, where moving symbols chase each other in a never-ending circle. These are called "ticker tapes," although they contain no tape, and no longer tick. They represent the information covering trades made on this exchange, the New York Stock Exchange, and the American Exchange. The NYSE is on the top line, the American in the middle, and the TSE on the bottom. It figures. These rolling symbols replace what used to be, on most exchanges, a huge board – it was called "The Big Board" in New York, and the phrase is still used to denote the NYSE. This is where trading information once was posted at the same time as clerks were entering it into machines that created an electronic signal. These signals, moving over telephone lines, would actually punch the information onto a ticker tape in brokers' offices. The symbols on the modern ticker move quickly, at a steady 500 characters a minute, enough to display the data from about fifty trades every sixty seconds, and, at first, they seem impossible to follow. (Actually, the same information is available on cable TV and on the data base of a number of computer services, but it is more interesting to look along the walls and realize that the data flashing along up there comes from the hand-waving, paper-tossing, and seemingly inane chaos on the floor beneath you.)

Most of the numbers and letters you see on the TSE tape reflect equity trading, since that is mostly what the TSE is about. Equity trading refers to the buying and selling of common and preferred shares, warrants, units, and options (we'll get into the last three as we move along; they are what is called "derived securities," that is, not the real thing, shares, but units formed from these). To one side of the tape on your left is another electronic screen carrying the Dow Jones news service ticker, which shows news bulletins from time to time, if they affect, or are likely to affect, trading. Such bulletins would include information about takeovers, stock splits, or a halt in the trading of a particular stock. At the end of the trading day, there is a summary of the trading thus far.

"The end of the trading day" has already become a misnomer; the trading floor is open from 9:30 a.m. to 4:00 p.m., but, in June 1991, in response to a lengthening of the hours in New York, first Montreal and then Toronto accepted an arrangement for extended hours. As I write this, most North American exchanges permit trading forty-five minutes before and forty-five minutes after the official close, at the stock prices established at the close. This is said to be for the convenience of some brokers, especially those who are cross-trading; that is, who have both orders to buy and sell the same security at the same price. In reality, these extended hours appear to be part of the process that eventually will turn the exchanges into twenty-four-hour-a-day casinos. Clearly, if stocks are being traded for investment, an hour or even a day doesn't matter much, since the stocks will simply be put into a portfolio, but if the purpose is to gamble, they do, especially since some Canadian stocks trade on foreign markets and vice versa.

There are two lines on the running ticker; the top line carries the stock symbol of a company whose shares have just been traded, and the bottom one tells you how many "board lots" were involved and the price. (Not all exchanges carry the same data in the same way on their tapes, but, once you have seen one ticker, it is easy enough to figure out any other one.) The stock symbol often consists merely of two or three letters, or a readily identifiable shortening of the name, such as ALCAN. These abbreviations are usually straightforward; Canadian Pacific Ltd., appears as CP, Bell Canada Enterprise Developments as BCED, American Telephone and Telegraph as Amer Tel & Tel. Sometimes, they are a little fanciful. Thus, a company called CHC Helicopter Corp. has chosen to identify itself as FLY. If the shares are common stock, just the stock symbol will appear; if there are have been a number of issues, the issue involved in this particular trade will be indicated, as in FLY.A or FLY.B. Preferred shares are indicated by the letters PR or P, and if there is more than one issue, again, it will be indicated, as in FLY.P. When Locket, Socket, and Trunk makes it to the TSE, we will call it LST.

The exchange publishes a symbol guide, a copy of which is available just outside the Visitors' Gallery, in which you can look up any of the 1,200 companies or 1,600 issues listed here.

The second moving line shows the number of shares traded according to board lots. The size of a board lot varies with the price; the lower the price, the larger the lot. Most often, a board-lot represents 100 shares, since that is the board-lot unit of any share on the TSE worth more than $1. If only one board lot was traded, no number will appear, just the price. For shares trading over $5 each, this is shown in eighths, quarters, and halves of a dollar, partly in memory of the "pieces of eight" that used to be involved, partly as yet another piece of the hokum and mystification that make market-players feel as if they are on the inside of some special rite. However, stocks that sell for under $5 are shown in cents, so that if a stock trading at $15 dropped to $4.50, it would go from 15 to 450, which you are supposed to realize is not a huge jump, but a horrible drop. Yes, I know, it doesn't make any sense.

A stock priced at 15⅛ would actually be worth $15.125, or fifteen dollars and twelve-and-a-half cents, while one priced at 15⅜ would be worth $15.375 and one worth $4.38 would appear as 438. Got it?

If someone bought 1,000 shares of LST for $31.50, the ticker would look like this:

.... **LST** ....
...............................**10.315** ....

If someone bought less than a board lot, the letter "s" would be used. Thus:

.... LST ....
...............................89s.315 ....

would represent the sale of eighty-nine shares at $31.50. It would actually be an "Odd Lot."

Not so hard, is it? Most of what you see in those dizzying columns of type in the business pages is the information off the tickers, long lists of stock symbols and the prices at which shares moved, plus historical information on how the stock has done – the high and low prices for the year and whether a dividend has been paid – and there is always a box explaining which symbols your newspaper uses. The nub of it is the stock symbol and the price.

Now that we have come this far, perhaps this is the place to look at how the ticker tape looks in a newspaper listing. The main table, under Toronto, or New York, or whatever, will have its own forms of shorthand, but must contain nine bits of information, ranged across the page this way:

Year								
High	Low	Stock	Div.	High	Low	Close	Change	Vol
8	420	FAS	1.28	7	6 1/2	7	−1/8	30500

This line summarizes the trading in the shares of Fairly Attractive Shares, Ltd. The first two columns, under Year, refer to the highest and lowest at which this stock has traded in the past fifty-two weeks; it has been as high as $8.00 a share, as low as $4.20. Next comes the stock symbol, FAS; these are always in alphabetical order, if you're looking for a particular stock (if you can't find it, either it isn't on this exchange, or it is listed under one of the special lists, such as Mining). The fourth column tells us that FAS has been paying dividends, and this is the annual dividend projected on the basis of dividends paid over the last twelve months. Very good, too. Under High (the second High), comes the highest price paid for the stock during this trading session (i.e., today), $7.00. Next is the low, $6.50. The last trade, at the close, was at $7, and this was down ⅛, or 12.5 cents, from the closing trade yesterday. Finally, the volume of trading for the session came to 30,500 shares. There will be more information beside some stocks, but the box with the table on the first page of the newspaper's listings will explain what these are – warrants, whether dividends were paid in U.S. funds, that sort of thing. The truth is that, compared to cricket scores, stock tables are a snap.

Returning to the ticker tape from which the key data are derived, we will notice that not every offer to buy or sell a share is consummated. This occurs, despite the fact that the theory of markets holds that there is a buyer for every stock, at some price. This theory led to the creation of what market-players call the "To Who" bird, since, if every stock is going to be sold, we have to know To Who? (yes, of course it should be To Whom; grammar is not a strong point with these birds). The To Who bird works in tandem with the "greater fool" theory, which holds that you can always sell a stock, even if you paid too much for it, because there is always, out there somewhere, a greater fool. Don't count on it.

Thus, some tightwad out there might want to buy 100 shares of LST, the company we launched in the last chapter at $30 a share, and have now, for this exercise, moved onto the TSE, but doesn't want to pay more than $29.125 each for them. He will phone his broker and pass along that request; if there is no one willing to sell at that price, called the "Bid," the lowest price for which the broker was able to find a willing seller, called the "Ask," will be listed. This non-transaction would look like this:

.... **LST** ....
.... **29 1/8B30 1/8** ....

This tells us that somebody wanted to buy at $29.125, and somebody else was willing to sell at $30.125. It will appear in the newspaper under the heading Bid and Asked and doesn't mean a hell of a lot, except that you could probably buy the stock the next day at about $29.50, which is halfway between the two.

What we ought to do now is to buy some stock. We called a broker before coming down here, and he opened up an account for us. We called a "full service," as opposed to a "discount" broker. The full-service variety provides advice, information, and pep talks; the discount broker simply carries out our orders. Since we used a full-service broker, he gave us, along with a lot of malarkey about investments in general, the information that there might be a "real opportunity" awaiting in the shares of Pitchman Allied Limited, whose stock symbol is PAL. We look up at the ticker, and can't find the damn thing anywhere. That's because there have been no recent trades. Never mind, there is a computer in the foyer, and when we tap in the letters "PAL," it tells us that the stock closed yesterday at 10¼. That is, the last transaction was at $10.25; we also learn that it had been as low as 4.50 and as high as 11.50 within the last few days. Very volatile, this baby.

We call the broker and tell him to buy us 100 shares if he can get them for ten bucks even. This is a "limit order." That is, we are only willing to buy at the $10 price. Otherwise, we would just tell the broker to buy 100 shares, and he would execute the order at whatever price the stock was trading when our order hit the floor. That would be called a "market order," and is the more usual trade. We're fussy. We also make it an "all or none" order, indicating that we want 100 shares; if there are only 60 available at the price, we are not interested in what would be a "partial fill." Finally, we place a time limit on the deal. There are three time limits: Day Orders, Good Till Cancelled, and Good Through Date, in which we give a specific day to close or forget it. In this case, we put in a Day Order. We are investing $1,000.

The broker writes up our order and telephones it through to

one of his company's clerks on the trading floor. In our case, because we are such small fry, we are eligible for a Minimum Guaranteed Fill, or MGF. While the exchange cannot guarantee that we will be able to buy an unlimited number of shares of any particular variety, with an MGF, if we only want a few, we can have them. What constitutes "a few" varies from stock to stock, but whichever floor trader is responsible for any particular stock will sell us some of his own, if necessary. Thus, we are guaranteed that our order will be filled, as long as it is kept to a minimum. The TSE, like all stock markets, is crazy for initials. In the exchange's language, the MGF is "To encourage client order flow," or, to put it another way, to make it easier for small investors to join the fray and lose their shirts. The size of order eligible for an MGF depends on the amount of trading done in that stock and its price; the order may be anywhere from fewer than one hundred to a few thousand shares. Chances are, our order will simply be typed into a computer and filled automatically through the Computer Assisted Trading System, or CATS. (When CATS collapses, as it occasionally does, all hell breaks loose, because brokers sending in orders have no way of knowing whether the bids they put in are on or off the current market for any given stock. This is known as the wonderful efficiency of the computer.) At the moment, about half the stocks listed on the TSE are available on CATS; they are, mostly, those in which trading is least active. The more active stocks, representing half the listings but four-fifths of the volume, are sold on the floor by what is called "open outcry." There is a great deal of open outcry around stock exchanges; only this brand is official.

Let us, instead, imagine that we bid for 1,000 shares – ten board lots – and PAL is not available through CATS. Now, our order will involve a floor trader, one of the people (they are mostly men – there are only a few token women) we see down below us wearing a distinctive jacket representing his or her brokerage house.

The brokerage house clerk calls our order over to a floor trade for his house, who goes over to the particular post where PAL shares are traded and says something like "Ten PAL at ten." (That is what he is supposed to say, but it all depends on how busy things are. He may say, "Hey, Charlie, I got some joker who wants to pay ten for that crummy PAL stock you've been trying to unload. What about it?") Someone else is willing to sell the stock, and has told his broker he will take anything over 10⅛. The registered trader in PAL stock will come back to our trader, either by shouting "An eighth," or pointing his index finger down – the signal for an offer one-eighth over the bid – or, if he is in the mood, by saying, "You're nuts. How about ten-and-an-eighth?" Since we gave our trader no leeway, he can't budge.

Let us assume the other side blinks, and we get our 1,000 shares at $10. The selling trader makes out a "Floor Ticket" in triplicate to record the sale, gives one copy to our trader, keeps one, and files the third with a TSE clerk, who types the transaction into a computer. The clerk calls our broker and tells him, and he tells us, that we have a "done deal." We are now, gulp, $10,000 into the market, and our trade will go out on the ticker this way:

.... **PAL** ....
.................**10.10**...............................

Once the order has been filled, we have five days to complete the purchase by paying up and collecting our share certificates. What a notion! Like most of the people here, we are "day traders," and will get out of the stock long before the settlement date arrives.

Later in the day, we see the stock begin to move. By golly, our broker had it right; it goes to $10.50. Should we hold, or sell? It is one of the axioms of small traders that you can't lose by taking a profit. At $10.50, our 1,000 shares are now worth $10,500. We can make a quick $500. Dump 'em. We call our broker, who tells us to hang on, because PAL is going to hit $12 before the week is out.

No, we say, get out. So he does, and sells our shares for $10.25 – the market sagged for a bit there, when someone reported that Saddam Hussein smiled.

Well, never mind, we have made $250, for no effort. No, we haven't. We owe the broker his commissions, on both buying and selling, and, since we used a full-service broker, he sticks us for 6 per cent of the $10,000, or $600 on the buy and $625 on the sell. It cost us $1,225, minus our profit of $250, or $975. We managed to drop nearly $1,000 on a successful trade. Funny that wasn't in the *How To Make Millions Without Risking a Dime* book we bought a while ago. Well, never mind, better luck next time. If we had used a discount broker, we might have come closer to breaking even, but then, the discount broker wouldn't have told us what to buy.

The registered trader referred to above is what the TSE calls those traders who have the right to maintain markets in a given selection of stocks. They are usually referred to as "market-makers." The notion is that somebody has to make sure the prices don't gyrate too wildly, and that there is someone to look after the transactions in widely traded stocks on the floor – roughly half the stocks listed on the TSE have designated market-makers, and are sold by open outcry. The market-makers hold an inventory of the stocks for which they are responsible, and that's usually where the guaranteed fill stocks come from. They set the opening price of each of their stocks each morning, usually very close to the previous day's close.

Traders make a good living by playing the spread between Bid and Ask prices on their own stocks; if someone is willing to sell PAL for $8, and the trader sees a Bid at $10, there is nothing to prevent him buying the stock for $8, selling it for $10, and keeping the change. They can also take a terrible drubbing if they guess wrong too often. If it seems rather strange that the same people who are flogging the stocks on behalf of clients are buying and selling them on their own account, well, it is, but it is all part of the "liquidity" which is said to be the stock market's fundamental grace.

Liquidity in this case is a word for describing the fact that you can, in most circumstances, get rid of your stocks quickly. The TSE calls liquidity "an obligation" of the exchange, which is a little like the car salesman assuring you that you will be able to resell the heap he is about to deliver into your hands. Cash is the ultimate liquid; Canada Savings Bonds are very liquid, because you can sell them any time a bank is open. If the real purpose of the markets were to create investment money, it would not matter if it took a few days to dispose of stocks, but since the real purpose is to keep the roulette wheel rolling, liquidity is next to godliness. If there were no one around to make sure all the stocks were absorbed, they would not be quite so liquid. Or, to put it another way, so marketable.

John Maynard Keynes put his finger on the problem with liquidity, as usual, in his *The General Theory of Employment, Interest and Money:*

> Of the maxims of orthodox finance none, surely, is more anti-social than the fetish of liquidity, the doctrine that it is a positive virtue on the part of investment institutions to concentrate their resources upon the holding of "liquid" securities. It forgets that there is no such thing as liquidity of investment for the community as a whole.

Liquidity, Keynes argued, perverts the purpose of the market and destabilizes it. When investments were primarily in private businesses, they were relatively stable for both the owners of the shares and the community as a whole. The business of business was business. But, as stock markets developed with their high turnover rates, transactions on the exchanges came to be, as they are today, almost entirely transfers of existing investments, rather than the creation of new ones, or even the elimination of old and inefficient ones. They serve secondary markets, not primary ones. The short term became the only consideration. The stock market does not reward shrewd calculations as to the long-term worth of any given company, but rather the best guess as to which way the cat will jump today or tomorrow. In the happy phrase of Benjamin Graham and David L. Dodd, who in 1934 wrote a remarkably prescient book called *Security Analysis,* a too-liquid market "substitutes financial reasoning for business reasoning." This is good for the folks who collect commissions on every trade, but not good for the community as a whole, since so much time, effort, and money is tied up in playing Old Maid rather than in productive enterprise.

The ticker that recorded our little foray into stocks also shows options and warrants. Warrants are certificates issued by the company giving the holder the right to purchase a certain number of stocks at a given price within a given period of time. They are usually given out as part of a new issue of shares, as an additional inducement. When we float our second subscription of LST shares onto the market, we will include a warrant with every share (like the Bonus Extra Value 10 Per Cent More! on the side of a laundry detergent box), awarding the owner of each share the right to buy another share at $30 any time within the next five years. It doesn't cost us anything, and it helps to move the stock. These warrants themselves become a negotiable instrument, and are bought and sold and gambled on like everything else.

There is also a brisk market in "rights," which are exactly the same thing as warrants – the right to buy a newly issued stock at a set price – except that rights are normally exercisable within days or, at most, weeks, while warrants may be good for years.

An option is the right – but not the obligation – to buy or sell a given investment, usually a stock, at *a specified price* within a set period of time. You pay a premium for this right, a fraction of the price, which varies with the length of time for which the option is open and the price at which it may be exercised. Usually, these options are sold in contracts of 100 units each.

Longer options cost more, as do those farther away from the current price. When you are buying the right to purchase the stock, the option is a "call," while the right to sell is called a "put," as in calling the stock to you, or putting it away. The price at which the contract will be exercised is called the "strike price."

All of this is carried on the ticker, with the stock symbol and the month in which the option can be exercised on the top line and the strike price, the number of option contracts traded, and the premium on the bottom line. If the contract is a put, the letter P appears on the top line. Thus, if there were twenty call-option contracts (each option is 100 shares) traded on LST for the month of June at a strike price of $35, and the premium was $1.85, it would look like this on the ticker:

.... **LST.JU**...................................
.............................**35.20.185**..................

For $3,700, the buyer of this call option would own the right to buy 2,000 shares of LST stock at $35 any time up to the end of June from the seller. (The $3,700 represents $1.85 times 2,000.) If, in the meantime, the price rose from $35 to $40, he would make a profit of $3.15 on each share, or $6,300 ($5 gained on the deal, minus the $1.85 per share he paid as a premium). If the price went down, he would simply not exercise the call, and lose the premium – $3,700. In short, the option adds enormously to the amount of money that can be gained and lost on trades.

A put option on the same trade would look like this:

.... **LST.JU**   **P**........................
.............................**35.20.185**..................

In this case, the buyer of the put paid $3,700 for the right to sell 2,000 shares at $35. He thinks the price is going to drop; the puts are another way to short the stock. If LST sinks to $30, he will be up the same $6,300 ($5 per share, because he has the right to sell shares for $35 to whomever took the other side of this transaction, that will only cost $30, minus his premium). At least, you will be saying to yourself, he can't lose more than he invested, as he might in any other shorting operation, because he doesn't have to take up the option.

There is another wrinkle in this game to take care of that: the "naked option." The person who makes the offer on the option is said to "write" it. For the writer, the option looks the other way around; thus, a person who writes a put is selling you the right to sell him a number of shares at a given price within a given time, and he or she who writes a call is selling you the right to buy a certain number of shares within a certain time. Got that?

Well, it can be done even without the shares, but it gets risky. If you write a call to sell shares which you don't own, you have a naked option. If the share price goes up, which will cause the person to whom you sold the call to exercise it, you will have to go out and buy the stocks at whatever price they have now reached. Similarly, if you have sold a put option, and the price goes down, someone has the right to sell you shares at a higher price than they are now worth. Although you may have paid only a few cents for the premiums in either of these cases, you could lose dollars per share. You may be naked in more ways than one.

Options, like most of these instruments, can be bought on time, and for a fraction of the price down, which gives them tremendous leverage and makes this sector of the market all the more volatile. You can gamble for thousands with an expenditure of hundreds. The *TSE Review* for April 1991 shows us that, in a typical month, the average call premium was $1.56 and the average put premium was $1.55. Many of the 148,788 contracts traded would have been on margin; so the actual cash involved amounted to pennies a share, although the dollar value of the trades reached $23.2 million in total. It's like being into the one-buck lottery ticket, except that, in the lottery, you can only lose your stake, not your shirt. Options, again, have very little to do with raising money. They are used to hedge other parts of the betting, and, in the vast majority of cases, the options are never exercised. The puts and calls are themselves sold back and forth instead. The number of puts and calls which have not been exercised, but are still outstanding at any time, are listed in the Trans Canada Options section of the stock tables under the heading "Open Interest."

In case this isn't complicated enough, the salesmen have invented something called "put warrants," the most popular of which, the Nikkei put warrant, is sold by a number of banks and other financial institutions. This doesn't buy anything, really, only the chance to gamble that the general run of stock prices in Japan will drop. The current level of the Tokyo stock market, as defined in an index called the Nikkei, becomes the strike price; the level at the time the warrant can be exercised is the settlement price, and the owner of the put warrant receives the difference, in cash, between the strike price and the settlement price on the day the option closes. There is a call warrant as well, and in most cases, the warrants are sold for whatever quick profit can be made, as soon as the market begins to move.

The most active options on the TSE are options on the Toronto 35 Index that we met earlier; you can not only buy the actual TIPs units, you can buy the right to buy and sell the units; in one typical month, April 1991, $10.4 million was gambled this way. The transactions do not take place at the eight trading posts, but in the trading pits of the Futures Exchange, off to your right as you look through the glass of the Visitors' Gallery.

Time for a look over there.

The ticker also carries the fortunes of the index trading units of the exchange, which are also sold in the pits – TIPs, the Toronto 35 Index Participation Units that we have already met, briefly. Each TIPs unit represents a portion of a basket of the shares in the thirty-five corporations that make up the index. They pay quarterly dividends, based on the dividends that are paid by the underlying companies and can be bought, sold, and shorted like any individual stock. The TIPs trade in lots of 100 and represent, at the time I write this, a minimum investment of about $2,000, which is nothing compared to the $1.5 million or so you will have to put up to buy a similar instrument in Chicago or New York. During 1990, TIPs traded a total of 49,406,262 units for a total value of $925,047,702. They are fast becoming a key part of the game.

The indices themselves, despite the millions that are made and lost on their advance and retreat, have no intrinsic value. Their role is supposed to be to track the ebb and flow of the markets by combining the changing values of a number of stocks to arrive at an index number. An index is not an average. To get an average, you add up a series of numbers and divide by the number of items you used. An index is historical: the base period is given a number such as 100 or 1,000, and the index reflects the change since that base was established in the combination of stocks that make up the index. Thus, the Consumer Price Index was given a new base of 100 in 1981, and today's CPI reflects the change since then.

Stock indices group stocks, weight them according to their importance, and relate today's result to the original base. The standard index, the one quoted most often on television and the daily newspapers, is the Dow Jones Industrial Average, which is actually not a very good indicator, since it covers only 30 stock issues, all of them industrial companies, like Bethleham Steel or General Electric. And, it isn't an average, it's an index. Standard & Poor combines 500 stocks representing 5 different groups – industrials, transportation, utilities, financials, and a composite index of all 500 stocks. The TSE 300 Composite contains 14 major groups (42 are industrials, while almost as many, 40, are in financial services). The TSE Index was reset at 1,000 in 1975 and, as I write this, jogs back and forth around 2,500. The narrow Toronto 35 Index, on which TIPs is based, comprises the shares of the best-known Canadian companies traded on the exchange.

The indices ought not to mean much, since the way the entire market moves should have nothing to do with whether we are going to make money in Locket, Socket, and Trunk. However, the market has become so tied together, with huge blocks of shares whisked around the world in a nano-second, that the indices have taken over much of what happens. When the Dow droops, shares that have nothing to do with it will fade away too, and when the Toronto 35 soars, we can probably flog shares in Locket, Socket, and Trunk. Even Over the Counter stocks will move up because the exchange is having one of its good days. This is known as the wisdom of the market.

Because the markets are so volatile, money managers have increasingly gone into what are called "index funds." These operate on the same principle as TIPS, except that they are managed by individual managers, not a stock market. That is, the funds buy a broad selection of stocks that mimic an index, such as Standard & Poor. If S&P has it, most of the index funds will have it. These funds now represent about 40 per cent of all institutional money available in the United States for stock investment, which means that most pension plans are into such funds. The advantage for the manager of such a fund is that he doesn't have to follow 500 stocks – he or she probably can't remember a tenth of them, anyway – he just sets up the computer to follow the index. In effect, the price and value of the shares is ignored, and the market play becomes the sole determinant of when to buy and sell.

Among the difficulties this creates is the fact that the funds are now so huge that they don't merely ape the market, they influence it. When a new stock is added to an index, its price will jump, whether deservedly or not (Reebok International shares jumped 6 per cent, adding $70 million to the worth of the stock, the day the company was selected as one of the Standard & Poor 500), and lobbying to get onto the various indices has become aggressive and expensive.

All of this frenetic activity is said to make the market efficient, or, to put it in the textbook phrase, "a stock is worth what the market will pay for it, no more, no less." If the price of a share gets out of line, the reasoning goes, someone will buy it, if it is too low – or will short it, if it is too high. Thousands of investors making these decisions day in and day out will squeeze prices into perfect "efficiency," to reflect the true, underlying value of the companies. The problem with this theory is that, as we all know, what spooks or gooses the market may be a wild rumour, and it will spook or goose almost every stock, no matter what the company itself is doing. The system would work if investments were made for business rather than financial reasons, but as it is, there are no real rules to follow except that, if a particular stock is going up, it will continue to go up until it is ready to come down. Then it will drop. Are you enlightened?

The huge increase in the trading of TIPs and other index instruments (Toronto 35 Index Futures Contracts jumped 50 per cent in 1990), does not make the market more efficient; instead, it reflects the view of the market-players that efficiency cannot be attained. Instead of trying to outguess the market, they give up and follow it. You can't beat the market by buying TIPs, because TIPs follow the market (although you might by shorting the units).

The large investment funds, like pension funds, use what is called "program trading," the buying and selling of securities according to a computerized strategy. Usually, the computers find and "arbitrage" discrepancies between index options and the stocks underlying those options, or between stocks in different markets. As you will remember, the term "arbitrage" covers the buying and selling of the same or similar commodities in two different places at the same time, to take advantage of a discrepancy in price. There may be such a discrepancy between the values of the stocks in an index and the index itself; if so, the computer can find it and buy and sell accordingly. Program trading may account for as much as 20 per cent of trading on any given day. It is, says Louis Lowenstein in *What's Wrong with Wall Street*, "a zero-sum game being played out for the sole benefit of the brokers" (who get the commissions as the trades surge back and forth).

Stock indices, options, rights, and warrants are all part of what is called "Futures" trading, a small portion of which, money and commodity futures, will engage our attention in the next chapter. They are bets. Sometimes, they are bets made to ease the pain if another bet goes wrong; most often, they are just bets. They are, in fact, the only form of betting that is treated with awe, although it is ten times as crazy as putting the rent money on a horse.

You could bet on anything – on the number of raindrops to hit a window, on the number of people who will be killed in car accidents over the next long weekend, over the exact size of the Gross National Product next May, or what number will show up next month under the listing TXO.S on the ticker, which represents Toronto 35 Index Options. Only in the stock market will your insatiable desire to play the numbers game be taken to heart, and saluted, and described as a boon to the economy. Louis Lowenstein puts it this way:

> The distinction between gambling and investment, it has been said, is that in investments everyone can win. No one loses, for example, when the owner of an apartment house receives from his tenants a fair rent. To read some of the promotional literature, one might think that index futures are also a place where everyone can win. Wrong. Futures, like other derived securities, are intrinsically speculative, a form of gambling in which *no one can win unless someone loses* [author's emphasis]. It is as if the landlord who built that apartment house did so not to collect rent from a tenant receiving real value, but to bet with a bookie on whether the building would be worth more this week than last.

The fact that no one can make sense of the markets, because they are so jerked about by all these games that their behaviour has become just plain silly, has bothered some of the finest financial thinkers of our time. To bring order out of chaos, these thinkers have constructed a great many theories to explain why stock prices whoop and swoop as they do, when economics cannot explain their behaviour. They manufacture a life for the stock numbers themselves, and look for patterns in the numbers which will, they say, be repeated. They put their faith in "technical analysis," which delivers a theory as to how the numbers will move in the future by the way they moved in the past. What is a little frightening about these people, the Christian Scientists of the market game, is that if enough of them follow the same system, it will become a self-fulfilling prophecy. Not much danger of that, though, because there are so many theories and so many ways of interpreting the theories that dart-throwers usually do better than "Chartists" – another name for these birds – every time.

The establishment of the Dow Jones index led to a strong belief in stock-charting, even before the turn of this century. As long ago as 1906, an American writer, Thomas Gibson, was dismissing the approach as "untrustworthy, absolutely fatuous, and highly dangerous." He might have added "and durable," for the Dow theory is still with us. The theory holds that the stocks of highly capitalized companies, the industry leaders, will tend to trade within a narrow range and, if they start to trend up, then they will break out of this range on the high side, and make new highs. When they dip again, they will not go down as far as they were before they went up. If you chart all this, you can find a "trend line" that will tell you where the stock should go next, namely, upward. If the pattern reverses itself, and the upward trend fails to make a new high, while the downward swoop goes below "the neckline" – the last low – then, folks, we have a new trend line. The Dow theory produces "shoulders" and "support levels" and "resistance levels," "double bottoms" and "head-and-shoulder formations," which can only be followed by the faithful and upon which millions and millions of dollars are gambled every day.

Then there is the Elliott Wave, which argues that the market simply repeats the mathematics of the Fibonacci series, the work of a thirteenth-century arithmetician. Find out where you are in the Elliott Wave, and you will know where the market is going next, and where to place your bet. Why should this be the case? Well, because, that is what happened in the past. In short, you can use footprints to predict the future. In a more sceptical world, the Chartists and Elliot Wavers would have a tough time. If Jimmy the Greek were to give his odds for next weekend's basketball game based, not on the relative strengths and weaknesses of the players, but on what the raw numbers of scores in the past suggest will happen next Saturday, he would soon be Jimmy the Broke. Move him over to the NYSE, though, and he can make a fortune as a stock analyst.

The terrific advantage of these theories is that, when the True Word doesn't pan out, we can always say that, well, we must have misinterpreted the chart. It is a theory borrowed from Ouija boards and palmists. About twenty years ago, a friend of mine who reads Tarot cards, announced, after running me through the decade, that I would be blind in a year and dead in eighteen months. When this did not come about, she became very cross with me; she claimed that the mistake must have occurred because I gave her the wrong time of day for my birth. Otherwise, I would be dead, because the cards are never wrong. This woman would do well as a stock analyst.

Thus, when Robert Prechter, one of the New York Elliott Wave gurus, predicted that the prices of thirty key stocks would go up in late 1987, and they came tumbling down instead, he had an explanation ready. He had begun his analysis with numbers from 1982, when he should have been measuring from 1974, he explained. Now that he thought about it, yes, by golly, when you re-oriented the Wave to 1974, it showed a sharp drop in 1987. Right again. Another Elliott Waver concluded in mid-1991 that we were currently either "in mid-1928" or maybe "mid-1929," which meant that calamity, desolation, and collapse were within either eighteen months or six months. If he can just hold on long enough, he's bound to have a winner one day.

Opposed to the Chartists and Wavers are two other groups, the Fundamentalists and the Random Walkers. The Fundamentalists look at a company – its past, its earnings, its management – and what the market generally is doing in that area of activity. They can be blind-sided by events, and, because they are trying to apply reason to a market which is not rational, they don't have much fun either. The Random Walkers, however, have it over everybody. They say that the past means nothing in stock analysis, and that the future price of any security is no more predictable than the path of a series of random numbers. Paul Samuelson of MIT and Henry Wallich of Yale have both testified on behalf of Random Walk analysis before the Senate Banking Committee. A couple of senators, thus influenced, threw darts at an NYSE stock-list (quite a popular pastime) and did better than a number of stock analysts. This caused George W. Goodman, editor of the *Institutional Investor,* who writes money books under the pseudonym "Adam Smith," to comment, "Everybody had better gird up, because if the random walk is indeed Truth, then all charts and most invest-ment advice have the value of zero, and that is going to affect the rules of the Game."

I don't think George-Call-Me-Adam need worry. The longing to believe in a market where you can place your bets according to double bottoms and heads-and-shoulders and complex mumbo-jumbo, rather than blind luck, is so strong that I imagine we are stuck with the Chartists and program-trading and all that stock-driving hype for some time to come.

I say this despite the fact that I, personally, am a Dartist. The great advantage we Dartists hold over Chartists is that darts don't take much work, don't cost anything much, and are shown, by empirical evidence, to work as well as anything else.

Remember what all this was supposed to be in aid of? In the words of the TSE:

In our free enterprise system, corporations are the engines that drive the economy. As companies expand and prosper, Canadians gain the benefits of a stronger economy and a higher standard of living. In order to grow, however, companies need money. One way they can raise that money is by issuing shares. People who buy a company's shares become partners of the firm and participate in its fortunes.

Square that, if you can, with the view from the Visitors' Gallery, where you have just begun to calculate how much money you can make by shorting shares in BCED because there is a juicy rumour floating around that Iraq is going to blow up again.

It is as if we set out to create a place to sell tomatoes and have, instead, wound up with a market that sells, not tomatoes, but the right to buy and sell tomatoes, their stems, their leaves, skins, roots, and smell, tomatoes of the future, tomatoes unplanted and ungrown, and the land they haven't been planted or grown on, along with a side-bet on whether the farmer who hasn't planted them has a moustache. We can even, by shorting tomatoes, buy the rights to the future prosperity of tomato slugs and the hope that the whole crop will be wiped out by pestilence, making us rich.

That should give free enterprise a boost.

CHAPTER SEVEN

Congratulations! You Are Now the Owner of 112,000 Pounds of Sugar. Or, Back to the Futures

Commodities

Robert Hocker told a federal court in Wyoming that he didn't even know what a commodity was when a broker for First Commodity Corp. of Boston phoned in 1983. But after listening to the broker's tales of huge profits to be made in silver, the unemployed oil-field worker sent the firm more than $55,000. First Commodity took 39 per cent of his money in fees the first day, then lost most of the rest in volatile futures markets. Mr. Hocker eventually got back $1,387.64, about 2.5 per cent of his original investment.

– *The Wall Street Journal,* July 1985.

$

The place is a cock-pit, and was deliberately designed that way. You expect, at any moment, to see fighting birds come hurtling out of the corners to meet in the middle, flashing spurs and screaming fury. Along the walls are monitors, carrying quotes from the Chicago market, including the prices of everything from pork bellies to metals. A larger, electronic board tracks quotes from the operations here in western barley, flax, canola, soybeans, rye, and oats. There are two pits sunk into the floor, and two trading desks, one at each end. A gaggle of men is standing at the top of the pits, telling jokes; one of them is reading a newspaper. Two businesswomen in their mid-thirties, visitors from Portage La Prairie – who were in the huge office building in the middle of Winnipeg on other business and saw the sign inviting them to check out the exchange on the fifth floor – are bemused by the lack of activity.

"When are they going to do something?" one of them asks me. She plainly thinks the traders are a shiftless lot.

"In about two minutes," I reply. We are about five minutes from the exchange's closing time, and the traders are waiting for the final quotes of the day to make their moves. Suddenly, they jump down into the pits and begin shouting, waving their arms, and transmitting hand signals. The frenzy of activity keeps up, with clerks dodging around to collect the trading tickets, until an electronic beeper goes off, and the session is over.

"Boy, that didn't last long," says one of the visitors.

"Like sex with my husband," says the other. And we all file out, decorously.

We have just come out of the viewing gallery over the Winnipeg Commodity Exchange, one of the score of North American venues where commodities and futures contracts are traded. Through these places move the vast quantities of grains, oils, and other agricultural products that serve most world markets, as well as metals, foreign currencies, and the bits of paper that represent all these goods, and have become saleable products themselves. There are only three futures exchanges of any consequence in Canada – in Toronto, Winnipeg, and Montreal – and each specializes in a narrow range of products.

The Toronto Futures Exchange, which operates out of one corner of the main TSE floor, sells index futures, contracts on government Treasury bills and long-term bonds, silver contracts, and U.S. dollar contracts. Paper.

The Montreal exchange sells lumber and gold futures. Here in Winnipeg, the emphasis is on agricultural products, mostly grains and oils. There are much larger commodity and futures exchanges in Chicago, New York, Minneapolis, Kansas City, and Philadelphia. Coffee, cotton, and sugar are the big sellers in New York, while, if you want beef, Kansas is the place for you. Grains are sold mostly in Minneapolis, foreign currency contracts in Philadelphia, and, if you want a mess of pork bellies, head for Chicago. We have come to Winnipeg because it is, after all, our own, and because what we see here is very much the same system followed in every major commodities market from Singapore to Paris, Tokyo to Zurich.

The pits at the Winnipeg Commodity Exchange are deeper and more impressive than the pit at the Toronto Futures Exchange. They are constructed in a series of hexagons; each hexagon consists of a step, running all around the pit and set about ten inches below the next and smaller in circumference; the closing ring descends to a small floor at the bottom. A tiny amphitheatre. The traders stand on these steps, or wander up and down them, singing out in a language wondrous to hear: "One May rye at a half" or "Sell one July flax at an eighth." The traders seem to pay no attention to each other. They walk up and down, bellowing away, until suddenly two of them will huddle together, twiddle their fingers at each other, nod, and mount the stairs to where exchange officials sit at recording posts. A deal has been done, and within seconds it will appear on the board above. When the place gets busy, it gets noisy. The *Winnipeg Free Press*, reporting the visit of a group of British journalists to the pits in 1925, quoted one of them as saying it was not an elevating experience, "with the men barking like dogs and roaring like bulls in a most undignified and excited manner." It hasn't changed.

The exchange is the only private futures market for grains in Canada, which would be more impressive except that by far the largest quantity of grain is sold through the Canadian Wheat Board. Winnipeg is also a futures market for precious metals, and its annual turnover runs to more than $10 billion. It has been around for more than a century, having started as the Winnipeg

Grain and Produce Exchange in 1887. A generally admiring book by Allan Levine, *The Exchange: 100 Years of Trading Grain in Winnipeg,* nonetheless points out that its rich history of skullduggery, wild gambling, and outright theft left a bad taste in the mouths of many farmers, who saw their crops disappear into its commodious maw, with very little return. Indeed, the rascality of the exchange – now, Levine assures us, only a memory – was one of the reasons for founding the Canadian Wheat Board in the first place.

A National Film Board documentary on the place, called *Paper Wheat,* caught some of the flavour in a song that contained the memorable lines: *It's free enterprise, American Dream, / We'll sell you down the river, but we'll never lose steam.*

Commodities are sold both for immediate use – "cash," or "spot," sales – or for future use and "hedging" – the term for coppering your bet by buying something at different rates for different delivery dates in search of an acceptable average. There are exchanges like this all over the world, linked by the electronic wizardry of our age. The main non-money products traded in Canada (we will come to money later) are oats, barley, flax, canola (which used to be rapeseed), potatoes, and cattle on the food side, and gold, copper, silver, lumber, plywood, and heating oil among the non-foods. This doesn't mean we can't buy all the other products available – they are as close as our broker's telephone – just that such wonders as hides, Indiana broilers, African cocoa butter, and Omaha hogs are sold through other exchanges.

Each commodity exchange specializes, and it is very tough indeed to gain new listings or to persuade customers that it would be a good idea to buy orange-juice contracts through Toronto. Winnipeg is a grain exchange; Chicago is strong on beef, shell eggs, soybeans, live hogs, and frozen pork bellies; New York is strong on cotton, orange juice, sugar, coffee, cocoa, hides, and platinum. London is the world's busiest metals market – and it is here that traders set the price for gold, twice a day – but London also deals in cocoa, sugar, coffee, and a host of other commodities. Each exchange acts as a listening post for the others, and if the price for a cocoa contract, which the exchange has decreed represents ten metric tons of the stuff, changes on one market, the others will soon adjust as arbitragers buy it one place and sell it another at the same time to make a profit.

The first written records of futures trading date from 1690, in Japan, where tickets were issued against rice growing in the fields. This was often, literally, seed money that allowed the planting to take place. Before long, a market was established in the tickets themselves, as well as the rice, and we were off. The process spread to Europe and then to North America, where the first North American grain exchange was established in 1848. The Winnipeg Grain and Produce Exchange didn't become a major grain exchange until 1904, when it established the first futures markets for wheat, oats, and flaxseed.

These exchanges grew out of the common need of both producers and users of commodities of all sorts. Let us suppose, for example, that you are in the business of growing canola seed, which will be made into oil for margarine, and you plant two hundred acres of the stuff. When you put your seed in the ground, you do a little figuring, and you work it out that with seed, fuel, mortgages, labour, and other costs, you are going to spend $5.00 for every bushel of canola seed you bring to market. You call up a grains broker, who can tell you that canola is selling for $6.50, which means that you should make a handsome profit. (The newspapers carry commodity prices, but canola, which is sold at 100 metric tons, or about 6,500 bushels, a contract, is hard to work out; easier to make a phone call.) But what if the price falls? What if it goes down to $4.50 a bushel? At that price, you will lose with every bushel you sell. Wouldn't it be nice to know, in advance, that you could get at least $5.50? The only way to do this is to sell your crop now, even before it is grown, at current prices, through a futures contract.

For buyers, the logic works in reverse. Suppose, this time, that you are a manufacturer of chocolate bars. Your bars are made of sugar, nuts, cocoa, shortening, and artificial flavouring and are guaranteed to rot the teeth out of every kid in the country. You mean to sell them for forty cents to the retailer, because that is what everybody else is selling them for, and you hope to make money from it. What you make will depend, in large part, on how much you pay for ingredients. These prices will vary, while the amount you can charge for your chocolate bars will not; you can't sell the things for forty cents one week and thirty-seven the next and forty-two the next. The changes in packaging and whole-saling alone would put you out of business in a few weeks. You must know, in December, what you are going to pay for your ingredients next May, and the only way to do that is to buy May's supplies now, through futures contracts. The same logic applies to everything from orange juice (sold in 15,000-pound contracts) to coffee (37,500 pounds a contract) to lumber (150,000 board feet) to pig iron (sold by the gross ton).

Commodity futures grew out of a real need, which still exists; it is too bad the process has become so screwed around by gambling – as it has.

The size of the trading units are usually determined by the amount that can be delivered in a truck, which is why they are so huge. Pork bellies (which is really just the name for bacon, before it is cut) come in 36,000-pound shipments, most grains in 1,000 or 5,000 bushels and, if you ever actually have to accept delivery of a sugar contract, you will discover that you have purchased a min-imum of 112,000 pounds. (Will that be one lump, or two?) Each commodity has a price quotation unit; canola is sold in cents and eighths of a cent per bushel, sugar in tenths of a cent per pound, unleaded gas in 42,000 U.S. gallon units, and gold and silver in troy ounces.

Finally, each commodity is linked to a series of dates, which, for agricultural items, are tied to the production cycle of the item.

The delivery months for rye, for example, are October, December, May, and July. Rye is normally sown in September, lies dormant throughout the winter, and is harvested in July and August. If the rye costs $4.00 in August, and is to be used in December, it will have to be stored for three months, adding costs for storage facilities, insurance, and bank interest. Purchased on the spot in August, the price would be $4.00, but for December delivery, it would be somewhere around $4.40, unless someone started speculating, in which case it might be twice or half as high.

Now we are in a position to make some sense out of the open outcry calls. "One May rye at a half" was a bid to buy one contract of 5,000 bushels of rye for delivery in May at $4.50. (The board listed rye at $4.00, and the half adds fifty cents; only the last unit is cried.) "Sell one July flax at an eighth" was an offer to sell one contract of flax for July at $5.35 ⅛; the currently listed price for July flax was $5.35 ¼, so this is a slight drop in price.

To keep some sort of control on fluctuations, daily limits on swings in price are set for each commodity. Most grains have a day limit of ten cents a bushel, sugar usually is limited to five-cents-a-pound swings, and so on.

So far, so good. We have constructed a system that satisfies the needs of both buyers and sellers and assures each of an acceptable price in the future. Enter the speculator. What is being sold on the floor of the exchange is not the commodity itself but a slip of paper representing a contract to deliver the item on the day specified. If you buy a contract for cocoa dated May 1, it does not mean that on that fateful day a truck will dump 30,000 pounds of the stuff on your driveway; it means that in a warehouse somewhere, one contract is assigned to your name. You can sell that contract at any time up to the delivery date for whatever you can get for it; you can gamble on it.

What is more, you can gamble with money you don't have. The margins on commodities are entirely a matter between buyer and seller and a 10 per cent margin is common. In *Anyone Can Make a*

Million, Morton Shulman showed how this could work in practice:

> As an example of how this low margin requirement can produce spectacular profits, examine the situation if one had bought sugar futures just before the Cuban crop failure a few years ago. At that time sugar prices jumped all the way from two cents a pound to twelve cents. Each contract (they were then of 11,000 pounds) which had been worth $2,200 zoomed all the way up to $13,200. If $200 had been deposited as an initial margin, it would have grown to be worth $11,200 – an increase of over 5,000 per cent.

If there was one lesson learned in the Great Crash of 1929, it was that 10 per cent margins were the road to ruin; so, we don't sell stocks for 10 per cent any more, just twenty-ton loads of pork. As we will see, the margin on some financial instruments is now 1 per cent. In the sugar deal Dr. Shulman writes about, something actually happened to allow the speculator to make his huge profit: the Cuban crop failed. But in real life, there need be no such real event. It is enough if speculators *think* something is going to happen.

The effect of commodities gambling is exaggerated because of a leverage technique known as "pyramiding," another form of the old Ponzi game. Take the example of Shulman's sugar speculator who laid out $200 and made a profit of $11,200 on paper. He could now reinvest that profit in more contracts. These are now worth $13,200, so his 10 per cent down payment would come to $1,320 per contract; he could buy seven more contracts and, Shulman calculated, he could make $5,000,000 by pyramiding his original $200 within six months, if only more sugar crops would get ruined, and the price would keep rising.

And what would happen, in the meantime, to the supermarket price of sugar, or cocoa, or coffee, or anything else caught up in this whirl? It would soar, of course, and onto it would be added all the new mark-ups of all the middlemen and retailers, which are based on a percentage of the original price, and the poor old consumer would be paying it all. The ten-cent jump Shulman's gambler made eventually translated into a hike of more than fifty cents in the store.

Commodity futures can be turned into puts and calls, just like any other instrument, adding yet another element of volatility – and, as usual, everything that goes up can come down just as fast. Shulman's happy hustler made $5,000,000 in six months; he could lose just as much just as quickly. If he had bought sugar when it was twelve cents, putting $1,320 down, and it went down to two cents, he could have lost $11,000 on his $200 investment; and if he tried to recover by plunging in deeper, he would have discovered that the wonderful thing about leverage is that it works both ways.

These markets make no more sense than stock prices, and are driven just as relentlessly up and down by Chartists and Elliott Wavers and others of their ilk. I once had a long chat with a man in the Winnipeg Commodities Exchange who was investing heavily in silver because he had seen, on one of his charts, the coming approach of a "complex head-and-shoulder bottom," which he took to mean that if he got in and out fast, he could buy when it was down and sell when it was up. I reminded him that the Hunt brothers of Texas had managed to lose $900 million on silver futures, but he said that this didn't worry him, because he didn't have $900 million.

"Neither did the Hunt brothers, as it turned out," I reminded him. You don't have to have it to lose it, in commodities or options.

I have two objections to the way commodity speculation affects food products, to deal with that subject first: One is moral and the other practical. Yes, I know it is foolish to attack anything that has to do with money on the trifling grounds of morality, but the point is worth considering. Robespierre, the French revolutionary, a man whose views I am normally inclined to shun, said it all in debate on December 2, 1792, when he said of French food speculators: "They have given great weight to the profits of merchants and owners, and almost none to the life of mankind."

It seems to me quite wrong that speculators, who don't do a damn thing but huddle over their charts muttering incantations and who clutter up the galleries of exchanges and brokers' offices, should be able to make money out of driving the price of foods up and down through the exercise of superstition, luck, or planted rumours. They did not produce the food, nor process it, nor market it; they have simply latched onto it as a means whereby they can enrich themselves at the expense of others. The poor of the world have no part in this game, but they are its victims.

The defence offered by the speculators is a curious one: namely, that's the way it works, baby. The case was put in a pamphlet called *Before You Speculate,* produced by the Chicago Mercantile Exchange:

> Sometimes speculators are accused of making markets unstable by virtue of their speculation, but it is not necessary for them to prove they earn their profits; if they do anything, by stabilizing or destabilizing prices, they earn the opportunity to profit merely by being in the market. Without the speculators, futures markets could not function; therefore, if the futures markets operate for the social good, the speculator who makes the operation possible must also contribute to the social good.

Or, to put it more clearly: if you own a knife, you are entitled to hack off your chunk of flesh where you find it; knife-makers have to live, too. That being the case, your bloody operations are, in the end, a boon to mankind.

Pausing only briefly to say that there is no evidence that futures markets could not function without speculation of the kind that now marks them, I note that naked greed has never had a shakier defence than the argument that it is bound to work out, in the end, for somebody's social good.

In Canada, futures wheat markets function very well indeed without the intercession of the speculator. In 1943, the Canadian Wheat Board was given sole marketing responsibility for wheat. The exchange would like to get it back, but it is on shaky political ground. Allan Levine, in *The Exchange: 100 Years of Trading Grain in Winnipeg,* argues that the place has been given an undeservedly bad name, although he admits that most of the charges of market manipulation have been met by flat denials — and by hiding the records. He says the exchange might be called "a house with closed shutters." It is also a house with fewer voters than there are on the farms, and the farmers, by and large, blame it for all the woes that attend swerving prices.

The Canadian Wheat Board is the sole agency allowed to handle wheat, oats, and barley shipped from province to province, or sold outside Canada. The producers deliver their grain to the local elevator and are given a government-guaranteed initial payment. Then, if the board gets more than the floor price when it has sold the entire crop, the farmer gets a second payment. Growing the wheat is a gamble, selling it is not. There is no such thing as a futures market in the three grains handled by the wheat board, and flour millers and other large consumers of wheat manage without it very well.

In the United States, wheat is a commodity like any other. In Canada, dozens of crops, from peas to pork, are sold on futures contracts without going through a gambling exchange. In short, it is no answer to the moral issue of gambling on food to say that it is either a necessary evil or a contributor to the social good; it is neither.

My other objection to commodity speculation is practical, not moral: it is that the exchanges in the United States which dominate commodity prices are, on the whole, appallingly run and regulated. The opportunities for graft, pilferage, manipulation, and all the other forms of hanky-panky that prevail in stock markets all over the world reach a kind of zany zenith in the commodities game. Particularly damaging is a form of wash-trading in which the speculators sell contracts back and forth at ever-increasing prices. It is widespread, costly, and almost impossible to prove. As in all the other exchanges, the commodity traders are essentially self-regulating, a hyphenated phrase meaning "forget it." When soybeans began to rise in value in the 1970s as a result of a shortage of protein caused by the failure of the fish crop off Peru, market manipulation drove the price from $3 to $12 a bushel in short order, which pushed the prices of every other grain up, as well. The speculators were not providing a market, they were making a killing; in many cases, they were making hundreds of killings, as food was pushed beyond the reach of impoverished people in the Third World. The U.S. Commodities Exchange Authority, after due deliberation, pronounced that it could not "rely to any great extent on exchanges carrying out their responsibility for maintaining adequate surveillance over the trading activities of floor brokers." Then it bowed out. I surrender, dear.

There was another investigation after the crash of October 1987, which was not left to the home talent, this time, but was instead conducted by the FBI. This resulted in a cluster of plea bargains, a handful of convictions of minor personages, a few fines paid, some name-calling among the politicians, and then, according to a 1991 book on the subject, *Brokers, Bagmen and Moles: Fraud and Corruption in the Chicago Futures Markets,* by David Greising and Laurie Morse, "business continued as usual."

Greising and Morse argue that cheating the customers is simply an accepted way of life in the pits, both by the brokers and the institution itself. Sadly enough, James M. Stone, who tried mostly in vain to clean up the markets while chairman of the Commodity Futures Trading Commission during the Carter administration, agrees. In a thoughtful article in the *Boston Globe,* he commented, "Infractions against customers, I was often told, have little or no influence on the price discovery process, nor do they seriously undermine the commercial hedging activity that takes place through futures."

Or, to put it in language we can all understand, the car salesmen agree that it doesn't matter if you roll back the odometer on that secondhand Chevy, because we're going to charge the poor sap the same price, anyway. It will not affect the market.

Stone rejects this argument, and puts his finger on the nub:

> Futures trading is like oil in the machinery of real commerce. A little lubricates the machinery; more begins to gum it up. The core problem at the futures exchanges is that they have gone past the optimum levels the free market would create if the regulatory and tax framework were rationalized. An excess of speculation, like gaming everywhere, tempts the cheaters and nurtures the fast-buck artists, then forces them into political activity to protect their franchises.

What this means, for the ordinary investor, has been put succinctly by Andrew Tobias in *The Only Other Investment Guide You'll Ever Need*: "If you speculate in your commodities . . . *you will lose your money* [author's emphasis]. In fact, it is even possible to lose more than you bet. I could tell you a lot more about commodities, *but this is all you need to know.*"

The last phrase is a bit of a cop-out. We don't have to play the markets to be hurt by the results of speculation; I think that as a society we do need to know a great deal more than the fact that futures markets are an almost sure-fire way to get rid of unwanted cash.

To blunt the knife-edge of risk, many investors join commodity funds (which Tobias dismisses just as quickly: "With a commodity fund you pay dearly for the privilege of having someone else lose your money for you"). These are set up in much the same way as mutual funds, which I deal with in Chapter Nine, and have the advantage that you can lose only your investment, not more, unlike the situation in other futures contracts. You buy units in the fund and turn the whole business over to a professional manager, who takes his cut off the top and then goes out to gamble with what is left. Some of these funds make money, most do not; they have nothing whatever to do with the legitimate business of markets. They are sold by aggressive pitchmen, often by calling cold to telephone lists of potential customers all over North America. They are assured, like Mr. Hocker, the victim at the top of this chapter, that they are in the hands of "trained professionals." So they are, but their profession is fleecing, not investing.

The Chicago Exchange is pressing forward with improvements. Not improvements to cut the cheating, silly, but ways to move the quotes faster. A new electronic trading network is being installed, with a guarantee that computers from around the world can pour in their orders in no longer than three seconds. And there is a project to design a hand-held, electronic order system, like a cellular phone, so the floor traders can roam the pits and punch in their orders on the spot as they see other trades go down.

The commodity exchanges are getting bigger and busier, but they are not getting better.

There is slightly more to be said on behalf of the currency side of the exchanges, the financial futures markets. It is inevitable that, given the ready flow of money around the world at different rates, people will want to speculate on what will happen in the future, both as a hedge to cover the need for dollars, or guilders, or whatever, to spend in foreign markets, and for speculation itself. Again, these markets are incredibly volatile, and require very little real cash to start a truly spectacular gambling run. For Treasury bills, for example, on the TFE, contracts worth $100,000 can be purchased for as little as $1,000 down, and gold certificates, traded in U.S. dollars, can be bought for 25 per cent down. Treasury bills are not much of a gamble. They are sold by the federal government at auction every Thursday afternoon, and do not fluctuate much. Gold, however, does fluctuate, and so do the dozens of currencies from all over the world that money-market speculators buy and sell in million-dollar lots.

The real gamblers in the money markets are the banks, who need all kinds of foreign currencies for their overseas operations, and who buy and sell the stuff by the tens of millions, trying to make a lot by making a little on each trade. As with other commodities, there are spot trades and futures; you can buy a million marks now, or buy the right to buy or sell it – or any of a score of financial instruments, from U.S. Treasury notes and German government bonds to Japanese yen and Swiss francs – at some fixed date in the future. Japanese yen, in case you want to tuck some away in your stocking for Christmas, sell in contracts of 12.5 million yen, so that a rise or fall of 0.0001 per yen works out to $12.50 (U.S.) per contract. This is a game for large institutions with huge amounts of capital to invest, and it is, like so much of market activity, essentially a zero-sum game. Everybody loses, everybody wins, and then somebody says, let's all go jump on the Canadian dollar, or the Deutschemark, or the Eurodollar. These activities certainly affect the economy as a whole – and therefore each of us as individuals – but mostly, the money markets are a game played by big boys who can look after themselves.

It is kind of interesting for the outsiders, however, when one of the gamblers comes up snake-eyes. At the 1991 annual meeting of Allied Lyons PLC (PLC stands for "Public Limited Company"; it is the British equivalent of "Co. Ltd."), a number of angry shareholders wanted to know how the conglomerate – which owns, among other companies, Tetley's, Baskin-Robbins, Dunkin' Donuts, and a batch of distilleries, including Corby Distilleries of Montreal and Hiram Walker of Windsor, Ontario – managed to show a loss of £147 million ($269.7 million) in foreign currency trading during the year. They did not find out. Allied Chairman Sir Derrick Holden-Brown told them "The necessary remedial action has been taken," and advised everybody to forget about it.

"The shareholders have not been given all the facts," complained one shareholder, but instead of replying, correctly, that they never are, Sir Derrick gave him the straight-arm. "I have taken great trouble to keep our largest institutional shareholders informed; their view is that it should be put into the past," he said. Institutional shareholders are the pension funds and other large stock-buyers; they get more information than the slobs who only have a few thousand dollars on the line. At the meeting in London, there were more rumours floating around than there are almonds in Jamoca Almond Fudge ice cream, but, beyond a hint that the entire bundle had been dropped on one series of currency gambles – "A little snowball can become an avalanche very quickly indeed," Sir Derrick said, mouthing a motto that ought to be embroidered on the pillow of every futures trader – no hard information emerged. No doubt we will learn more when Sir Derrick writes his memoirs, which were moved perceptibly closer by the blunder. He retired a year ahead of time. Still, Allied Lyons managed to make a pre-tax profit of $876 million, despite dropping nearly $270 million on currency trading. The lesson we learn from this is that if you are looking at an income this year in the billion-dollar range, you are probably able to mess around with financial futures, and if not, not.

To let us in on the action at a slightly lower level, we now have money-market funds, which are mutual funds. In essence, they are a reflection of the fact that large gamblers have taken over the operation of currency speculation.

CHAPTER EIGHT

Gentlemen Prefer Bonds

The Bond Markets

There are probably only two alternatives. One is that a bond will be paid back in worthless dollars. Government will infuse geometrically increasing numbers of dollars into the economy in a desperate attempt to keep debtors from defaulting. This will lead to hyperinflation, and bonds could then be repaid for [the] face amount, but the face amount will only have nominal purchasing power. This has been the fate of debt in numerous countries; it is why long-term debt does not exist in places like South America. The other alternative is that your bonds will not be paid back at all.
– Douglas R. Casey, *Crisis Investing*, 1980.

$

Two of the most important sets of financial instruments available are not traded on Canadian stock exchanges, namely mutual funds and bonds. They can be bought and sold through any financial adviser, including your broker and your corner bank, but not through the exchange. Corporate bonds are sold through U.S. exchanges, though, so it is probably only a matter of time before that is the case in Canada, and there is already a move afoot to have mutual funds traded on the TSE, possibly on the grounds that there are still some potential customers out there with a jingle in their pockets – or in fulfillment of some other great social need.

If bonds are not part of the exchange, they are, nonetheless, very much part of the market, and their transition from safe, acceptable, even dull instruments of investment to the wildest cards in the pack shows how it is possible, if the best and brightest financial minds are put to work on a problem, to screw *anything* up. When we begin to delve into their innards, you will find it hard to imagine that such innocent-seeming, straightforward instruments could be the implements of so much rascality, but we must never underestimate the ingenuity of a hustler on the make.

While it is the stocks that get all the press, bonds represent much more money; every day, several times the volume of dollars represented by stock transactions is traded in bonds, although they are not nearly so visible, because the figures are not compiled daily, as they are in stock trading. Governments cannot issue stocks, but they can and do float issues of bonds. Indeed, virtually every government and the vast majority of corporations issue some bonds, and some have dozens of issues outstanding. As with stocks, there are two markets: the primary market created by the first issue and the secondary market created when already-issued bonds are bought or sold.

Bonds, as we have already seen, are debt instruments, as opposed to equity. They are IOUs issued by governments and corporations. If you buy shares in Locket, Socket, and Trunk Co. Ltd., you own part of it; if you buy a bond issued by LS & T, you have simply loaned money to the corporation. Or the government. Or Ontario Hydro. Or to whomever issued the bond. You will receive interest on the bond annually and, at the end of the time shown on its face, you will get the principal sum back as well. With Canada Savings Bonds and other "cumulative" bonds, you may leave the interest in, to compound, and take the whole whack at the end.

All perfectly straightforward. The bond certificate, usually printed in a very fancy way on good paper, to make it harder to forge, carries the details. These include the issue date, from which interest starts, the maturity date, the denomination, or par value, and the rate of interest paid. Bonds mature at any time from one to thirty years, or even more; short-term bonds are those maturing in three years or less, medium-term, in from three to ten years, and long-term, in over ten years. As the bond ripens, its status changes: what was a long-term 1995 bond in 1978 is now called a short-term bond. The par value of most corporate bonds is $1,000, although there are "baby bonds" of less than that.

Many bonds have a "call" or redemption feature, allowing the issuer to pay off the issue, with notice given to the bondholders. This, too, will be shown on the certificate, as will whether it is a "bearer bond" – it belongs to whomever holds it – or "registered" – the owner's name is recorded, as on a Canada Savings Bond. Bearer bonds carry a series of coupons representing the interest, which becomes cashable on the date shown; with registered bonds, a cheque is usually sent out by the issuer of the bond automatically. Some bonds are "registered as to principal only"; the bond will carry coupons, representing the interest payments, and these can be detached and sold as with a bearer bond, but only the registered owner can cash the bond certificate itself. There is even an instrument called a "strip bond," in which the bond is sold entirely separate from the interest coupons. These instruments are also known as "zero coupon" bonds. A zero coupon bond pays no interest while the loan is outstanding; instead, the interest piles up annually, as with a cumulative bond, and, to make up for this, the bond is sold at a deep discount to the face value. The interest, plus the selling price add up, at maturity, to the par value of the bond. Either the coupons, the bond itself, or both, may be sold. Issuers like these bonds because they can keep the money longer than if they had to make annual interest payments, and investors like them because they get more bond for the money. The trick, however, is that the interest which has not been paid, but is accruing, is taxable in the hands of the investor, year by year. Just because you don't get it doesn't mean you don't owe the government.

Corporate bonds, which, behind their bland faces, represent the really great opportunities for chicanery, come in nine main varieties:

1. **First mortgage bonds:** The company owns real estate, and borrows money backed by these assets. If it gets into trouble, the bonds are backed by the right to convert the assets into cash to pay off the bondholders.

2. **Second mortage bonds:** We have already issued first mortgage bonds, but we have assets worth more than the amount covered by these, so we go to the market again.

3. **Debentures:** A debenture is a bond backed only by the borrower's word, not by any specific asset. Our company is sufficiently well-established that it is not necessary to pledge any particular assets for us to issue a debt instrument. Moody's, which rates corporations, has given us an AAA rating, and that ought to be good enough for the likes of you. There is another version of the debenture, called a "subordinated debenture." In this case, the bonds are junior to another debt of the corporation; they are riskier, and pay higher rates. The parallel is with a second mortgage.

4. **Collateral trust bonds:** A bond issue protected by a portfolio of securities held in trust by a bank. If the market value of the securities drops, the bank will be required to sell them to redeem the bonds.

5. **Convertible debentures:** These are debenture bonds that can be turned into common stock at the option of the bondholder, at a rate set down on the bond. We may issue LS & T convertibles which allow the holder of a $1,000 bond to convert it into thirty shares of stock at any time. If the stock goes to $40, it will make sense for bondholders to switch their bonds into stock. There are

advantages on both sides of this arrangement. For the bond-holder, it represents a chance to make a capital gain on the stock, with no additional risk. For the issuer, the conversion of bonds to stocks reduces the debt of the company without costing anything. It means there are more stocks out, that's all. When you run across the phrase "fully diluted" in the business pages, this does not refer to watering the chairman's whisky; it means that there are convertibles outstanding and the number of shares issued on a fully diluted basis refers to the number of shares there would be if every convertible were converted.

6. **Extendable and Retractable bonds or debentures:** We can extend the term, or shorten it, anywhere along the way.

7. **Floating rate debentures:** The interest rate is not fixed, but moves up and down with the markets.

8. **Corporate notes:** These are, in effect, simple IOUs on the corporation, and may have any term or denomination that investors are willing to accept.

9. **Income bonds or debentures:** These do not automatically pay interest, but pay only when the company is doing well enough to afford it, just as dividends are, in theory, only paid out of profits.

I have listed these in the general order of their seniority in the event of trouble. That is, the first mortgage bonds are at the top of the list as a charge on the company's assets in the case of bankruptcy, and income bonds – not much used these days – at the bottom. All of them come ahead of the dividends paid on shares as a call on the corporation's revenue. The rate of interest paid on each of these instruments will reflect directly the amount of risk; first mortgage bonds are safer than second mortgage bonds, and therefore pay less interest, and so forth.

Bonds, even more than stocks, are responsive to general interest rates, since it is only the "coupon," or interest, payment that is guaranteed, more or less. When the bond is first issued, its interest rate is set, based on the interest paid on other instruments at the time. In Canada, we see this happening under the public view every year when the federal government makes its guess as to what level at which to set the interest on Canada Savings Bonds. If the rate is too low, everyone will cash them in and buy Guaranteed Investment Certificates; if it is too high, not only will the taxpayer have to pay too much in interest charges, but the high rates will tend to distort all other money-market instruments, which is to be avoided, if possible.

But the bond itself can be bought and sold at prices that rise and fall with the general rate of inflation and the interest rate as set weekly by the central bank. As the interest rate rises or falls, the bond prices fall or rise, i.e., inversely. Much speculation (gambling) is based on nothing other than the expectations of what the central bank may do.

Consider the case of a company that issues a bond with a par value of $1,000 for a ten-year term at a time when interest rates are running, generally, around 9 per cent. The issuers of the bond, having consulted their oracles, decide that interest rates seem to be dropping, the bond market is sound, and, all in all, 8 per cent looks good to them. So, they issue $100 million worth of $1,000, 8-per-cent bonds, maturing in ten years.

Interest rates go up. The bond is going to pay $80 in interest the first year, but nobody with money to invest will hand out the full value for a bond paying less than general interest rates. Therefore, anyone who bought the bond and now wants to resell it in the secondary market will have to offer it at a discount. The bond is no longer worth $1,000; it will sell, let us say, for $900.

Now take a situation in which rates drop. In this case, the bond carries higher interest than the new issues coming on the market; it becomes worth more and it is said to sell at a "premium." That is, if interest rates fall to 6 per cent, a bond paying 8 looks pretty good; it will sell for, let us say, $1,140.

So, what seemed so simple is not so simple after all. The interest rate does not, it turns out, determine the value of the bond.

Rather, what the buyer looks to is its "yield," which is the term used to describe what you will actually get from the thing, and which can be readily compared with other investment possibilities. To calculate the yield, divide the amount of money the bond will pay in interest by the current price (not the face value). Thus, a $1,000 bond paying 8 per cent would give the holder $80 in the first year; its yield is 8 per cent. However, when interest rates go up, it loses value; now the $1,000 bond can only be sold for $800. It will still pay the same $80 in interest, because that was the original deal, but now the yield becomes $800 divided by $80, or 10 per cent. As the selling price of the bond goes down, the yield goes up, and vice versa, because the interest rate remains steady.

If the interest rate drops, and the bond becomes, as in our example, worth $1,140, the yield becomes $1,140 divided by $80, or 7.01 per cent. A bond purchased at its face value is at par; a bond purchased at a discount provides a yield higher than the interest rate shown, and one purchased at a premium provides a yield lower than that shown.

You don't need to go through the mathematics if you want to buy a bond. Yields are shown in the daily newspaper under the bond listings. Thus, if we see a N S Power bond with a coupon of 11 per cent and a price of 97.125 in the *Globe and Mail* listings, we know that Nova Scotia Power has issued bonds at $1,000, paying 11-per-cent interest, and that these are now worth $971.25 (bond prices are always quoted in cents on the dollar). The yield is listed for us, 11.326, which means that we'll receive an 11.326-per-cent return on our investment if we buy one today. Tomorrow is another matter.

We cannot easily calculate, and the newspaper will not tell us, the "yield to maturity" of a bond, because it depends on the interest rate as a proportion of the original price, the purchase price of the bond today, and the length of time remaining to maturity – the day it comes due. A broker can tell us, though, because he will, or should, have it on a chart.

Once we know about yields, the link between bonds and stocks becomes clear. When interest rates rise, bonds become more attractive. Why fool around in the stock market if you can make 20 per cent, risk free, on a Canada Savings Bond, or even a corporate bond? When interest rates fall, stocks become more attractive because you can pile up more gains faster. Why buy a bond at 8 per cent when you can buy a stock paying a dividend of 7 per cent and with a built-in capital gain? (Income from bonds and income from dividends are taxed at different rates, adding another complication, and a discrimination against bondholders.)

So, the potential investor looks up the yield of a bond, compares it with the Price/Earnings ratio of a stock, and makes his choice accordingly. This will often, but not always, mean that when bonds are up, stocks are down, and vice versa. This does not help much, though, since what is happening today doesn't tell us what will happen tomorrow. In deciding to buy either, the investor is looking at two factors: the "credit risk" – the chance that the company will go broke – and the "market risk" – the chance that the investment itself will become worth more or less.

In the past, bonds were always seen to be safer than stocks, because they are backed by the corporation's assets, in one way or another, not just the hope that the company would make a profit this year. Thus, bond yields could be lower than P/E ratios of the actual dividend rate, and still do well, because they gave the conservative investor a reasonably safe return. On the other hand, lower tax rates on dividends and expected capital gains can make stocks attractive.

No more. The complications of modern life mean that bonds are no longer really safe, because so many other demands precede them in the case of trouble. Property taxes, real-estate taxes, the GST, and income taxes all go in to dinner ahead of bonds and debentures, followed by any holiday pay owed to workers, pension-fund payments that have not been kept up-to-date, accounts payable, and secured short-term notes (which have usually been allowed to build up as the cash flow dried up); then, and only then, come the various issues of bonds and debentures. Bondholders are better off than stockholders, but when you've said that, you've said everything.

The effect of inflation also undermines bonds. A bond you buy for $1,000 today, which pays you back $1,000 in ten years, will probably be worth less than half that in current purchasing power. Thus, as with stocks, the real play in bonds consists of buying and selling them over and over again, according to the latest market swings. They have become part of the casino.

There are some bonds that are still the preferred investment of the cautious market-player: those issued by governments and such quasi-government bodies as Ontario Hydro, B.C. Power, and Quebec Hydro. Treasury bills, which are a form of bond (they are called "bills" because the term is less than one year) are safest of all. They are described in more detail in Chapter Fourteen. These are investments you will normally buy to hold to maturity. The rest are passed, like the Old Maid, before the hand ends. On the other side, companies have learned not to let them mature, but to keep rolling them over (i.e., issuing new bonds to pay off the old), thus avoiding the dreadful moment of truth when the borrower actually has to give the lender back his principal. It is this development that brought about the transformation of the workaday bond to that street harlot, the junk bond.

Very often, really good ideas are quite simple – the safety razor, for example; unfortunately, really bad ideas are quite simple, too. The junk-bond craze arose when a number of market-players, led by Michael Milken, then a trader at Drexel Burnham Lambert, one of the key Wall Street firms, noticed that bonds that were eschewed by the financial establishment because they seemed so chancey, very often paid off, despite the odds.

Up until the early 1980s, the bond market lived and died by the rating codes of Moody's and Standard & Poor. In Canada, Dominion Bond Rating Service in Toronto and Canadian Bond

Rating Service in Montreal both provide independent bond surveys to subscribers to their services, but the keys in this business, which is very much an American business in its main operations, are Moody's and S&P. An AAA rating from Standard & Poor described a bond that was "of the best quality, offering the smallest degree of investment risk." An AA bond was "of high quality by all standards." And so on, down to C, the lowest-rated class – "Very poor prospects." A D stood for "In default." Under Standard & Poor ratings, only bonds above BB+ are "investment grade" (the Moody equivalent is Ba1). Therefore, no respectable investment house would back these "fallen angels," as they were known in the early 1970s.

However, an academic, W. Braddock Hickman, had published a study in many volumes called *Corporate Bond Quality and Investor Experience,* which seemed to show that if you held enough crummy bonds, the reward would outweigh the risk. Sure, some of the bonds would go sour on you, but those that didn't would pay several percentage points in interest over other bonds.

Michael Milken had read the Hickman study, and believed it; all he needed was a chance to cash in on it, and that came when a surge of "M & As" – mergers and acquisitions – began to bubble through the North American markets. Takeovers had been around forever. It was only a question of how they would be paid for that gave Milken his opportunity, and revolutionized the bond business.

In recent years, takeover deals have been financed by cold, hard cash, rather than by issuing bits of paper alleged to be worth cash. Somebody else's cold, hard cash, mind you, but real, crinkly dollars nonetheless.

People like cash, especially in takeover situations – and for very good reason. Takeovers that are financed by the issuance of securities are subject to regulation, a process that not only exposes the buyer to a lot of irritating questions, such as whether or not he and his gang have any money, but slows the process down. When the corporate raiders begin to move, they don't want anyone looking over their shoulders, and they don't want to have to issue a preliminary prospectus and wait six weeks before closing the deal.

So, if you were planning to grab the company that somebody else had spent a few decades building, you would go to the bank and borrow a whole whack of money, use that to take over the target firm, and then, once in charge, pay off the debt with the cash flow of the firm you just acquired. Or, you would break up the company, sell off its parts, and keep the change. This is the classic takeover, and has been going on, using various techniques, for centuries. However, the actual financing arrangements go through bouts of fashion. In the 1880s, bonds were the usual instrument for financing takeovers, although you will recall that when J. P. Morgan formed U.S. Steel, as we saw in Chapter Two, he financed the deal by issuing one of the most outrageous bundles of watered stock in history, and did very nicely.

In recent years, dollars have been the instrument of choice, but in the 1960s, when one of the great merger movements was under way, the takeovers were nearly all financed with convertible preferred shares. They were the funny money of their time. Because many conglomerates, like ITT, were selling at very high P/E ratios, they could use their stock as inflated currency to pay for target firms. To use another of Wall Street's sayings, "You don't mind paying $800 for a cat, if you're selling $900 dogs." Because the preferred shares were not common stock, they could be issued almost without end without diluting the rest of the stocks; only when they were converted did they have to be reported. A change in accounting practice ended this advantage, while a series of tax changes, favouring debt over equity, helped to swing the action over to bonds, used to finance the cash transaction. Thus bonds became the funny money of the 1970s and 1980s, when the next bout of merger mania hit the markets. Interest paid out of existing earnings was a deduction from earnings. Dividends were not.

Milken's firm had a small, weak M & A department. He restructured it by setting up mergers which were acquired by issuing junk bonds – high-risk, high-yield debts – as a major part of the financing package that made the necessary money come welling out of bank vaults. Of course the bond issues were shaky, but who cared? They paid 15, 16, and 17 per cent when other, certified, Standard & Poor rated bonds were paying 10 and 11 and 12. As to paying them off, that didn't matter, because – and here was the other brilliant idea – you just kept rolling them over. If you had borrowed $100 million for a takeover, you covered the debt by issuing $100 million worth of ten-year, 16-per-cent bonds and, long before they became due and payable, you issued $150 million of fifteen-year, 17-per-cent bonds, and used that money to pay off the first batch. As long as you kept the balls in the air, no one could come to harm. Connie Bruck, in *The Predators' Ball,* a book that examines the rise and fall of Michael Milken and his junk-bond raiders, quotes one of the early Milken backers as explaining, "Of course you have to do the exchange (viz., of new bonds for old). Otherwise the bonds will come due!" We don't want that.

Milken had invented a way to print his own money. It didn't matter how much you spent, because you were never going to pay it back. It didn't matter that the interest rates you paid were far in excess of anything the company you had taken over could afford, because the real excitement, and the real money, came to the traders during the takeovers themselves. Fees of anywhere between 2 and 4 per cent were paid for "investment advice"; this was real money, not funny bonds. It meant that in a $10-billion deal – and such deals became common – the lawyers, investment houses, and freelance analysts who pronounced the deal to be all that anyone could wish, walked away with somewhere around $400 million in fees. Not bad, for building a pyramid. In a number of cases, rival investment houses or legal firms were paid millions in investment advice just to keep them from working for the other side.

It was our old friend Carlo Ponzi's game, in a new and virulent variation. It worked, for a time, because the investment bankers who had been the cool kings of Wall Street were now hurting for business. Deregulation had swung many of their depositors, large and small, over to the savings and loans banks, where interest rates were much higher. (This would lead, in due course, to the savings and loans banks falling over a cliff, but my, it was fun while it lasted!) The banks became active, eager participants in the acquisitions game; they needed the business and the fees, and to hell with the risks. When the takeovers were friendly, prices could be kept reasonable, but when the target company's management kicked, more money had to be poured in to satisfy them – or to persuade shareholders to sell their shares, no matter what management said. This was not a problem, since the money was going to come from the suckers, pardon me, investors, on whom the various partners unloaded the bonds.

Then, there developed a healthy business in greenmail, which means, as we have seen, taking a run at companies that you didn't really intend to take over, and then selling the stocks you had acquired back to management for two or three times what you paid for them. Donald Trump bought shares in Holiday Corporation, which definitely did not want him as a major stockholder, so it bought him out for a profit – to Trump – of $35 million. Then he bought 9.9 per cent of the shares of Bally Manufacturing; if he had bought 10 per cent, U.S. law required him to hold on for six months. Bally bought him out for a $30-million profit. It began to look like a pretty good business.

The Belzberg brothers of Vancouver greenmailed four U.S. companies within one three-week period. All this took money, and at one point Michael Milken assembled a war-chest of $100 billion that he could call on at any time for whatever investments, real or threatened, he cared to contemplate. The money would come from junk bonds, backed by airy nothing.

It had previously been a prudent rule of investment to make sure that the company issuing the bond was making enough profit to ensure that it could always pay the interest when it came due. To meet the "acceptable investment quality" standard of the Canadian Securities Institute's handbook, *How To Invest in Canadian Securities,* an industrial corporation has to be able to show that, in the past five years, it earned enough to cover interest payments "at least three times." It was also a rule of thumb that total debt outstanding should not exceed 50 per cent of equity. That is, a firm whose shareholders' equity is $10 million shouldn't borrow more than $5 million, because too much debt weakens the company's credit rating, increases interest charges, cuts the amount available to pay out in dividends, and, in times of trouble, may topple the firm into bankruptcy.

All that went out the window. Ted Turner of Turner Broadcasting boasted that he didn't even bargain over price when he bought MGM, the Hollywood movie and TV giant, and the income shown on the balance sheet in this and a score of other major takeovers didn't cover the interest payments even once, much less three times. Some companies built up debts that were 100 times their equity, a level of imprudence not seen since 1929. It didn't matter, as long as the bonds were never allowed to come due. Then it did.

That, in short, is what happened to Robert Campeau, the Canadian who moved south to take America by storm. Campeau Corporation, in a hostile takeover in 1986, bought control of Allied Stores Corporation for about $4 billion. At the time, Allied had about $700 million of debt and $1.3 billion in equity, a ratio of roughly 1:2. Its income was sufficient to cover interest payments from about 2.4 times in poor years to 3.8 times in good ones, and the firm made $160 million in profit after taxes, a return on equity from the department-store business of about 12.5 per cent.

Overnight, the debt load, caused by the huge price paid to acquire the company, jumped to $3.8 billion, interest charges soared to $465 million – more than four times its income – and a solid, long-established company became a financial cripple. The takeover was made possible by a junk-bond issue arranged by First Boston Corporation, and most of the proceeds from this issue went, not to reduce the debt, but to pay back bridge financing that First Boston had advanced to Campeau to tide them over through the takeover. First Boston was the banker, the underwriter, and the financial adviser, which made life interesting for investors who drifted up to the firm's wickets looking for advice on prudent investment.

Anyone foolish enough to buy these bonds soon came to regret it, but this was just the beginning for Campeau. He went on to buy Federated Stores, which owned Bloomingdales, among other retail giants. He paid more than $6 billion, again covered by the issue of bonds, and the debt-load proceeded to sink his entire empire, when various issues actually came due and a wary market could not be persuaded to substitute new bad paper for the old bad paper. Even selling off chunks of what other people had built up over years couldn't raise enough money to cover the payments, and the end result, among other things, was the destruction of entire chains, and the job losses of thousands of people who had put years into the firms, and had not been consulted.

In the midst of his buying spree, Campeau condescended to visit Canada to tell the folks at home that they were doing things all wrong, and that the federal government should get its debt-load under control. Very soon after that, the first twinges of recession hit North America and sent his company to the bankruptcy courts. He and Campeau Corporation, which finally dumped him as chairman, are currently suing each other in a series of actions that will no doubt go on for years – and spin-off yet more money to the lawyers and advisers. Not for the investors, though; the people who bought these bonds will be lucky to emerge with a fraction of their original stake. So much for the safety of bonds.

The intermeshed interests represented in the dealings of Campeau and First Boston Corporation was typical of most junk-bond deals arranged by the raiders whose leader and exemplar was Michael Milken. The junk bonds spawned elaborate networks, as investment banks issued written assurances that they were "highly confident" that the money required for a pending takeover bid would be forthcoming. Milken and the other junk bond raiders would use these letters to persuade their bands of investors to buy the junk. The deal would close; everyone would be paid a few million for helping out, and it was on to the next. Within six years, Milken's firm had created a $40-billion market and made fortunes for Milken and his cronies.

When the deals began to sour, Milken hired PR men and paid off journalists to produce stories that all was well, that his junk bonds were holding up remarkably well. None of it was true. The financial pages duly, and wrongly, showed that Drexel bonds were defaulting at a rate of no more than 1.5 per cent a year. In fact, to take a typical crop of the bonds, Drexel sold $784 million of junk bonds in 1981; by 1989, 54 per cent of them were defaulted, or had been switched to avoid default. No one bothered to check the records until nearly a decade later, while Milken sailed on.

The pace grew frenetic with the arrival of the LBO, or Leveraged Buy Out, in the early 1980s. In an LBO, a small group of investors, usually but not always led by the management of a firm, buys out the public shareholders in a technique known as "taking the firm private," i.e. from a widely-owned, publicly-traded corporation to a narrowly-held, private one. Then, if all goes well, the firm is sold back to the public again, at twice the price, and the deal's backers clean up. The financing is arranged by using the firm's assets to provide security for a bank loan and then piling in junk bonds to make the package so attractive that the shareholders will gladly part with their stocks.

Suppose the company to be taken over is worth, by the usual measures of P/E ratio and book value, about $15 a share. It is easy enough to finance that, but why should the shareholders sell? The trick is to offer them $20 or more, and finance the difference with junk bonds. Then the whole tottering edifice is owned by the minimal equity put in by the takeover artists. It is the huge difference between equity and debt that put the leverage in LBOs; you could buy a company worth $100 million with $1 million, and you could probably even borrow that.

One of the most illuminating of these LBOs was one that didn't quite come off as originally planned. This was the attempt, referred to earlier, by Canadian-born F. Ross Johnson to "take private " the giant cookie, candy, and tobacco conglomerate RJR Nabisco, of which he happened to be president and chief executive officer at the time. Johnson and a gang of allies proposed to get a block of underwriters to issue billions of dollars worth of junk bonds, with which they would buy the controlling shares of the maker of Oreo cookies, Shredded Wheat, and Winston's cigarettes, among other things. According to Bryan Burrough and John Helyar, whose *Barbarians at the Gate: The Fall of RJR Nabisco,* details the takeover bid, Johnson was motivated in the first place by the notion that just making an LBO bid would juice up the company stock, which was trading rather listlessly when the process got under way in the fall of 1988.

However that may be, had the deal worked as Johnson planned it, the end result would have been to give himself and his cronies a corporation worth somewhere in the neighbourhood of $20 billion, bought with its own assets, which could then have been run, dismembered, and sold off, or sold back to the public again. If the plan didn't work, Johnson expected to make $2 billion for his gang in speculation on the RJR Nabisco stock.

We have come a fair distance from conventional notions of business, I think it can be said, when the chief operating officer of a company sets out to use its assets to grab it for himself. One of the more riveting of Johnson's quotations in the book consists of his Three Rules of Wall Street: "Never play by the rules. Never pay in cash. And never tell the truth." This should also be embroidered on all the doilies in the financial district.

When you think about it, the attempted takeover wasn't even

smart. Inevitably, as soon as word leaked out, other bidders leapt into the fray, sprayed monopoly money around, and the price of the shares skyrocketed. Then it became clear that Johnson's personal share of the take would amount to a minimum of $100 million; not a bad fee for breaking up your own company. What we like to refer to in financial circles as "adverse reaction" set in. The board of directors, at least those not in on the action, were mad as stink, and did their best to see that anybody but the Johnson gang got the company.

Time magazine ran a cover story called "The Game of Greed," with a picture of Johnson and the caption, "This man could pocket $100 million from the largest corporate takeover in history. Has the buyout craze gone too far?"

The answer to that one was easy. "Oh my, yes."

During the frenzy, money was scattered to the winds by executives who, on the proper occasion, liked to lecture us all about government waste and the follies of piling up debt. There is a scene in *Barbarians at the Gate* where Johnson, about to go out to do a little shopping, says to his secretary, "Get me about an inch of 50s."

He meant, of course, $50 bills, for walking-around money.

One investment counselling firm was paid $25 million to keep its services unavailable to a rival bidder. Corporate jets crisscrossed the country, bearing the conspirators. Johnson had thirteen jets in the company fleet, more than some nations. Nothing was too good for the boys – limousines, lavish meals, sumptuous homes and apartments, and the appropriate female companionship, nearly all of which wound up on the business tab, and got deducted from taxes. All the millions that were wasted in this crackpot game had to come out of the hides of the taxpayers and/or the shareholders, the investors foolish enough to back the junk bonds – and the employees. Nobody, including the authors of *Barbarians at the Gate*, gave much thought to the thousands of employees whose lives were torn apart by all this nonsense. To make up for the waste, workers who had been on the company payroll for decades were fired out into the street, part of the new corporate dedication to being lean and mean. Del Monte was broken up and sold off, and 2,300 Reynolds Tobacco employees lost their jobs as their small contribution to the operations of debt financing.

Just as neglected were the shareholders; the ones who, in theory, rule over the corporation. Their only role was to provide the seed money for the game of greed to begin.

In the end, Johnson and his group were outbid by another gang, led by Kohlberg Kravis Roberts & Co., another LBO specialist, which paid $25 billion, thus wasting, at a minimum, $5 billion – but no worry, it has just been added to the debt-load. Because he sinned, Johnson was ushered out the door, with a pay-off of $52 million.

That'll teach him.

The RJR Nabisco case led to a good deal of disillusionment with the machinations of the bond hustlers, but the real break came with the revelations that spilled out, day after day, with the unwinding of the Security and Exchange Commission's cases against Michael Milken, Ivan Boesky, and other Wall Street luminaries. The first open break came in 1986 when officials at Merrill Lynch, the giant stockbroker, received a letter from Caracas, Venezuela, charging that some of the firm's brokers were trading on inside information. That tip led to a wider investigation, which showed that almost everybody's brokers were trading on inside information. In fact, the entire, monumental structure of junk-bond trading seemed to depend on the information exchanged among insiders.

To understand what was going on, you have to know that in investment houses, because the firm is likely to be dealing on several sides of almost any given operation, conflicts of interest are almost inevitable. In Drexel, Milken's company, you had salesmen out flogging stocks and bonds to customers, market managers out buying stocks and bonds, analysts telling the folks which stocks and bonds made a good buy, cross my heart and spit, and Milken's group, over in Mergers and Acquistions, working for fees to help various other firms in their takeover raids, and financing the whole thing by selling bonds.

Conflicts were avoided – and are still, in theory, avoided – by a series of "Chinese Walls": the lads in sales are not supposed to talk to the lads in M & A, a few feet away, about what is going down today. There were a number of people who actually believed in these Chinese Walls, and still believe in them, just as there are people who believe that, if you clap your hands hard enough, Tinkerbell will come back to life. They are not numerous, especially since the trials of the past few years showed that the Chinese Walls are made of crêpe paper. Information, the most precious commodity on Wall Street, was traded even more briskly than the bonds, and traded from investment house to investment house. Ivan Boesky, who ran an arbitrage partnership, actually lugged briefcases full of cash around to pay off contacts for information.

The first one arrested was Dennis B. Levine, who was from Milken's firm, and he strapped on a tape recorder to help prosecutors gather evidence. (He was sentenced to two years in prison, served about half that, and re-emerged as a consultant and lecturer on ethics.)

On November 14, 1986, it was announced that Boesky had pleaded guilty to insider trading and agreed to pay fines of $100 million. Moreover, it was announced, he would cooperate with the authorities in prosecuting other charges against other Wall Street figures. Must have made for some interesting conversations in the executive loos on Wall Street.

As these cases dragged through the courts over the next five years, the world discovered that the junk-bond raiders were not so darn clever after all. Mostly, they were cheaters, who violated all the rules – including and especially the quaint notion of Chinese Walls – to make a killing. In *Barron's*, the weekly magazine, Michael Boylan, the president of a firm called McFadden Holdings, trilled that "Drexel is like a god in that end of the business and a god can do anything it wants." This was framed, in bold print, in the office of one of Milken's colleagues, and kind of gives you the feel of the way the junk-bond raiders operated. Gods don't have to obey the law. The game was rigged, and had been rigged from the beginning.

There was much lamentation in the land, strong editorials, and repeated assurances that these bad boys were not at all typical of the way matters are usually arranged on Wall Street. These assurances became harder and harder to accept as the details emerged, even though the guilty pleas of most of them kept much of the information under wraps. Milken, who was originally charged with scores of felonies, ended up pleading guilty to six. They included conspiring with Boesky and fund manager David Solomon to manipulate prices, rig transactions, and evade taxes and regulatory requirements; securities fraud; violating SEC reporting requirements; mail fraud; assisting the filing of a false tax return; and helping to file false information with the SEC.

Milken, as the most active and visible villain, was fined $400 million in all, then had to cough up another $500 million to settle various lawsuits brought against him by the federal government, fellow employees at Drexel Burnham Lambert, his old firm – which was forced into bankruptcy – and the firm itself. The Associated Press story reporting the settlement in late February of 1992 calculated that Milken was left with a measly $125 million, but I can't work that out, since he was previously reported, by the same news agency, to have cleared $1.2 billion. Let us say simply that, when all was said and done, Milken was cleaned down to his last few scores of millions, as well as earning a stretch in quod.

Thirteen of his colleagues, involved in many of the major firms on Wall Street, received sentences that ranged from probation to three years in jail.

It now appears that those who pleaded guilty – most of them – made a mistake. In mid-July, 1991, an appeal court threw out the conviction of John Mulheren, Jr., one of those Boesky testified against. He had been convicted on four counts of securities fraud and conspiracy in November 1990, and was sentenced to a year and a day in jail, along with a fine of $1.68 million. However, the appeal court ruled that the government had failed to prove that Mulheren's somewhat lively stock machinations amounted to manipulation, because the government could not show "beyond a reasonable doubt" that his intent was to manipulate prices. If that ruling stands, it may be difficult if not impossible to obtain any future convictions on charges of manipulating stock in the absence of a direct statement from the accused that he was not merely investing in a lively and interesting way.

In the wake of the scandals and, more crucially, in the wake of the market collapse of late 1987, junk bonds withered on the vine, but as soon as the markets picked up, so did the junk-bond business. By mid-1991, the market in junk bonds had hit $227 billion (U.S.), not far off its glory days in 1986, and I write this staring unbelieving at an article in the *Financial Post* which notes that among the junk-bond issues recently oversold is one involving Federated Department Stores, Robert Campeau's glass jewel. There is, apparently, a sucker reborn every minute.

If the record of the transformation of the bond market shows anything, it is that nothing we read about how the business world is supposed to operate helps us to understand the skullduggery that actually shapes market decisions. For example, I cannot find anywhere, in any economic text, an explanation for the fact that, at gatherings of traders, investment bankers, and consultants hosted by Michael Milken every spring in Los Angeles, the common practice was to provide the visitors with comely women whose lot in life is to be friendly to strangers for a previously negotiated fee. Drexel paid the fee, presumably on the grounds that this tax-deductible expense would help the customers evaluate their portfolios. ("I've got to hand it to these guys," one newcomer to this practice noted. "I've never seen so many beautiful wives!")

This annual orgy went under the name "The Predators' Ball," which is where Connie Bruck got the title for her book on Milken. The women were paid, Bruck reports, "varying amounts, depending on how pretty they are, and what they'll do."

I don't want to appear prudish, but it seems to me there ought to be some notable distinction, in any well-regulated sector of the business community, between conducting an information seminar and procuring hookers for a bunch of fat old men.

Barbarians at the Gate finishes with a wistful passage in which the authors wonder what R. J. Reynolds, the founder of RJR, and Adolphus Green, the founder of Nabisco foods, would make of what had happened to their companies:

> They would turn to each other, occasionally, to ask puzzled questions. Why did these people care so much about what came out of their computers and so little about what came out of their factories? Why were they so intent on breaking up instead of building up? And last: What did all this have to do with doing business?

It is hard to see that anything was learned in the junk-bond trials except that there is a lot of money to be made, any way you want to do it. In 1987, while the scandals were just beginning to unfurl, Morgan Stanley & Co., a giant New York investment house and the latest version of J. P. Morgan's firm, bought into Burlington Industries. Over the next three and a half years, it collected $176 million in fees and dividends from Burlington, while the textile giant was sinking ever deeper into debt, its junk bonds trading at thirty-three cents on the dollar. Then Morgan Stanley backed out, leaving Burlington with $2.2 billion in debt – having, of course, made sure to collect all its fees, including $64.6 billion in underwriting fees for the junk-bond issue. Waves of layoffs and the sale of much of the company's most modern operations were another part of the cost of what the *Wall Street Journal* called, "the fee binge."

We are beginning to see a pattern here; the market develops an instrument to meet the legitimate needs of investment finance, and the hucksters immediately grab the new instrument and turn it into trash. Read on.

CHAPTER NINE

The Feeling Is Mutual

Mutual Funds

Until the 1930s, small investors were at millionaires' mercy. Many millionaires pooled their money, bought huge blocks of particular stocks, drove prices sky high, then promptly sold out . . . leaving the overpriced stocks to tumble in the hands of unwary investors. Today, every aspect of mutual fund trading is tightly regulated.
  – *Wall Street Journal Guide to Understanding Money and Markets,* 1990.

$

Millionaires, as demonstrated in the quote above, tend to be rascals. They will pick on a poor investor, who has no way to fight back. You put all your money in Fare Thee Well Finance, Inc. shares, and it turns out that the stock only looked so good because a half-dozen insiders were wash-trading. When the dust settles, so does the stock, and there you are. Joe Kennedy, the father of a future president of the United States, was one of these rascals; he cleaned up by bilking ordinary investors and became rich and

179

respectable, while those he bilked were poor and therefore disreputable, so that their complaints about him could be, and were, dismissed out of hand. The answer to this age-old dilemma has always been the same one-word solution: Diversify. Spread the risk, sons and daughters; they can't all be crooks out there. If you own oil shares, and oil prices plummet because somebody forgot to turn off the tap over in Saudi Arabia, don't worry, your bank stocks still look good. If the banks seem to stand on shaky ground, due to having loaned a few more billions to Brazil and Iran than was really prudent, take heart, your real-estate shares are holding up well. If real estate comes unstuck, there are always those preferreds in Ma Bell, or IBM, or General Motors.

Trouble is, it takes so dang much money to diversify. By the time you have spread yourself across the market for safety's sake, you have either laid out far more than you can afford or bought so few shares in each market sector that you would have been as well off to leave the money in a sock, at home. The shares of IBM went up fifty cents overnight. Fantastic, I'm a dollar richer. Wouldn't it be nice if you could diversify your investments, and at the same time tap into really seasoned, professional investment advice, instead of having to rely on that pimply-faced kid down at the broker's office who looks as if he just graduated from high school?

You can. Ladies and gentlemen, fellow sportsmen, roll up, pay out, and fear nothing. If you sincerely want to be rich, but don't want to lose your socks and underwear along the way, plunk down your doubloons in a mutual fund.

That, at least, is the idea. In a mutual fund, you do not buy the shares in individual companies; instead, you buy units in an investment fund, which is a company or trust engaged in the business of managing investments for other people. You do not need to be a millionaire. Indeed, with a modest investment you can own bits – small bits, but bits – of more companies than most millionaires, since the average mutual fund carries about one hundred different kinds of shares in its portfolio.

According to the *Wall Street Journal Guide to Understanding Money and Markets,* mutual funds were invented in 1924 by an American. Shows how much they know. In fact, the Foreign and Colonial Government Trust was formed in 1868, in London, to invest the savings of others in lightbulb companies, steel firms, and railways, and did very well. Robert Fleming, the grandfather of Ian Fleming (the inventor of James Bond), started a similar fund in Scotland soon after.

These funds were of the "closed-end" type, not very common these days. In a closed-end mutual fund, the sponsoring trust only issues only a certain number of shares or units. When the fund is established, the income from the sale of the units is invested in a portfolio, which is often specialized – ASA Ltd., a typical closed-end fund, buys and sells only South Africa gold-mining stocks; Japan Fund deals in the securities of Japanese firms. When you put in your money, you get back certificates not very different from those you would receive from the South African gold mine or the Japanese electronics manufacturer, and the trust gives you payments from the dividends on the stocks, or interest on the bonds that it holds in the mutual interest of all the members of the trust. If you want to get your investment back, you can sell your holdings to someone else, but the fund itself will not redeem them, normally, unless and until the entire trust is wound up. You pay a commission, sometimes without knowing it, when you join and when you sell your shares, and your investment, minus these fees, goes to the sellers of the fund's stocks. Management fees paid along the way keep the fund going.

While there are more than 650 mutual funds in Canada (and another 3,200 in the United States, for our cross-border shopping), only about twenty of them are closed-end funds, led by names such as Canadian General Investments and Worldwide Equities Limited, and they trade on the stock exchanges and on the Over the Counter market. In the United States, there are about seventy closed-end funds, also traded on the exchanges and OTC.

There are a couple of variations on the closed-end fund, such as the holding company – firms like Canadian Pacific Enterprises and Power Corporation and the *Caisse de Dépôt et Placements* in Quebec. In the holding company, the managers of the fund try to influence the workings of the companies whose shares they own; in the usual closed-end fund, they simply hang on to the shares or sell them, but never interfere. It would be simpler if holding companies were called "busybodies" and the others "holding companies," but we have already learned that, in the world of finance, nothing is ever made simple. In the United States, there are "dual-purpose" funds, which are set up with a specific expiration date on their units. These have two classes of stock: preferred shares, which receive all the income from dividends or bond interest, and common stock, which gets no interest or dividends, but divides all the capital gains – presuming there are capital gains – in the underlying stock when the fund expires.

However, the typical mutual fund is the open-end fund. In this case the sponsoring fund, instead of using a finite sum of capital, will continue to create and sell new units until the cows come home or the market quits, whichever comes first.

To make this work, the fund itself promises to redeem the units for cash, on demand, from the investors; this creates a continuous market and makes for an arrangement that is more liquid than the closed-end fund. It has, I think we can say, at least one redeeming virtue: namely, that it will always redeem your shares. The first open-end fund for which I can find any record was the Massachusetts Investment Trust, which was formed in 1924, and it did well, as do all mutual funds, when stocks were rising, but took a terrible beating in the Great Crash.

However, it did better than the closed-end funds, such as the famous, later infamous, Goldman, Sachs Trading Corporation, which we have already met, briefly. This one began, in late 1928, with a million shares, which sold for $104 each. After it merged with another fund, the Financial and Industrial Securities

Corporation, by February 7, 1929, the shares had rocketed to $222.50. It later turned out that much of this gain was due to the fact that it was buying its own shares at ever-higher prices, to help them on their way. In turn, two new trusts appeared, the Shenandoah Corporation and the Blue Ridge Corporation. Goldman, Sachs begat Shenandoah and, exactly twenty-five days later, Shenandoah begat Blue Ridge; between them, they spun out more than $250 million in securities in less than a month, backed by nothing much more than a touching faith. Each had a ratio of debt to equity of about 20:1, which gave the original trust marvellous leverage. Thus, Goldman, Sachs, which owned about 40 per cent of Shenandoah, which owned almost all of Blue Ridge, stood to gain, if the market went up by 50 per cent, by a factor of 122. One hundred and four dollars invested in Goldman, Sachs would be worth, in that event, $12,688. Not bad.

Alas, the market did not go up and, before long, the units were available, to anyone who would buy them, for $1.75.

This took some of the bloom off the rose, and investors in closed-end trusts were suddenly confronted with the drawback to their investment: they could not force it back on the issuing fund as prices dropped, and still save something from the wreck. They had to try to flog their units to an unenthusiastic general populace.

Thus, when, in due course, mutual funds began to rise again from the ashes of the Depression, it was the open-end funds that prospered most, and still do. So much so that, by and large, most references you read to mutual funds mean open-end ones, and, unless otherwise noted, that is the way I will use the term from here on in. Mutual funds, in this sense, are not sold on exchanges in either Canada or the United States; you buy directly from the fund itself, or from an independent agent, viz., a "financial counsellor" or broker. They are the easiest form of security to get your hands on; simply fill out the coupon in the newspaper or at your bank (banks have leapt enthusiastically into the game) and then the trick will be *not* to buy. You will get a telephone call from a salesperson, very nice too, followed by a personal chat, with charts to show you how you can't go wrong and how you owe, positively owe it to your loved ones to get your money down quickly, with the glad news that you don't have to buy your units all at once, you can put so much down per week (they will even, for your convenience, make an automatic deduction from your bank account). Before you are signed up for sure, you will receive a prospectus, describing the fund and its past performance in what looks like a straightforward and frank fashion, but is often somewhat gamey.

You sign, send in the cheque, and you are in business. There is no trick to buying mutuals.

The advantage of the closed-end fund is that professional managers have a given pool of capital to work with; if they know their business, they can often do better than open-end funds. With the standard mutual fund, the promise of redemption is always there, which is why these funds, aided by aggressive salesmanship, expanding markets, and a certain amount of rascality in some of the sales pitches, have grown so rapidly.

Canadian mutual funds today have more than $50 billion in assets under management, a greater-than-tenfold increase in the past decade (the U.S. figure is $1.4 trillion; their mutuals are growing at the rate of $1 billion a day), which is more of a tribute to their salesmanship than their performance. Their proliferation in recent years has led to their division into an incredible array of types, and more will probably spring from the ground between the time I write this and you read it. What follows is a brief survey of the main kinds, and how they fare:

1. **Income or bond funds:** These invest mainly in government and corporate debt securities, with some investments in shares and mortgages. They are the most conservative funds. In the five years ending June 30, 1991, they averaged a return of 8.08 per cent annually, without accounting for management fees, which would have wiped out up to a quarter of your gain. You'd have done

much better to leave your money with a trust company in a long-term note. It would have given you an average return of 9.82 per cent, with none of the funny math that makes the mutuals look good. Virtually without risk.

2. Money-market funds: These are the darlings of the banks and trust companies, the fastest-growing of the funds, with assets at the end of 1990 of more than $4.5 billion. These funds, particularly those run by the big financial institutions, are about as safe as any mutual-fund investment can be, because most of the money goes into Treasury bills or, in the case of U.S. money-market funds, into U.S. Treasury bills. Management fees are typically lower than with other funds, since there is not a hell of a lot for the gang to do, and a 1-per-cent charge is common. You merely have to ask yourself why you should pay anyone else a fee to tell you that a Treasury bill is a safe investment? You also have to ask yourself why you should put your money into a mutual fund, with no government deposit insurance, such as covers your bank account, when you can make a better return in a trust-company certificate guaranteed by the government.

Money-market funds had an average return, again by their strange reckoning, of 9.56 per cent annually over the five-year period ending June 30, 1991 – not as good as a five-year Guaranteed Investment Certificate with a trust company.

3. Real-estate funds: The money goes, mostly, into conventional first mortgages, although commercial properties are sometimes included. These funds were in big trouble a couple of years back, but have begun to recover. Over the five years ending June 30, 1991, they averaged 9.42 per cent annually. Not quite as good as a Canada Savings Bond, which has no management fees to bear, and no risk to bear, and which made, during this same period, an average annual return of 9.82 per cent.

4. Balanced funds: They buy a number of bonds and other fixed-income securities for safety, then take wing on common stocks for "growth potential." They vary widely in returns. The best performing of these funds, Altimara Growth & Income Fund, gained, by its own math, 10.24 per cent annually over five years, but Altimara's other balanced fund – called Altimara Balanced Fund – actually lost 0.27 per cent annually over the same period. The group of balanced funds averaged a meagre 6.00 per cent. An ordinary, guaranteed savings account in a bank earned 6.75 per cent in the same period.

5. **Equity funds:** The bulk of the assets are in common stocks, in pursuit of capital gain, which moves rather fast. The best-performing Canadian equity fund in the five-year period ending June 1991, Imperial Growth Canadian Equity Fund, had an annual rate of return of 13.72 per cent, minus fees. The worst, Corporate Investors Stock Fund, Ltd., lost 7.38 per cent; which means that if you put in $1,000 a decade earlier and left it in, you wouldn't have a whole lot left, by the time annual management fees came off your investment.

6. **Dividend funds:** These invest in preferred stocks, mostly, with some common stocks, but, for income from the dividends of "blue chip", i.e., so-far-respectable stocks, not for capital gain. The average annual return for these over five years ending June 30, 1991, was 5.96 per cent, a good deal less than you would have made putting the money in a fixed-term deposit with a chartered bank (7.83 per cent annually), even before we mention the fees.

7. **Specialty funds:** Japanese stock funds, energy funds, precious-metals funds. They have no independent track record, but show up in the equity-fund listings.

8. **Ethical funds:** These make investment decisions that avoid, for example, companies that trade with South Africa, or those that make tobacco, or those that pollute. Whatever. The best known of these in Canada is the Ethical Growth Fund, launched by Vancouver City Savings Credit Union in 1986 with the sale of 2,000 units at $5 each. The fund is now valued at over $50 million and its return on investment over the three years to December 31, 1990, was 10.42 per cent. It has a "green screen," and will not invest

in the arms or nuclear industries, or firms that are known to damage the environment. This appears to be one of those have-your-cake-and-eat-it-too funds, where shrewd investment practices live side-by-side with ethical considerations. Just before the October 1987 market crash, the fund turned most of its assets into cash, and escaped comparatively unscathed. Just the same, when markets drooped in 1990, it suffered the same fate as most mutuals, and lost 3.14 per cent. As a group, equity funds lost 12.83 per cent that year.

There is not a single one of these funds, as a group, that has done as well as you could do with your money in other, safer investments. There are certainly some funds that have done better than the group, some that have even done better than, say, a five-year GIC, although, as we get into the mathematics of the thing, you will see that all these figures must be treated with caution. The trick is, of course, to find out which fund is likely to do so well in the next five or ten years that it is worth the extra risk for the extra, possible, return. In my judgement, none; but then, I am a cautious soul, and I know something about the background of these funds.

While writing this chapter, I have consulted fifteen texts of the "How To Make a Million" ilk. All of them, with varying degrees of enthusiasm, push mutuals, despite what seems to me to be an abysmal track record, taken all in all, and none of them ever mention the built-in drawback to the mutual fund as a financial instrument. This drawback is perhaps best illustrated by example, so, if you find yourself cornered in your living room one night by a mutual-fund salesperson with coloured charts and a missionary zeal, lean forward, tap him or her on the knee, and whisper three words: "Fund of Funds." You may draw only a blank stare, but never mind, if the salesperson is that ignorant, tell him or her about "people's capitalism," Bernard Cornfeld, Investors Overseas Services (IOS), and the Fund of Funds.

Bernard "Call-Me-Bernie" Cornfeld was a psychology major

at Brooklyn College who was introduced to mutual funds in 1953 by Walter Benedick, a man who had attended the same summer camp where Bernie had gone as a member of the Socialist League for Industrial Democracy. No kidding. Cornfeld's dream was to make the socialist nirvana come true by sharing the wealth – beginning with himself. The man who showed him how to do this had started his own mutual fund, Investors Planning Corporation, and put an ad in the *New York Times* to recruit salesmen. Bernie applied, and the rest is history. Cornfeld became a mutual-fund salesman, and, more importantly, an organizer of mutual-fund salesmen, first in the United States and then in France and, when France got too inquisitive for him, in Switzerland.

He formed his own corporation, Investors Overseas Services (IOS) to sell, first, units in other mutual funds such as Investors Planning Corporation and the Dreyfus Fund, at that time the world's hottest-selling mutual, and, later, his own Fund of Funds. The money was made on commissions paid by the funds for moving their products. He inculcated a missionary zeal in his sales-men, convincing them that they could all become millionaires by allowing the little people to tap into the market leverage of the mutual fund. The Fund of Funds purported to be a mutual fund that invested in other mutual funds; in fact, it was an instrument to create millions of dollars in commissions and administrative fees, all of which poured into IOS, which was, for most of its existence, closely held by Bernie and a group of associates. It was, not to put too fine a point on it, a gigantic swindle, made possible in part by the fact that Bernie had moved his operations offshore to Geneva, far from the Nosy Parkers over at the Securities and Exchange Commission. For years, the Swiss authorities didn't care much what Bernie and the boys did, so long as they didn't do it in Geneva, and frighten the horses.

Thousands of fund-floggers combed the world, calling them-selves "financial counsellors" and drawing in the savings of millions of individuals, who heeded the missionary cry of "people's capitalism." But most of their capital was creamed off on the way past by I O S – which meant Bernie and the boys – in management fees and "front-end loading" and other tricks.

Front-end loading refers to the practice of deducting a fee from the investment before it goes into the mutual fund. It is still widely practiced, and one simple rule to follow is never buy a mutual fund with a front-end load. If you invest $1,000 in a mutual fund, and the usual front-end load of 8.5 per cent comes off first, you are not investing $1,000, only $915, and if the fund winds up claiming a return of 10 per cent for the year, you will get $91.50, not $100, which is just over 9 per cent, not 10. To return you $100, or 10 per cent, of your investment, the fund would actually have to make a return on its investments in shares and bonds of about 11 per cent, and that assumes, wrongly, that there are no other charges. In fact, its return would have to be around 20 per cent to cover other costs. One of the many ways mutuals get into trouble is by taking flyers on unproven stocks or junk bonds to try to bump up these figures.

In the case of the Fund of Funds, the front-end loads often swallowed the entire amount of the original investment, and investors who wanted to withdraw found themselves locked in; they were charged both a front-end load for joining and a "back-end load" for leaving. There was nothing left of their money if they withdrew, so they kept paying in, and soon there was nothing left at all. The crucial point to cling to is that front-end loads are taken from the customer before *anything* is invested. Win, lose, or draw, the fund manager gets his.

Money raised for the mutual funds was used by I O S to finance its own shenanigans, which included floating dubious stocks, buying a bank, and manipulating stock prices. Massive illegal currency transactions kept the money spinning, and the sales force, and Fund of Fund pamphlets and reports, consistently mis-represented the performance of the fund, to keep the suckers coming. In theory, the Fund of Funds was an organization to provide investment guidance; in fact, the money was often used to buy shares that IOS itself was selling, and which no one else would buy. Then the boys unloaded $100 million in IOS shares by deliberately misrepresenting its own business and the state of its affairs. In its crowning achievement, IOS floated a gas-and-oil exploration venture in the Canadian arctic, which flopped, then paid itself a fee of $10 million, which came straight out of the Fund of Funds, to "revalue" these now-worthless investments. In addition, the insiders paid themselves "performance fees," which again were charged to the Fund of Funds by IOS and amounted to as much as $500,000 annually for some of the main figures in the scam.

The fundamental swindle in the Fund of Funds was that it held itself out to be a trust on the side of the little people, when in fact all the benefits accrued to a handful of insiders. Even most of the salesmen wound up with miserable takings, for all their hustling and lying, because their commissions were shared with their bosses on a scale that increased the higher they reached in the company. It was like the prize money doled out in the British navy to keep the captains hustling in the eighteenth and early-nineteenth centuries; the booty was divided with the admiral – Bernie – at the top, even if he was nowhere near the scene of glory, then with the captain, then with the other officers, and finally only a pittance was left for the people who trimmed the sails and fired the cannons.

At its height in 1969, the Fund of Funds controlled $2.5 billion in investments, and 85,000 salesmen, all on commission, scoured 100 nations in a constant struggle to feed the company maw. The font, IOS, listed fifty-five principal subsidiaries and redirected money into, among other things, a Hollywood movie that flopped (it was called *Snobs*). There was a vigorous branch of IOS in Canada, along with two mutual funds for it to sell, the Regent Fund of Canada and the Canadian Venture Fund, both of which turned out to be Bermuda Triangles, into which money vanished mysteriously.

Cornfeld was, like so many of his kind, fêted, saluted, and gloried over by the financial press and the world of finance in general – until the moment Swiss authorities woke up long enough to clap gyves on his wrists. As soon as stock markets faltered in 1970, the company had begun to collapse, and it became apparent that so much of the real money had been looted that it could not cover its nakedness; the units could not be redeemed. By then, Cornfeld had sold most of his own holdings to other employees of IOS who sincerely wanted to be rich.

Cornfeld was forced out, and the operation wound up in the hands of Robert Vesco, who managed to strip off more millions, and with whom a number of police organizations have been anxious to exchange words since he decamped, first to Costa Rica, and later to Panama.

Bernie was arrested by the Swiss police on securities charges in April 1973. He spent eleven months in custody and then was released on $1.5-million bail. He wasn't brought to trial until 1977, in Geneva, on the limited charges of having defrauded 350 former IOS employees by selling them stock which he knew to be worthless.

And guess what? Bernie made a deal under which he would pay $3 million to these stung employees, whether convicted or not. And then guess what? As they were called one by one to the stand, the former employees testified that they were sure Bernie had no intention of defrauding them when he stuck them with the stock. After a trial that went on almost two years, the Geneva judge acquitted Bernie, who immediately began a vain attempt to take back control of IOS. He told reporters at the end of his trial that he reckoned his net worth at $4.4 million, which was a lot more than IOS was worth by then.

When he could not get his company back, he went to Los Angeles, where he bought the house that had once been owned by Douglas Fairbanks, Jr. He started a new business, in the food industry (which L.A. wags wanted to call "Food of Foods"), and became a guru for consultation on financial matters. One of his more acute observations is contained in *An Oral History of Finance,* published by William Morrow in 1988: "I had some interesting cell mates."

Yes, but why? Why would a man, a group of men (women were mere objects) of obvious energy, talent, and ambition get caught up in a game that was bound, in the end, to unravel? I think there were two reasons. One was that, as in every pyramid scheme, the originators did very well. A few went to jail, some wound up bankrupt, but others, especially those who got out before the collapse, got to keep their millions. Bernie certainly did. Nothing was lost save honour. The other reason was that they became trapped as the process went on. To keep the swindle going, it was necessary to keep pouring more and more money into the funds, for reasons that become obvious when you look at the mechanics of any mutual fund.

These funds, although they purport to be for the benefit of the small investor, in fact work best, from the fund's point of view, with large investors. That is because it costs just as much to look after an account with only a few hundred dollars in it as one that has millions. The gimmick that is generally used to keep the money coming in is the "investment program" or "contractual plan" you will find in the ads of so many mutuals. You sign up to pay so much per month, reassured by the assertion that you can take your money out at any time. And so you can, but, even if there is no penalty down in the fine print for doing so, you are likely to be killed by the administration charges and management fees levied against the fund along the way.

Moreover, mutual funds have to keep expanding, just to keep their ever-increasing fixed costs covered, because the way the "investment counsellors" who sell the fund make their money is as a percentage of the investments they bring in, or the "trailer fees" they get for talking anyone who wants to sell out of redeeming his shares. The instant the flow is turned off, their income plummets. More customers beget more costs and, now that the amount of money that can be skinned out at the start of the plan as a front-end load is controlled by law in most countries (at 8.5 or 9 per cent), there are bound to be a great many customer accounts that do not cover their administrative costs, certainly not at first.

Then the dilemma of the redemption feature comes into play. If the markets are rising – the only time mutual funds can generally prosper – the customers whose investments have now shot up in value will, in a great many cases, want to cash in. Very wise, too. So, a rising market helps bring in investors, but it also sends a good number of them streaming out again, and all the weary work to do over.

The case of a falling market is much worse. Mutuals die in a falling market, in part because they cannot sell short, so they can't take advantage of an expected fall in share values to clean up. This is a provision of law in most countries, and for very good reason. The money you put into a mutual fund represents your entire gamble, but, as we have already seen, in short-selling, you can lose far more than the original investment; indeed, you can lose several times what you put into the pot. There is no mechanism that would allow the fund to go back to its customers and say, in effect, "Sorry, folks, but we blew more than we had in the kitty on Take a Chance Mining. Pay up." For the same reason, mutuals cannot buy on margin.

These and other restrictions mean that, as soon as the market trembles, the mutuals are in trouble. There is not much that can be done but wait out the storm and/or resort to creative accounting to make the fund look more attractive than it really is, in order to move the product even in these tough times.

Bernie and the boys developed a breathtaking expertise in picking the right time period in which to measure performance. They measured IOS from October 1962, when it and its subsidiaries had just been through a disastrous shrinkage of nearly one-third its value. Measured from that nadir, the books looked pretty good, whereas, if they had measured from the beginning of IOS, any investor could see that he would have done better to leave his money in the bank.

These games are still played, only they have become formalized and accepted. For example, the funds are allowed to sell themselves on what is called "effective yield," a fiction that makes it appear that the fund is doing better than it is. Effective yield is the average daily yield of the fund over a period of seven days – any seven days the fund chooses – pro-rated to cover a period of one year, and assuming that all returns remain the same for that period, and that everything within the fund that might be distributed to the owners is instead reinvested and compounded. It is a fiction that will make, for example, a money market fund appear more attractive than putting the same cash into a Guaranteed Investment Certificate, when the reverse is the case.

A more accurate measure is "current yield," which shows the average daily yield, *without compounding*, for a period of seven days, and then annualizes that figure. It is still fiction.

Shrewd investors will pay little attention to these short-term measures and look at much longer terms (while realizing that past performance may tell nothing about the future). Even here, the going can be tricky. After the market fall of October 1987, a number of mutual funds took to showing longer terms because the shorter ones looked so bad. For the year ending June 30, 1991, the average yield on 160 Canadian-equity mutual funds was *minus* 0.19 per cent, and the three-year average was 3.98 per cent. It's rather hard to convince a pensioner that this is a better bet than a dreary old bank account. Ah, but if you talk about the average gain of the stock market since 1929, you can come up with a much better figure.

Even the funds that averaged 10 per cent – below the return on an absolutely risk-free Treasury bill – managed to show returns that looked like 12 per cent. Some of them did it by neglecting to mention the management fees, and a lot of them did it by lying.

Or, to put it another way, as the *Globe and Mail* did in its February 1991 *Report on Mutual Funds*:

> Although the Ontario Securities Commission says that company marketing arms and brokers should behave ethically, it admits that it is impossible to deal with the possible expectations raised during a consultation or conversation with a prospective customer who may be considering an investment.

Even if the fund-floggers were suddenly stricken by a collective compulsion to tell the truth during a "consultation or conversation," it would be difficult to tell how any given fund is doing, because of the commissions and management fees.

The funds have to go through brokers to buy and sell the stocks they deal in to make money, and the brokers have to be paid commissions. This is usually done, as we saw above, by charging the client what is called a "load fee," either at the front or back end.

We have already seen how front-end loading can distort your investment in a mutual fund, and this may incline you to leap into one of the funds that carries the proud banner, "No Load!," but look before you leap. The front-end load, or its back-end equivalent, have drawbacks, all right, chief among them the fact that it is the mutual-fund company itself that decides what the level should be. It can be anywhere from 2 to 9 per cent of the investment, and you can bargain for a lower fee if you have a larger pool of money to put into the pot. But at least you can see it. Or, most of it. And at least it only hits you once, not every year. When investors began to scream as front-end loads ate up their gains, the mutual funds, or many of them, switched to charging back-end loads that decline the longer you hold your shares. You could be charged, say, 4.5 per cent if you wanted to get out in the first year, down to 1.0 per cent after five years. The trick is, though, that you will usually be charged on the basis of the market value of the fund when you cash in, not when you bought in, so, if you happen to make money along the way, more of it will be taken away from you when you actually want the cash – and you don't know, in advance, how much.

The funds that don't charge any load fees have to get money somewhere, and they do it through higher management fees, charged on a regular basis against the account. You can't see them. What is more, these fees, charged for looking after your money, include wages and bonuses for the salesperson and, quite often, the trailer fees paid to brokers or other sales reps for keeping you on the hook. Pardon, for servicing your account. Every year, the sales representative gets a fee if you don't cash in. If you do, no fee. It is this same sales rep who is supposed to give you advice as to when to buy and sell. Surprising how seldom they tell you to sell; even more surprising that you are expected to pay them for their "service." If a mutual fund advertises itself as a "No Load" fund, chances are it makes up the difference with higher management fees; otherwise, it has no income from which to pay the commission sales on stock transactions.

Management fees in Canada average 2.08 per cent of your investment annually – it takes money to create all those ads telling you what a swell deal awaits. (The management-fee figure is from the ROB's *Report on Mutual Funds* of July 19, 1991.) If you consider that the return on equity funds currently averages about 5 or 6 per cent, you can see that about a third of your take is going to vanish, and the numbers you read in the newspaper, or hear from the honeyed lips of the salesperson, may mean very little.

The numbers used in the ads mostly relate to periods when management fees were lower, because, as the customers began to kick more and more about the visible front-end and back-end loading fees, most mutual funds switched over to the invisible management fee, hiking the take there to make up for dropping the other loads. Then there are deferred sales charges, RRSP fees – for those funds that are eligible – switching fees, if you change funds within the same company, and termination fees. In most cases, by the way, the fund can change its management fees simply by giving you notice, and since all the funds tend to jump their fees at the same time, you won't get much satisfaction out of going elsewhere.

The good mutual funds pay better, on paper, than some other investment instruments, but wind up, usually, leaving the individual investor worse off. The bad ones don't even look good on paper. The truly safe ones charge you a fee to buy government paper that you can buy without their help, and the truly risky ones will clean you out with much the same panache as those rascally old millionaires, back before the 1930s.

And how can you tell them apart? We are back where we started, with so many products being pushed at us by so many hustlers that we need ten hours, a Ph.D., and access to more information than we are likely to obtain readily, to make an intelligent investment decision. Royal Trust alone has thirteen mutual funds to flog, including one that does nothing but invest in units of other Royal Trust mutual funds. These range all the way from the staid Canadian Money Market Fund to the highly volatile European Growth Fund, where you can be blind-sided not only by changes in stock prices, but by the machinations of the Canadian dollar.

When you go to look these up in the newspaper, under Canadian Mutual Funds, you will hit a line that looks like this:

Fund	Load	RSP	Dist	Value	Chg
ROYAL TRUST GROUP					
yEuro Growth	N		D	7.23	−.05

We'll come back to that little "y" in a minute. The other information identifies this fund among all the other Royal Trust funds, tells us, under Load, that there is no front-end load, leaves a blank under RSP to indicate that this investment is not eligible for inclusion in a self-administered Registered Retirement Savings

Plan (if it were, it would say "R"), tells us – "D" – that it is distributed by the fund sponsor rather than – "I" – independent agents, puts the Value of the units at $7.23, and lets us know that this is a drop of five cents from the last time the units were measured. I pause to point out that Royal Trust is one of our largest and oldest trust companies, and ask you whether, as a prudent investor, you wouldn't rather put your money into one of its Guaranteed Investment Certificates, at a fixed, known percentage, which will increase your money in a guaranteed way covered to the last dime by deposit insurance, than sock it into a mutal fund which has dropped the value of your investment, but gosh, not by much. And which carries no guarantees or insurance whatever.

The little "y" at the beginning, by the way, indicated that this value is not current, it is just the last value measured. If we want the current value, we have to call Royal Trust Mutual Funds, where we can get today's rate.

Which won't mean a damn thing to us, anyway. The value is, officially, the "Net Asset Value Per Share Or Unit," or NAVPS. This is the total value of this particular fund's holdings, divided by the number of units that have been issued. This is the price at which the units are sold on the market. We now know that a unit of Royal Trust European Growth Fund is worth $7.23, as of the last measurement, but whether this is good or bad we do not know, unless we have been following the action, or unless we want to trust that friendly voice on the telephone that says this really is a very good price with "tremendous potential for growth."

If we want to know whether this value is going up or down over time, the best way to find out is to look up the value currently shown, go back, say, one year by checking old newspapers in the library, and compare these two figures. We will find under these circumstances that a fund advertising "Annual Growth Rates of 17.2 per cent!" is just kidding. The gains, minus all the service charges and management fees, we will almost certainly find, are under 10 per cent.

You think I'm joshing you. You think mutual funds wouldn't be allowed to carry advertisements telling you that they have made their clients a fortune, when they haven't. Don't take my word for it; let's look it up. We have before us the *Globe and Mail* of July 18, 1991, which carries a special section called *Report on Mutual Funds*. Investors Group, Canada's largest mutual-fund group, is showing a year-over-year gain of 6.63 per cent in this mutual-funds round-up, for its Canadian Equity Fund. Not bad, considering what was happening to a number of other funds. However, when we check the NAVPS for this one, we find that the units are buying and selling for $6.41, and when we go back a year, we find they were selling for $6.25. They haven't gained 6.63 per cent in our hands, only in the fund's; our units are worth 2.56 per cent more than they were a year ago. A chequing account pays more.

I don't complain that any of these methods of measuring the funds are wrong or illegal. Indeed, my complaint is that they are perfectly proper and perfectly normal.

Actually, we can probably figure out all the wrinkles in any given mutual fund by reading the prospectus we got when we bought it – if we can understand it. My guess is that not one purchaser in a hundred can or does, or the funds wouldn't sell except to a handful of real gamblers. What we buy isn't the prospectus, but the sales pitch.

To soften your sales resistance, mutual-fund sellers have worked out and memorized lines of patter that range from the fanciful to the downright misleading, and they are egged on by such plums as free trips to Hawaii for the fund-floggers who do well. Major appliances are given out as prizes, too. How seriously do you think you should take the investment counselling of an investment counsellor to whom you represent a stretch on the sand at Waikiki or a shelf in his or her next refrigerator? He wouldn't fib, would he?

Bud Jorgensen of the *Globe and Mail* came upon, and

reprinted, a company memo written by Marketing Specialist Meri Rawling-Taylor of the brokerage firm Wood Gundy, designed to whip the company's financial consultants into fighting trim to sell Mackenzie Financial mutual funds – of which there are at least eighteen. Staff who reached Level 1 in fund-flogging, Ms. Rawling-Taylor wrote, would get a trip to sunny California, while Level 2, even higher, would bring a trip to New Zealand. Moreover, sales staff could win more points by steering clients into funds that paid higher commissions. Selling someone $100,000 worth of a fund with a 7-per-cent commission earned 75,000 points, but if the client could be persuaded to sign up for an 8-per-cent commission fund, the reward was 100,000 points. Win 500,000, and take wing. "Rev your engines, full force ahead all the way to KIWI LAND!!" wrote Ms. Rawling-Taylor, not one to spare the capitals or exclamation points. "Put the pedal to the metal and just keep thinking QUALIFY! QUALIFY!"

Thus armed, the brokers go out and help retirees to make the crucial decisions that will determine how much money they have to live on for the rest of their lives.

The handing out of free vacations has blown up in the face of one of the nation's most aggressive mutual-fund movers, Mackenzie Financial Corporation. Mackenzie, the industry leader in incentive bonus trips to faraway lands, was told by Revenue Canada that all these junkets are taxable benefits, and asked Where are the tax payments? Mackenzie replied that, well, these were really working trips, and therefore not taxable benefits, although it did offer to make a "voluntary payment" in lieu of taxes. No doubt, a few years from now, some tax court will make a ruling. In the meantime, the Ontario Securities Commission jumped into the fray and proposed a ban on trips to exotic spots as incentives for the fund-floggers. The Investment Funds Institute, which represents most of the Canadian Industry, begged to differ, and, after a lot of back and forth, the OSC came up with a "voluntary guideline," restricting trips among Investment Funds Institute members to "legitimate sales meetings and educational seminars" held in Canada. Your fund-flogger will not win a trip to Hawaii, if his company chooses to abide by this rule, only to Halifax. Incidentally, Mackenzie Financial Corp is not a member of the Institute. Other incentives to egg on the fund-floggers remain in place.

It is nice to think that sales personnel juiced up with incentives would refrain from pressing the units of a positively smelly mutual fund on old-age pensioners; anything is possible. But the fund may start out all right and then turn smelly, as was the case with United Services Funds, an equity-based investment trust from San Antonio, Texas, which was relieved of $9 million or so by stock promoters Edward Carter and David Ward. Between them, the two men controlled fourteen companies, mostly hollow shells, that traded on the Vancouver Stock Exchange, where the rules have traditionally had that amiable flexibility that allows full scope to the imaginative stock-seller. One of their companies, Tye Explorations Inc., a mineral exploration company with evanescent assets, was urged from 41 cents a share to $3.35 during twenty-six days in 1985, by the two men buying and selling back and forth among 126 accounts listed in different names. At $3.35, the stock was unloaded, for a total of more than $2 million, to United Services Funds, the way having been first prepared by a bribe to the fund's manager, to show him what a good stock it was.

In all, the fund wound up with $26 million worth of Carter and Ward shares that were not worth, collectively, a bucket of warm water. When the facts began to come to light, Carter told a lawyer from the fund that he would buy all the shares back, which gained him just enough time to transfer millions of dollars from his accounts to a bank in the Bahamas, from which it mysteriously disappeared. An Ontario judge, sentencing Carter in October 1990 to seven years in jail, grumbled that, "Somewhere on this planet Mr. Carter has hidden a substantial amount of money. He has engaged in a deliberate secretion of assets to enable him to retain the proceeds of crime." Well, I guess.

It is not true, as the *Wall Street Journal* would have us believe, that "every aspect of mutual funds is closely regulated." Nor is it true, as *How To Buy Stocks* argues, that "There is obviously less risk... in owning an interest in 50 or 150 different companies than in just one company." If the mutual-fund manager is taking a bribe to buy bum stocks, the risk rises appreciably, no matter how many companies are involved.

Mutual funds were supposed to save us all the hassle, by giving us skilled practitioners to make decisions for us – for a fee. It turns out that we need skilled practitioners to tell us which skilled practitioners to hire, and what their advice means. So, guess what the gurus want us to do now? Gordon Pape, in his *1991 Guide to Mutual Funds* gives us the answer:

> And don't put all your mutual fund eggs in one basket. A carefully-selected, well-diversified portfolio of mutual funds will reduce your risk and increase your chances of finding some big winners.
>
> In the end, that's what investing is all about.

In a word, Diversify. Isn't this where we came in?

CHAPTER TEN

I Went to a Broker, and Now I'm Broke

Brokers

I am in a non business. Inventory is never a problem for me, yet my inventories are unlimited. Seasons are never a problem, yet style-changes in my business would give Yves St. Laurent a spastic colon. Selling my merchandise is easy because it sells itself. Dreams of glory always sell themselves. Men and women lie, cheat, steal, kill and commit suicide over my merchandise. It makes them miserable and it makes them joyous; it makes everything possible and everything impossible. If I pedalled LSD, the illusions I sell could put me in jail; if I sold my body I wouldn't last long . . . if I sought through politics the power I now hold over men's emotions, I could be voted out of the White House and end up scribbling my memoirs for some library yet to be built. But I can have it all. I *do* have it all and I don't even pay for my secretary or my long-distance calls. I'm a stockbroker and the name of my game is greed.

– "Brutus," in *Confessions of a Stockbroker*, 1972.

One of the really well-worn stories of the brokerage business pconcerns a young man who is being introduced to the business from the vantage point of one of the big Wall Street firms. A senior partner beckons him over to the window of a New York skyscraper and gestures down to the river below.

"Look down there," he says, "in the harbour. That big white yacht belongs to J. Pierpont Morgan, the blue one next to it to Mr. Goldman of Goldman, Sachs, and that's my yacht over there, the brown one. Do your job well, my son, and some day, you'll have a yacht down there."

"Ah, I see," says the neophyte. "And where are the customers' yachts?"

Brokers laugh at this story; they ought to blush. The term "broker" originally referred to wine retailers, who broached wine casks and sold the contents. Early in the seventeenth century, it began to be used to describe any agent in financial transactions. Today, it describes the people who alone have the right to sell registered stocks and bonds, and to collect a commission thereon. They also sell commodities, options, futures, RRSPs, annuities, mutual funds, money-market instruments such as Treasury bills, and even the humble Guaranteed Investment Certificate. Brokers are called by many names, some of them suitable for family viewing, such as retail representatives, financial consultants, institutional salesmen, securities salespersons, account executives, investment executives, portfolio salesmen, or, occasionally, brokers.

The firms they work for are called investment dealers, stock brokers, securities houses, investment firms, broker-dealers, brokerage firms, brokerage houses, or securities dealers. Same fella. These firms are also the underwriters for securities issues.

There used to be a sharp distinction between investment dealers and stockbrokers. In the first place, investment dealers did their business mainly in bonds, and brokers in stocks; in the second, the dealers acted as principals in securities transactions, while the broker's role was to serve as agent. The dealer owned the securities he sold, and he made money on the difference between the buying and the selling price. The broker didn't own the shares, but made all his money on the commissions he earned from the buying and selling. No longer. Now, in the words of *How To Invest in Canadian Securities,* "Most firms today deal in both bonds and stocks and act as both principals or agents *though never in the same transaction.*" I didn't put the emphasis in there; it came from the folks who compiled the book for the Canadian Securities Institute, which happens to be owned by the Investment Dealers Association of Canada. Same fellas.

This sentence refers to the Chinese Walls we have already met, which are intended to sort out conflicts within these meshed institutions – and sometimes do. This sentence also ignores the fact that, quite legitimately, market-makers (the floor brokers charged with maintaining orderly markets in a number of stocks) buy and sell from their own portfolios as a matter of routine. They are not allowed to charge commissions when they deal in their own stock, except – and it is an exception as wide as a barn door and as deep as a well – that on U.S. exchanges there is an exemption on block trades that are being made because the firm is getting out of that particular share. As Martin Mayer puts it in *The Markets,* "Few brokers see anything improper in putting out a buy recommendation for a stock in which their firm holds a position it will be winding down for a profit."

In short, they tell you to buy something their firm owns and they want to sell, which is one definition of acting as principal and agent at the same time.

In fact, some brokers may go even further, and deliberately bet against their customers by shorting the stocks they are flogging. It is illegal, but that is not the same as saying that it is uncommon. A broker can achieve the same goal of covering all bets, without breaking the law, if he follows the example of a man described by C. David Chase in *Mugged on Wall Street:*

> He divides his clients into two groups. He tells the first group the market is going to hell and to sell, or sell short.

He tells the other half the market will rise and buy, buy, buy. He's an old-timer of fifteen years making an annual salary over $100,000. He could be your broker.

John Saunders, a *Globe and Mail* reporter, calculated, in an article published in July 1990, that "Something like 60 per cent of the trading now is done by brokerage firms for their own accounts, a risky but expanding side of the business." We are asked to believe that these are all arm's-length transactions when the time comes to move the stuff on to the customers, and some of us do believe – just as some of us believe that babies come from Eaton's.

The most glaring example of the conflicts inherent in the brokerage business can be seen every day in the heart of the stock markets, at the New York Stock Exchange. It is the practice in U.S. stock markets that only traders who do business with the public, as opposed to institutional traders, may stand on the top ring of the financial trading pits, so that they can see signals from telephone clerks relaying orders. But anyone on that ring may and can buy and sell for his own account before fulfilling public orders, and anyone who understands the hand signals can do the same. In short, as Martin Mayer remarks in *The Markets*:

> Virtually no public order for an S&P (Standard & Poor 500) contract (or a gold or silver future at New York's COMEX, for that matter) is ever filled at a price more favorable to the customer than the price of the most recent trade. If the possibility of such a price arises, a member of the exchange takes the money and runs.

The blatant unfairness of this led to a suggestion that traders on the top rung should not be allowed to buy and sell on their own accounts, but this was quashed, proving, Martin notes, the difficulty of "taking an acorn away from a pig."

In a subtler variation of this, called "front-running," the trader places an order for his or her own account, knowing that a large pending order from a customer will move the market one way or the other. How can this be detected?

The public cannot tell, in any event, whether what the brokerage does is based on inside information, instinct, or shrewd guessing. Gordon Capital, a Toronto firm that revels in the adjective "aggressive," sold a bundle of call options in the stock of LAC Minerals near the close of the trading day. And guess what? The share prices fell the next day, making this a very shrewd move. And guess what else? Trading in the stock was suspended that very day, because of an announcement that there would be a new share issue from LAC, for which Gordon's corporate finance department just happened to be one of the underwriters.

Gordon Capital is the prime example of a firm that likes to be in on the action – sometimes on all sides of it. While acting as an advisor to Unicorp in the hostile takeover of Union Gas Company, Gordon sent out an advisory to its institutional clients, suggesting that it would be a good idea for them to sell Union Gas shares at $13, which happened to be what was then being offered. The Ontario Securities Commission launched an investigation into the arrangement in which a broker was offering advice on a deal it was itself pulling together, but nothing came of it, except that Gordon was required to send out a letter explaining that it was not exactly a disinterested party.

Gordon was also unusually active in a deal described by Erik Nielsen in his autobiography, *The House is Not a Home.* Nielsen reports that he became concerned, as deputy prime minister, when he was investigating the activities of Sinclair Stevens, a colleague in the Mulroney cabinet, and discovered that Stevens had close ties to Gordon Capital. As a cabinet minister, Stevens was working with the firm to sell to the public the government's shares of the Canada Development Corporation, while Gordon was helping to obtain capital for York Centre Corporation, Stevens's ailing firm. Moreover, Gordon was a major player in the CDC shares it was selling. To top it off, Stevens intervened to get the price of the CDC share-offering set where Gordon wanted it set, at $11.50.

Could one company act in so many different directions at once? Apparently so; Stevens was bounced from the cabinet for a series of conflicts of interest, but Gordon went on its merry way.

If Gordon is an investment house that likes to be thought of as aggressive, I know of none that wants to be hailed as "timid." There are scores of brokerage houses in Canada, ranging from firms with more than two thousand employees, like RBC Dominion Securities, to those with a handful of workers, but the business is dominated by about a dozen firms – the figure shrinks yearly, as they merge together – centred in Toronto and Montreal. Despite the inroads that recession and amalgamation have made in their ranks, brokers are not an endangered species; there are eighteen retail representatives – the ones who actually get you on the phone – for every 100,000 people in Canada, according to a count done in 1991 by Technimetrics, a financial consulting firm. This is fewer than in the U.S., where there are 22 per 100,000, but enough to be getting on with. According to the same survey, in 1991 Toronto had 997 retail representatives, Montreal 799, Vancouver 595, Calgary 365, Edmonton 123, and Winnipeg 127. Behind these busy talkers stands an impressive army – even if it is shrinking these days – of support staff, from analysts and managers to clerks and foot-sloggers. The TSE's broker-members had 21,600 employees at the end of 1990. A considerable business.

There are two major kinds of brokerage operation, full-service brokers and discount brokers, and they are very often owned by the same company. The full-service broker supplies investment advice, tips, and, in due season, sympathy to the client, for a commission that will range anywhere from about 6 to as high as 15 per cent of the price of the shares bought or sold. The discount broker simply puts the deal through for you and takes a commission that is usually, but not always, much lower. You can negotiate with the broker, if you are buying a large block of shares, to pay a smaller commission, since there is no more work involved for him in selling you 100,000 shares of B.C. Telephone at $47.50 than in selling you 100 shares of Take a Chance Oil Wells at eleven cents. This is another way of saying that the small trader – you – pays far more by way of commission than the larger traders with whom he or she has to compete. On "block trades" – 50,000 or more shares at a whack – large institutions may pay 1 per cent while you pay 5 per cent. Since this difference may determine whether you make or lose money on the deal, it has a sharp edge for most small traders. It may be one of the reasons, although it would be cynical to say so, why the exchanges are so anxious to help us little guys trade. The exchanges are owned by the brokers.

Incidentally, the broker can change the commission charge without telling you until you get the bill, although he is supposed to warn you when you place your order. The company he works for makes the decision, and he is supposed to keep you informed. If he doesn't, too bad.

"Shop around," the experts tell us, but this may not help if you already shopped around and got the lowest rate – before it went up. We are not talking about peanuts here. To start with, the discount brokers have minimum commission schedules that run from $25 at this writing (the Bank of Montreal's discounter, Investorline) to $45 (the Toronto-Dominion Bank's Green Line) on trades of under $2,000. Then there is a table of fees for each transaction, made up of a base fee and a per-share charge that rises with the price of the stock.

At Scotia Discount, you will pay at least $55 for the purchase of 1,000 shares at $6 a share, up to $85, if the shares cost $50 or more. The equivalents at Marathon Brokerage, one of the major discount houses, are $75 and $95. Not are, but were. Were when I wrote this. They may be higher now. What this means is that when you get that hot tip to buy Snake Eyes Preferred, you should spend a few days on the phone nailing down the commission price before you swing into action; by which time it will be too late.

Never mind, go to a full-service house. There you will pay $195 on 1,000 shares at 6 per cent.

Marathon Brokerage runs an ad in the newspapers at frequent intervals, which compares its own prices with those of full-service brokers. The ad shows that, if you buy 1,000 shares of a stock at $19.25 and sell it at $20, the full-service broker will charge you $418 to buy and $425 to sell. This not only makes your margin of profit disappear, it means that you lose $93 on your coup. At Marathon, you pay only $80 to buy and the same to sell, so the shares for which you paid $19,330 (with commission) bring in $19,920 ($20,000 less commission); you make $590 instead of losing $93. This is a highly educational ad, but one of the things it teaches us is that we can make money on a trade and lose it on commissions, if the difference between buying and selling prices is narrow enough, no matter where we deal.

Moreover, something the ad doesn't tell you is that, because of the minimums the discount houses impose, you could pay more commission buying cheap stocks from them than you would at a full-service house. To buy 50,000 shares of a 9-cent stock at a discount house would probably run you $290, made up of a $40 minimum, plus half a cent commission on 50,000 shares; you could do the same deal at a full-service house for between $155 and $162.

One more moreover. The broker gets different commissions for pushing different stocks, and his company can use these rates to whipsaw the broker, who in turn will take the right line when dealing with the customer. A broker who is going to get 15-per-cent commission for selling the shares of Watch My Smoke, Ltd., or 6 per cent for IBM, is going to be inclined to push the former on the Widow Brown. In the same way, his company may sweeten the pot if he can get rid of the dud stocks in its own portfolio, and the Widow Brown has no way of knowing that the broker's strong recommendation that she buy Watch My Smoke has nothing whatsoever to do with the worth of the company, and everything to do with the richness of the commission.

In one of the more eyebrow-raising of these cases, which came to light in late 1990, it developed that Durham Securities Corp. Ltd. of Toronto had acquired nearly all of the shares of two companies, Aatra Resources Ltd. and Bayridge Developments Ltd., and then sold the shares to customers in Ontario. This had the great advantage that neither of the two companies had to release financial statements or other disclosure documents, because the customers were in Ontario, while the stock was issued in British Columbia. Considering the state of the companies, this could be called a necessary prerequisite to selling the stock.

Richard Stevenson, a salesman at Durham, told an Ontario Securities Commission hearing that he earned $200,000 in 1989, almost all of it from pushing the shares of Aatra and Bayridge. He was paid 15-per-cent commission on the sale of either, but if a client wanted to unload the stock, the broker got no commission. In fact, if the client dumped his shares within sixty days of buying them, the broker lost the commission he had made selling them. You can guess how often customers were told it was a good time to sell.

Bayridge shares went from fifty-five cents in January 1989 to $6.50 in March 1990, at which time the OSC issued a cease-trading order in Ontario, because the company was in violation of regulations. Then the stock became worthless. Aatra shares went from thirty-five cents in August 1989 to $3.95 in March 1990, when trading was halted in Vancouver. This stock, too, became worthless.

So, while the brokers got 15 per cent, and the brokerage house sold its own shares on a rising market, the customers wound up with a lot of dud stock. We call this "the level playing field."

The organization of most large investment houses follows a similar pattern. There are five major divisions, and it is among these that the Chinese Walls are said to have been firmly placed.

1. **Selling:** The heart of the business is the sales department, which, in any large house, is divided into two sections; an institu-

tional section, to service major financial institutions and large organizations, such as pension funds, and a retail branch, to serve individual customers.

2. Underwriting: This department advises corporations and governments on the best way to raise money in the markets; it then helps to float the issue and undertakes to support the initial offering at the price agreed upon with the client. Often, it does this by actually buying the shares and reselling them. The gang in sales are not supposed to know that the gang over in underwriting are pushing Take a Chance Oil and that, if it cannot be unloaded, they are going to have to eat it for dinner.

3. Trading: The bond-trading department buys and sells bonds directly to and from other dealers and deals indirectly with the public through the sales department. The stock-trading department sells listed and unlisted stocks, options, futures, and so forth. The floor traders come from this department.

4. Research: This department analyses companies and government issues and prepares reports for the firm and its clients. The stock analysts you so often see quoted on Monday explaining what a terrific buy Take a Chance is going to be when it is launched on Tuesday, and explaining on Wednesday why it bombed, come from this department. They are not supposed to care that the company has a block of the shares. Stock analysts tend to specialize, and some of them are very good and thoroughly honest and incredibly knowledgeable, and some of them are stupid and ignorant and venal, just as in any other business. The only difference is that, in another business, you know that the guy in the checked suit whose first name is Honest is trying to shift Fords, because he sells for a Ford dealership. You don't know why the analyst wants to shift Take a Chance, any more than you knew why your broker kept telling you what an unparalleled opportunity existed in Aatra.

5. Administration: Where the drudgery is done and where, among other things, there is supposed to be a foot patrol to check the state of the Chinese Walls. This may be the place to mention that Sir Peter Tapsell once told the British House of Commons, "I have visited the Great Wall of China and it has this characteristic: It has never kept anybody in or out."

One department which is not formally acknowledged, but which ought to be in there somewhere, is **Promotion.** Stock promoters are not the same as brokers. Indeed, they are no part of the brokerage business, but they are, nonetheless, absolutely essential to it. They are the folks who beat the drums for Snake Eyes Preferred, either because it is their own company – at least until they can sell it – or on behalf of someone else, for fees and commissions, or, far more usually, by buying the stock when it first comes out, promoting it upwards, and then bailing out.

Unlike brokers, promoters are not licensed, trained, or regulated. If you want to be a promoter, stick up a sign and go into business. Your job will be to convince the public to buy, not just any old share, but the particular shares you have signed up to sell. It is done on the phone, in boiler-rooms, by letter. It is not an easy job, but when you consider that any given stock exchange really has only one product to sell, although tarted up in endless variations, you will see how important the promoter's role can be. "Canadian promoters," write David Cruise and Alison Griffiths in *Fleecing the Lamb,* "are now the reigning monarchs of the profession – especially on the dark side of it."

But that, of course, is in Vancouver. Their book is about the Vancouver Stock Exchange, where promotion is king. Or, as they put it:

> Someone still has to go out on the streets, into the back rooms and increasingly into the board rooms to convince people that the promise of gain (usually quick) lies in one stock or another. Someone has to promise investors that there will be a buyer for their stock when they want to sell. Someone has to get people taking about Urea High

Mining and make sure information about its "fabulous" new property becomes affixed to the market grapevine. That someone is the promoter. Some floor traders, who are close enough to the action to know, maintain that as much as 70 per cent of all trading on the VSE is generated in one form or another by promoters.

Well, that's Vancouver, of course. The closest guess I could get as to how much stock-trading activity in Toronto is the direct result of promoters was "quite a lot," which lacks the precision we all strive for. In any event, promoters have shaded, especially outside Vancouver, into the tribe of analysts, lawyers, consultants, and freelance market-players. The phrase "stock promoter" has a somewhat dodgy ring to it in most parts of the world, so promoters call themselves almost anything else. I have attached them to the brokerage houses, although they are never members of brokerage houses, because of their symbiotic relationship, and because, as Cruise and Griffiths put it, "Without promoters, the VSE and many brokerage houses would cease to function overnight."

You don't need promoters to sell IBM stocks, but you do to sell most of the Over the Counter shares that keep rolling into the market, year after year.

The presence of promoters makes explaining the brokerage houses a little more complicated, but it is nothing as compared to the recent, and regrettable, dominance of the industry by the banks. To help make life interesting for us all, the Canadian chartered banks leapt into the brokerage business after June 30, 1987. That was the day deregulation hit the industry, and banks and trust companies were allowed to jump in. It was an imitation of Britain's Big Bang of October 1986, when banks and foreign firms were allowed to join the London Stock Exchange. Now, every one of Canada's six largest banks has a wholly-owned discount-brokerage subsidiary, and five of the six have part or all of a full-service broker.

Without beating around the bush, it strikes me as absolutely insane that the bank that may be advancing the money to an underwriter to launch a stock issue may own the underwriter who sets the share price. The same firm provides the broker, who advises customers, not merely on whether it is a good idea to invest in stocks as opposed to Canada Savings Bonds, but on which stocks the customers should buy, all based on analyses done by his own outfit and knowing that – as is often the case – the broker owns shares in the brokerage house and/or the bank that is behind the whole operation. The same bank's customer-service department will advise the Widow Brown on where to invest her husband's insurance money, but never, for that would be wrong, by telling her to buy Take a Chance. It will introduce her to the brokerage house instead, if that seems to be what she ought to be considering, and the brokerage house will do the rest.

The customer who rolls up to the window at Nesbitt Thomson, one of our largest firms, may or may not appreciate that it is 75 per cent owned by the Bank of Montreal. ("What looks good these days?" "How about bank shares?") You ought to guess that ScotiaMcLeod is part of the Bank of Nova Scotia, and you might work out that the RBC in RBC Dominion is the Royal Bank of Canada, but there is no way to guess that Wood Gundy is in the grip of the Canadian Imperial Bank of Commerce and that Lévesque Beaubien belongs to the National Bank and two corporate partners. Wood Gundy, in turn, owns the retail business that used to be part of Merrill Lynch Canada, Inc. The Royal Bank's RBC Dominion is the result of six mergers, which swallowed some of the best-known brokerage houses in Canada, including Dominion Securities Co., A.E. Ames & Co., Pitfield MacKay Ross Ltd., Molson Rousseau, and Pemberton Securities Inc. of Vancouver. Oh, yes, and the largest discount brokerage in the country is easy to recognize: it is the Toronto-Dominion Bank's Green Line Investor Services Inc.

I am not arguing here that the brokers who work for bank-owned firms are acting against the best interests of their clients;

rather that they, and we, are put in an impossible position by this cross-ownership and its inevitable conflicts of interest.

It wouldn't be so dangerous if we could count on the independence of the stock analysts to guide us through these troubled waters. But we can't. We get some notion of the difference between the cool, arm's-length, Chinese-Wall approach seen in the texts and that found in real life through the story of the stock analyst who insisted on writing a negative report on the machinations of Donald Trump, before that mogul became de-moguled. Trump's new Atlantic City casino, the Taj Mahal, was too heavily weighted with debt to succeed, reported Marvin Roffman, an analyst for sixteen years with Janney Montgomery Scott Inc. of Philadelphia. He told the *Wall Street Journal,* in March 1990, that the casino "Won't make it. The market just isn't there." Trump demanded a letter of apology, and Janney Montgomery ordered the analyst to produce it, take a pay cut, and stop talking to reporters. When he refused these dicta, he was fired. The Associated Press, in a follow-up story from New York on March 27, 1990, quoted James Cramer, president of an investment-management firm, as saying: "Most people think analysts are independent, understand their industries and do tough analysis. It's just not true. Most analysts can't afford to be independent."

Incidentally, the Taj Mahal has been in financial trouble since the day it opened.

In Canada we do things more subtly. When analyst Douglas Cunningham wrote a scathing commentary on Rogers Communications Inc. for his employer, First Boston Canada Ltd., the firm simply refused to publish the report. Cunningham quit, and his new employer, BBN James Capel Inc., did publish the commentary, which advised investors to sell.

The Chinese Wall that really works is the one between the brokerage firms and the world outside, for brokers are instructed, in the name of client confidentiality, that they must never reveal on whose behalf they are buying or selling, even if it is themselves.

Thus, most of the cases of conflict of interest never come to light. Now and then one does, though.

In *Liar's Poker*, Michael Lewis, a former bond salesman for Salomon Brothers, describes in detail how he sold $3 million worth of AT & T bonds to a new client, who had the authority to invest $20 million on behalf of a German bank. The client was drunk when Lewis sold him the bonds, on which, Lewis had been assured by his own company's bond trader, "Your guy will make money." In fact, the bonds he was selling were in Salomon Brothers' own account; the company had been trying to unload them for months, but Lewis wasn't told that. The Chinese Wall was up. He only learned who owned the bonds when the transaction was announced over the brokerage public-address system, and Lewis was congratulated on selling "three million of our AT&T s for us, a great trade for the desk." The Chinese Wall was down. The next morning Lewis received a call from his client, who was now sober and whose bank was now $60,000 poorer, because the bonds had slipped in price, so he went back to the trader who had given him the hot tip and accused him of lying about the worth of the bonds.

"Look," the trader replied, "who do you work for, this guy or Salomon Brothers?" The Chinese Wall was up again, facing outwards.

Lewis remarks that the firm's operating principle was once put to him by the then-president, Tom Strauss: "Customers have very short memories." Lewis adds, "If that was the guiding principle of Salomon Brothers in the department of customer relations, then all was suddenly clear. Screw 'em, they'll eventually forget about it! Right." The client, in the end, lost $140,000 and was fired, while "I was a minor hero at Salomon for dumping a sixty-thousand-dollar loss into someone else's pocket." Lewis comforts himself with the thought that, "He didn't have to believe me when I told him AT&T bonds were a good idea."

What Lewis did to this client is known as "blowing up a customer," which is not as common as another technique known as "churn 'em and burn 'em." This is where the broker operates the client's account for him or her, saving all the bother of telephone calls, and proceeds to slosh sales back and forth, collecting a commission each time, until the client is broke. The technique is known as "discretionary trading"; you give the broker the right to buy and sell on your behalf after filling out a form that indicates the investment strategy you wish him or her to follow.

Whenever I hear of someone who has instructed a broker to operate the account according to his own best judgement, given the client's original instructions ("buy good stuff"), I am reminded of a Peter Arno cartoon in the *New Yorker*. The cartoon showed a shapely young woman in a skimpy sailor suit which has become somewhat torn and mussed. She is explaining to her room-mate, "He told me there was a storm coming up, and I like a fool let him lash me to the mast."

The customer who puts his or her whole faith in the broker is lashed to the mast, and the results are often dismal, even if no discretionary trading form has been signed and the client merely follows the broker's advice.

An elderly doctor opened an account with a member-broker of the Toronto Stock Exchange. He wanted someplace safe to invest his retirement fund of $140,000, and he had no doubt read all that interesting material put out by the stock-pushers that stocks are a better hedge against inflation than any old dull bank account. The broker ploughed most of the $140,000 into options and, in less than a year, drove the value of the physician's intended retirement nest-egg down to $23,000.

Do not think that the Toronto Stock Exchange let this rascally broker get away with it. When a complaint was laid, and duly pursued, the broker was fined $2,000.

A retired farming couple in Saskatchewan were led by their broker into stock indexes and options accounts and, first thing you know, the savings of a lifetime went down the drain. A

Toronto couple lost their entire investment pool of $155,000, while the broker they trusted to help them invest cleared $132,000 in commissions for himself and his firm.

Brokers are salespeople. That's all. The best of them are good, and conscientious, and worry a great deal about their clients, and the worst of them are unscrupulous thugs, but the great middle mass are just salespeople. The more business you do with them, the more money they make. The more you can be persuaded to buy and sell and buy and sell, the better off they are. If you buy and hold stocks, they don't make a thing beyond the original commission; how often, in the circumstances, do you think they will tell you just to sit tight? About as often as a shoe salesman will point out to you that you don't really need a new pair of brogues, why not just wear the old ones a while longer?

If there is anything that sets the brokers aside as a class, it is their greed. They work in a game that salutes greed, glories in it, makes it a positive virtue. Don't take my word for it; this is what C. David Chase, vice-president of E. F. Hutton, wrote in *Mugged on Wall Street:*

> This sounds crass, but avarice is essential in a broker's personality. Unless he has a continuous growing need – a second car, a growing art collection, twins, alimony, a second wife, a second husband – he or she won't be driven to increase their [sic] income. Therefore, brokerage firms hire people who have expensive tastes for expensive acquisitions. The broker who is satisfied with a certain level of income soon reaches a sales plateau. Too many like him will hamper the firm's growth.

There are many businesses in which greed is acknowledged, but few in which it is worshipped as it is in the stock-flogging game. The players are expected to keep up. When Martin Siegel was arrested, thus bringing on the first of the scandals that landed Ivan Boesky and Michael Milken in jail, it came out that he was earning $1 million a year at the same time that he was accepting suitcases full of cash for inside information. A fellow broker was quoted in the *New York Times*, asking, "How many yachts can you water-ski behind at the same time?"

Even the leaders of the investment industry are showing concern. Brian Steck, the outgoing chairman of the Investment Dealers Association of Canada, in his farewell speech to that group in June 1991, said:

> There is something fundamentally wrong with a member firm being able to hire an individual with no industry and investment experience (and after a relatively short course) immediately being allowed to advise clients on some very complicated issues.

It is interesting how many people, like Steck, who have seen the business from the inside, think brokers do a lousy job. *Report on Business* magazine, in August 1990, quoted Jack Lawrence, the chairman of Burns Fry, Ltd., saying, "About 30 per cent to 40 per cent of brokers do a disservice to their clients." He put most of this dismal record down to the "profit-minded aggressiveness" of the industry. I think some blame ought to be left for sheer dumb ignorance on the part of many brokers, who are turned loose to shear the lambs with about six weeks' training in the mechanics of the business and none in the ethics, if any, of the business.

Ah, but wait, the neophyte is not alone. He can call on all the collective experience of the firm, and the analysts who put out all those clever papers. But we have already seen that there are two problems here. The first is that the analysts are under a good deal of pressure to write reports that will lead the clients to buy – especially to buy the stocks the house would like to see moved. Michael Lewis found only two "sell" recommendations in his own firm in the first two years he worked there, which is quite staggering, when you think of the number of stocks and bonds a major firm would have under analysis at any one time. The second is that, even if the analysts escape being suborned, persuaded, or pressured, their overall track record as a group is deplorable. These are the experts who lose out to the darts. David Chase tells the story of an analyst who was asked why stock prices were rising. He replied, after due consideration, "I guess there are more buyers than sellers."

Chase says his experienced friends on Wall Street "don't buy many stocks or pay much attention to reports that originate on the Street"; in his view, personal experience is the only way to master the intricacies of the market. The problem with that approach is that it is the customer who is going to pay for all the mistakes that are made while the experience is being gathered. The customers are in the familiar dilemma of not knowing whether they would be better off in the hands of a rogue or a simpleton; sometimes they get both.

At least when your broker is selling you stocks traded on exchanges, there is some information available. In the Over the Counter market, not only are you flying blind – so, most of the time, is your broker.

He may be selling you a stock that his own firm is shorting, and he may or may not know that, depending on how high the Chinese Walls rise in his particular firm. When the stock crashes, the brokerage will have made money from it two ways: from the short-selling and from the commission it made when you were loaded up with the shares it was helping to undercut.

What can a body do? Pay a fee to a "personal financial adviser," who is supposed to be neutral, because at least he or she isn't making a commission on stocks being unloaded from his or her own company's bin of fading papers? The difficulty here is that there is no regulation of these personal financial advisers, no formal training required. Indeed, all anyone has to do to become one is to stick an ad in the paper or the yellow pages, print up some business cards, and start in. The only personal financial adviser I have known personally had to move frequently for non-payment of rent, was being pursued by Toronto Hydro for non-payment of bills, and was wanted by the cops for non-payment of parking tickets. He was thus in a good position to advise bewildered clients on the best way to handle their savings: Don't waste any of it on rent, electricity, or parking fines.

The fundamental dilemma is that the real organizers of the stock market are the brokers, promoters, and stock-floggers who are on the inside of the trading transactions and who can make money whether you win or lose. And they are the ones who run the exchanges and set the rules.

Never mind, they have to operate within a set of strict regulations laid down by law. Don't they?

We shall see.

CHAPTER ELEVEN

Standing on Guard for Thee.
Or Them.

The Regulators

And always remember the weak, meek and ignorant are always
good targets.
   – Advice in a memo to bond salesmen from Lincoln Savings &
Loan Association, 1988.

$

The entire securities industry likes to refer to "the burden of regulation," apparently somewhat akin to the "white man's burden,"
which has now gone so deservedly out of fashion. You might think
this is a little like the Mafia complaining of the undue cost to the
taxpayer of police salaries, but you would be wrong. In the first
place, the majority of people in the stock markets are honest –
although some only marginally so – and in the second, there is, in
fact, a great deal of regulation of the markets. There are commissions and agencies, and investigating arms and internal-confor-
mity groups, and postal officials and customs officers, and
monetary exchange bureaucrats and even cops, swarming all over
the place at every level from the lowly brokerage office in a small
Canadian city to the international stage.

Unfortunately, all this regulation doesn't seem to do much good, and there is a good deal of pressure, not all of it coming from insiders or crazy people, to forget the whole thing. Let it go. Cover the widows and orphans as best you can, and let the rest take their chances.

If we want to know why this mood of disillusion and despair exists, we need, once more, to look at the historical record.

During most of the development of the stock markets, as we have already seen, regulations were few and vague. No opium-smoking in the corridors and bury your own dead; that was about it. From time to time, when a particularly odiferous scandal broke, such as the South Sea Bubble, there would be a flurry of activity, and the passage of some legislation of the barn-door-closing variety. This ensured that the next scam would at least look a little different from the last scam, but did little else. Since the major players in government were usually mixed up in the scandal, indignation was likely to be kept under control, unless and until, as in the South Sea Bubble, the promoters themselves got hurt. It was generally felt that *caveat emptor* covered most situations, and if you got burned on the markets, chances were you asked for it, by getting too greedy.

All that changed when money became more plentiful in the hands of ordinary people, beginning early in this century, and the markets were no longer merely the playgrounds of the privileged. The testimony taken by congressional committees in the United States in the wake of the Great Crash genuinely alarmed and offended a wide sector of the populace. The systematic cheating, the trading on insider information, the manipulation of stock prices, and all the other games played by the promoters, brokers, and even bank presidents, cost hundreds of thousands of small investors their life savings and – it was widely believed – brought on the Great Depression.

Well, dammit, something ought to be done. And it was. Franklin D. Roosevelt, an activist politician if ever there was one, was the governor of the state of New York, where most of the abuses took place, and the state was then responsible for security regulation. In the 1932 presidential election campaign, his Republican opponent, Herbert Hoover, met some of Roosevelt's complaints about the chicanery that had flourished under his administration by pointing out that it had flourished under Roosevelt's wing, not his. The individual states had passed "blue sky" laws, so called because they were alleged to require complete disclosure of the information necessary to investors, i.e., a clear blue sky. If these didn't work, then it was the fault of the state laws, not of Washington. It was doubtful, Hoover said, that the federal government even had the constitutional authority to control the markets; that was a job for the states. Don't look at me.

At that point FDR riposted rather neatly that, since stocks crossed state borders, they came under federal jurisdiction. Besides, state regulation could never meet the problem. All the crooks had to do was to ride over the state-line and thumb their noses at the regulators (which is still the case in Canada); if you closed down a bucket shop in Manhattan, it would bob up a few days later across the river in New Jersey, and begin again. The answer, Roosevelt said, was control from Washington. If elected, he would introduce the requisite legislation. And he did.

His first reform bill, the Securities Act of 1933, called for the regulation of securities by the Federal Trade Commission, and it was based on the same principle as the state blue-sky laws. Disclosure to the glaring light of publicity would do the trick; investors, properly informed, would be able to decide between various investments. That established, the exchanges could be left to regulate themselves. This act, sometimes known as the truth-in-securities law, remains the philosophical underpinning of market regulation. Let 'em know, and let 'er rip. The result is that the overwhelming majority of disciplinary cases in both Canada and the United States are undertaken because someone violated a disclosure regulation. No one will come after you for selling shares in Missing Mines, Inc. to old Aunt Min, as long as you can show that you told her the mines were missing. After that, it's her lookout.

The 1933 legislation covered only new issues; it did not cover the reselling of existing securities, which, even then, made up most of the market. Accordingly, Roosevelt established a committee to examine how this could best be done, and to put together a report to make recommendations for the regulation of commodity markets. The Roper Report, named after FDR's Secretary of Commerce and the committee chairman, Daniel C. Roper, recommended a very mild form of regulation: the federal registering and licensing of the exchanges, and their oversight by a new agency. The necessary staff could be drawn from the staffs of the stock exchanges. Roosevelt didn't see the need for this; he thought the job could be done through the Federal Trade Commission, which already existed and had some experience in this line.

A number of congressmen, alarmed by the stories that were then unwinding before them, wanted much stiffer regulation than either the Roper Report or the president seemed to be contemplating. As the necessary legislation began its torturous way through Congress, they made it clear that they wanted the exchanges brought to heel, and they certainly didn't want them, in effect, to be allowed to staff any oversight agency, whether it was the FTC or something new. They wanted the regulations to extend to the links between banks and investment houses, too, and they wanted some of the prime movers and shakers on Wall Street to be faced with criminal charges if they ever got out of line again.

This radical talk – jail, forsooth! – brought all the big guns of the financial community into the fray. If any regulator, new or old, were given the power to control the markets, it would bring the return of Chaos and old Night. Washington would be able to dictate to every American corporation, the Wall Street lobbyists warned; industries would all be nationalized and capital formation would be doomed. One of the most vociferous opponents of any substantive reform was Richard Whitney, president of the New York Stock Exchange. Of course, this was before he was exposed as one of the more active crooks extant.

Whitney rented a house in Washington to lead the anti-regulatory crusade – a crusade that House Speaker Sam Rayburn later described as "the most powerful lobby ever organized against any bill which ever came up in Congress" – and rounded up the Hearst press to thunder that the whole thing was a Communist plot. "Much of the Administration is more Communistic than the Communists themselves," the Hearst editorials declaimed, although it was not explained what yardstick was used; presumably, the more you wanted to tinker with the New York Stock Exchange, the more Red you were. Whitney told a congressional committee that was holding hearings on the bill, "You gentlemen are making a great mistake. The exchange is a perfect institution." Republican Congressman Fred Britten of Illinois chimed in, "The real object of the bill is to Russianize everything worthwhile."

Will Rogers, the comedian, put his finger on the weakness of the argument raised by Whitney and his supporters. "Those old Wall Street boys," he said, "are putting up an awful fight to keep the government from putting a cop on their corner."

Whitney did his cause more harm than good, because of his insistence that the exchange was a perfect thing which could not be tampered with. A congressman asked him, "When does speculation become excessive?"

"That I cannot tell you," Whitney replied. He only knew that no attempt should be made to control speculation, because, "You are trying to deal with human nature."

The great J. P. Morgan, Jr. – son of the original – also put in a word on the legislation. "If you destroy the leisure class," he assured the congressmen, "you will destroy civilization." Asked for a definition of the leisure class, he replied, "Anyone who can afford a maid." (His pa was a snob, too. "You can do business with anyone," the senior Morgan had said, "but you can only sail a boat with a gentleman.")

Roosevelt was well aware of the public's view of Whitney and his lobby, and made it clear that he had no intention of backing down on the key point: that the exchanges must be licensed, with regulations drawn so that the licences could be revoked. However, he preferred the regulatory role to be assumed by the Federal Trade Commission, not a new outside agency. At this point, the financial community changed its stance. Let there be a separate agency, Wall Street argued; it would be much easier to develop friendly ties with a new body than with an existing hostile bureaucracy.

And so that was the compromise. The exchanges would be licensed, but the oversight job would be given to a new body, not the FTC. The Securities Exchange Act of 1934 set up the Securities and Exchange Commission, and gave it the task of registering the exchanges and the securities traded thereon. The disclosures principle of the 1933 act was extended to secondary markets, and a number of fraudulent, but common, practices, such as wash-trading, were made federal offences. The legislation also contained a clause, later shed, which we could do with today; it flatly forbade brokers to trade on their own accounts, because the testimony before the committee investigating the stock-market collapse had made it so clear how easy, and common, it was to abuse this practice.

The first chairman of the SEC was Joseph P. Kennedy. The fox was on patrol in the hen-house. Kennedy's qualifications included a good deal of experience on Wall Street, much of it in shady dealing, and the fact that he had contributed heavily to FDR's campaign fund. As for his Wall Street background, Robert Sobel, in his book chronicling the New York exchange, *NYSE*, pointed out that "most of the manipulations and schemes that resulted in the Kennedy fortune were now illegal under laws he was supposed to enforce."

The smelliest of the Kennedy deals was one in which he and a couple of co-conspirators bought into a glass-making company and then boomed the stock by floating a rumour that the company was about to clean up, because Roosevelt was going to end

Prohibition, thus creating a massive market for whisky bottles. The company did not, in fact, make whisky bottles, then or later. After a nice ride, the Kennedy gang, apparently realizing that the stocks were bound to fall when it became apparent that the rumour was unfounded, went short on them, and made another fortune on the way down, while the innocents, as usual, got shorn.

"Judged on its legal merits," writes Richard Ney in *The Wall Street Gang*, "this achievement should have sent Kennedy to Sing Sing, instead of the SEC."

As commissioner, Kennedy's stint was marked mainly by speeches meant to encourage the flagging financial markets, in which he stressed the Better Business Bureau motif; the SEC would protect the honest exchanges, brokers, and promoters from the machinations of the few crooks. Capital formation would flourish because the game was no longer fixed. This argument, coming from one of their own, impressed the business community.

Arthur M. Schlesinger, Jr., in his three-volume history of the New Deal, remarked that, by early 1935,

> It was already beginning to be apparent that the Securities Act and the Securities Exchange Act, far from destroying the security business, were offering it a new lease on life. . . . In a short time, few men in Wall Street would wish the repeal of this legislation which, when proposed, they had so desperately resisted.

(Schlesinger's version makes no mention whatever of the glass-company swindle.)

The exchanges were duly required to register and provide information about their activities, a process that led to the closing of nine of them, including a one-man operation run out of a pool hall in Hammond, Indiana, not far from Chicago. But the SEC, perhaps inevitably considering the collapsed state of the markets, was more of a cheerleader than a cop. This was regulation as we have come to know it – part nursemaid, part disciplinarian, part lobbyist.

After fifteen months, Kennedy left to follow other interests (he became U.S. ambassador to Britain not long after, from which vantage point he urged his nation not to get involved with the nastiness about Hitler, because Britain was finished, anyway), and the SEC took on wider duties, including, in 1938, regulation of the Over the Counter market and, in 1940, regulation of investment trusts and the registration and disclosure of investment companies and advisers.

In the 1940s and 1950s, the SEC almost disappeared from public sight; its staff was slashed, its funds shrank, and it became not much more than a training ground for Wall Street lawyers. A new and juicy scandal on the American Stock Exchange in 1960, which involved some of the most blatant manipulation of stock prices yet, caused another activist American president, John F. Kennedy, Joe's son, to enact new legislation to beef up the commission's mandate. However, the fire went out of that reform movement when the markets drooped in 1962. And so it goes: the SEC acquires new powers whenever a particularly stinking mess breaks over the markets, then sags back when the crisis passes. Headlines break, reform is promised, a couple of victims are singled out to walk the plank, and more forms are required to be filled out and filed at every level. Pretty soon, a new and even-more-lucrative scam has evolved around the new regulations.

The process always reminds me of the apparent futility of developing new sprays to control insects; the little buggers simply mutate into a new breed that is immune to the spray, and when the formula is adjusted, they do it again. Maybe the stock regulators should stop reading the Securities Exchange Act and tune in to Rachel Carson's *Silent Spring*.

It must be acknowledged, however, that within the mandate originally set down for it, the SEC is an effective organization. It certainly gathers and disseminates information; I have often been able to dig up material on Canadian businesses in Washington that I cannot get anywhere in Canada. (As I write this, an agreement to share this information on Canadian data bases is being negotiated between governments.) But its role is still that of the Better Business Bureau, not the cop. When it does take after malefactors, it is always on behalf of the purity of the turf, never because it sees anything wrong with making the markets into casinos. When it does move against those who break the rules, nine out of ten of its cases are closed by consent decree, which imposes no penalty, but merely admonishes the party charged to go and sin no more.

What do you think it would do for the extortion racket if the practitioners, when caught, were allowed to plead no contest, pay a fine, and walk away? Or to loan-sharking, if the hired knee-cappers were punished by having their names printed in the newspaper?

The SEC does not deal with the ripest sector of the markets, commodity trading, which comes under the Commodities Future Trading Commission, whose incapacities were discussed in Chapter Seven.

The five commissioners of the SEC are usually drawn from the ranks of brokers, corporation lawyers, or investment bankers, and I can't imagine any president appointing a commissioner who expressed the view, for example, that it might be a good idea if some of the frenetic activity on the exchanges were slowed down. They are, always have been, in favour of frenetic activity, and one commissioner, Joseph Grundfest, looked forward to the day when "pensioners and others come to understand the benefits of futures and options markets." This would mean, he noted, that "support for futures and options trading will build." So it will, along with the proportion of old-age pensioners walking around in barrels.

Not only are the appointed commissioners inclined to leave the market to its own devices, so are the hired help. The SEC staff is drawn from the ranks of lawyers, accountants, and Wall Street specialists. "The interests of this group," write Susan M. Phillips and J. Richard Zecher in *The SEC and the Public Interest*, "are sometimes different from the interests of other groups in the securities markets, including those of widows and orphans."

One of the most contentious issues considered by the SEC in recent years was the proliferation of non-voting shares, which negate the entire notion of shareholder control, and whose spread helped the Great Crash along its way. These shares went out of favour in the 1930s, but returned with a vengeance in the 1970s and 1980s, and helped fuel the takeover frenzy that led to Son of the Great Crash in October 1987. (If you have to buy only the 5 per cent or so of a company's shares that have voting rights in order to control it, your investment has an instant leverage of 20:1; takeovers become a snap.) Because the essence of these shares is to allow the investor to gamble without any control or responsibility, the New York Stock Exchange initially would not accept non-voting share issues, and major exchanges, including the TSE, followed suit. However, the American Exchange allowed such issues, and pressure built for the NYSE to do so as well, for fear of losing business.

The SEC waded into the debate, firmly on the side of non-voting shares, which are now trading on all the major exchanges. There is nothing surprising in this. The SEC exists to serve the exchanges and the corporations who are issuing securities; it doesn't stand on guard for thee, it stands on guard for them. It just wants to make sure they play by recognized rules in order to retain, in one of the favourite phrases of the business, "investor confidence."

The corporations and exchanges who come under its purview see it as a terrible busybody, but the truth is that if it weren't for the show-trials staged by the SEC from time to time, the supply of suckers to feed the maw of the exchanges would have dried up long since.

Whatever its weaknesses, the SEC has always been a major instrument for forcing information out into the public arena, but, first under President Ronald Reagan and now under President George Bush, it has been cut back severely in its capacity to perform even this role. Deregulation is in, which means that, once more, the SEC staff and budget have been slashed at a time when thousands of new securities are coming onto the market every year.

On paper, the SEC has more power than ever, but in fact, outside its information-gathering role, it is increasingly irrelevant, an expensive institution whose major task appears to be to provide symbolic reassurance that all is well within the markets, so the customers will keep coming. I think we can catch the flavour of the thing with one fact: When Ivan Boesky was finally caught, the SEC allowed him to sell $447-million worth of shares from his own portfolio, so he could afford to pay his $100-million fine. More than that, his arbitrage partnership was allowed to unload $1.32 billion in stocks before the case was made public. The then SEC chairman, John S. R. Shad, explained that to have named Boesky as a criminal before allowing him to sell would have caused "a serious decline in the market." Of course, when the announcement came, prices did plummet, but not for our Ivan. Other speculators lost about one billion dollars, but Boesky sold his shares before the little crash he caused. Thus, he departed as he came, coining cash out of insider trading, but this time, with the blessing of the regulator.

What would it do for the embezzlement game if the chief embezzler were to be given a few days more alone with the books, so he could cover his legal expenses, before being marched off to the hoosegow?

While Michael Milken, the most notorious stock-market crook of our generation, was awaiting sentence, Benjamin J. Steen, a Los Angeles lawyer, made a point of more than passing interest in an article he wrote in *Barron's*, entitled, "Why Michael Milken Deserves a Stiff Sentence":

> Two of the last three chairmen of the SEC, John Shad and Roderick Hills, until just weeks ago served on the board of directors of Milken's firm, Drexel Burnham Lambert, and were directors when Drexel engaged in some of its most

ethically questionable acts of fraudulent conveyance (and were fabulously well-paid for their services even after Drexel entered bankruptcy, leaving the pension funds of teachers and janitors owed millions.)

It creates an atmosphere.

Canada, too, has a national securities body – a clawless, toothless wonder called the Canadian Securities Administrators, which has no legal existence, no corporate entity, and no public accountability. Instead, it is a banding together of administrators from the provincial securities bodies, which police the markets in conjunction with the stock exchanges and such other self-regulating bodies as the Investment Dealers Association and the Investment Funds Institute of Canada, the body that looks after – to the extent that anyone looks after – mutual funds. The Canadian Securities Administrators was Canada's response to the Great Crash; it was formed in 1936. Nothing so radical as the SEC was ever contemplated here.

In part, this was because the Americans were looking after all that, weren't they? After all, many of their stocks trade on our markets and many of ours on theirs; in either case, the requisite paperwork is done and submitted to Washington, which is why, if you really have to know what the president of a publicly traded Canadian company makes, you get on your bike and head for the SEC building on 5th Street, N.W., in Washington.

There was also a constitutional problem to get over – the British North America Act firmly assigned property rights to the provinces – and there was no Canadian disposition to shove past constitutional niceties on behalf of small investors. The cabinet of R. B. Bennett, the first to wrestle with the aftermath of the Great Crash, included ten businessmen, four lawyers, three doctors, a civil engineer, a farmer, a labour representative, and a journalist. Bennett looked and mostly behaved like the cartoon of Capital in a left-wing newspaper, and was the largest shareholder in Imperial Oil and the E. B. Eddy Match Company. He was not one to interfere with the markets, and if he had ever inclined that way, one of his largest campaign donors, Ward Pitfield, a Montreal broker and president of the Conservative Party there, would have had something to say.

Bennett was succeeded by Mackenzie King, whose cabinet consisted of a number of the nation's most powerful corporate presidents and directors. His minister of finance, Charles Dunning, later controlled more assets than any other Canadian corporate director.

Whatever the reasons, Canada has never contemplated a federal securities watchdog until recently, and has been content to blunder along with the securities commissions in the provinces in which there are stock exchanges – Quebec, Ontario, Alberta, and British Columbia.

Of these, by far the most active is the Ontario Securities Commission, which is aggressive in pursuing those who violate disclosure regulations, but which, like the SEC, apparently sees its main role as making sure that investors have information. When Gordon Capital, which makes up to 90 per cent of its annual profit through the activities of its own floor traders, was found "grossly derelict" in its supervision of its staff in 1989, the OSC hit it hard, in OSC terms. A Gordon trader had accumulated 40.3 per cent of the convertible preferred shares of ITL Industries Ltd., twice the level at which it was required to announce a takeover bid. The investigation showed that Gordon had no procedures in place to ensure that its traders were following the rules, or even knew them, and, because the brokerage firm had a history of violations, it was punished. Two years after the violations, Gordon was suspended from trading on its own account for ten days. The OSC's concern was, as James Douglas, the commission's counsel, noted during the hearings, to protect "the integrity of Ontario's capital markets."

The most active stock market in the nation is in Toronto, so most firms who trade publicly want to be listed on the TSE. The drawback is that this may bring them under the purview of the OSC. You can fleece the folks in Alberta and Saskatchewan more cheaply and easily by staying out of the OSC's reach, or by running for the border if you get caught. Then you will only have to deal with provincial securities legislation, which, in every province, covers three main facets of regulation: timely disclosure of pertinent information; registration of the people and firms who sell securities; and investigation and prosecution of those who violate the regulations.

There is nothing in there about looking after the interests of the bathers ahead of the sharks.

To date, the OSC, the nation's largest stock regulatory body, has only prosecuted one insider-trading case successfully, and none has been prosecuted successfully in British Columbia, home of our most malodorous market, the VSE. The innocent reader may conclude that this indicates that our markets are clean, just as the innocent reader may choose to believe that a cardboard pyramid, placed beneath the bed, will ensure marital bliss. Objective information suggests that the odds are against either. Among the happy coincidences in Canadian markets: Genstar shares jumped $11 in the two trading sessions before the Vancouver firm was taken over by Imasco. There were also price hikes just before takeovers were attempted or gained at Daon Development Corp., Union Enterprises Ltd., the Bank of British Columbia, Canadian Tire Corporation, and Standard Broadcasting. All were investigated, without result.

The fundamental task of protecting the widows and orphans is left to the exchanges. When your broker takes you to the cleaners, you can take him to the exchange, by laying a complaint. But here's a funny thing; if he has ceased to be a broker, the exchange can't do a damn thing.

The Toronto Stock Exchange launched disciplinary actions against fourteen brokers after the messy and expensive 1987 bankruptcy of Osler, Inc., a high-flying Toronto brokerage firm. The TSE wanted to take action against Len Gaudet, the firm's president, two other company executives, and eleven brokers, for 440 infractions of exchange rules. However, the Supreme Court of Canada held that, in the case of David Hugh Chalmers, a stock salesman who quit his job when he learned that the TSE was investigating him on the basis of a complaint from a former client, the exchange no longer had jurisdiction.

What do you think it would do for the bank-robbing industry if all you had to do, when you heard the police siren wail, was to turn in your mask, gun, and threatening notes and begin life anew as a trainer of performing elephants?

The Supreme Court decision finished, in all, twenty-six cases against brokers who had left their jobs, including those in the Osler bankruptcy, and made something of a mess of the entire notion of disciplining traders who overstep the bounds. Not that the disciplining ever amounted to much; in 1990, the TSE levied a total of $71,000 in fines against transgressors – slightly more than what some of them spend on caviar. The TSE has the right to soak the malefactor up to $1 million per offence.

But hey, you have the right to lay a complaint, and the TSE has a Central Complaint Bureau ready, willing, and eager to receive your information. What will come of it is something else. In a study jointly conducted by the Canadian Shareowners' Association and Consumer and Corporate Affairs Canada, and released in *The Canadian Shareowner* issue of May-June 1991, 67 per cent of "seasoned" investors surveyed believed that they had one or more justifiable complaints about the actions of a broker or the issuer of securities during the previous five years. But very few of them actually launched a formal complaint, either because they didn't know how to go about it, or didn't think it would do any good. On the second ground, they were right. Only 16 per cent of those who did launch such a complaint were satisfied with the way it was handled.

If only one in five of the people who believe they got stung kicks up a stink, and if only one in seven of those is happy with the result, I think we can guess that there is a lot of unsung stinging going on out there. *The Canadian Shareowner* concluded:

> One undesirable result of this type of experience with complaints is growth in the perception that securities legislation and regulations are ineffective in protecting individual investors. Such a view is likely to discourage the maintenance and growth of individual investor participation in stock markets.

What a pity. Still, when you can see that the rallying cry of the regulators is *caveat* bloody *emptor* even after all these years, the wonder is that *anybody* buys stocks.

To test the notion that insider trading, condemned in theory, is embraced in fact, an investigative team from ABC-TV sent Mark Lukasiewicz, a producer on the program *PrimeTime Live,* to Vancouver, a city with a reputation for mountains, sea views, and stock swindles. This produced a rather embarrassing program in which a broker named Françoise Otto appeared to be releasing insider information and offering to manipulate the market on behalf of an investor. The president of the VSE, Don Hudson, acknowledged that this is what appeared to be going on, but when the exchange brought charges against her as a result of the program, the broker was cleared on the grounds that ABC-TV wouldn't turn over its unedited tapes to the committee working for the exchange. In a twenty-three-page decision, the VSE's investigation committee concluded that, "In the view of the Committee, ABC set out with an intention to 'expose' the Exchange. The program was biased, one-sided and unfair to all persons involved."

Actually, ABC's sin may not have been so much that it set out to expose the VSE, as that it succeeded.

Never mind. Ottawa will fix. Recently, the federal government claimed a right to establish a regulatory agency at the national level. The 1991 Speech from the Throne contained a reference to the possibility, and a background paper obtained by Ken Rubin for the *Financial Post* lays out the case for a national agency. It is based on the globalization of securities trading, and the rapid and voluminous transfer of all sorts of financial products across provincial and international frontiers.

The paper argues that Canada must have a single body to speak to international institutions and to deal with cross-border cases involving, for example, the SEC in Washington. Moreover, the paper argues, with the major role now played by banks in the securities industry, more than half the trading done in Canada is conducted by institutions that are themselves regulated by Ottawa. It would seem logical that their securities activities should come under federal care as well. One case the paper cites is worth a look, for what it says about the fundamental problem that regulators face.

William Bennett, the former premier of British Columbia, and his brother Russell, were shareholders in Doman Industries, a forest-products company founded by long-time family friend Herb Doman. Louisiana Pacific Corp. of Portland, Oregon, had entered a takeover bid for Doman Industries, which didn't do the stocks any harm. Then, suddenly, on the morning of November 4, 1988, the takeover bid was withdrawn, and, very shortly thereafter, the share price collapsed. Between the time a telephone call from Portland to Doman's office in Duncan, B.C., informed him that the bid had been killed and the time the share price plummeted, there was a telephone conversation between Doman's office and the office of Russell Bennett, in Kelowna. That was followed by a telephone call to the Bennett brothers' brokers, and the sale of their shares. This saved them several hundred thousand dollars.

A pension fund from the Canadian Broadcasting Corporation, which had bought some of the shares and did not get a chance to unload them, lost heavily when the price dropped, and the fund filed a civil lawsuit, which was settled out of court, with no details ever being revealed. Then police in both British Columbia and Ontario – the shares also traded in Ontario – charged the Bennetts with insider trading. In May 1989, a provincial court in British Columbia acquitted them. The Bennetts testified that the timing of the phone calls was coincidental. They were not tipped off, and the fact that they saved a few hundred thousand, while others lost, was just the result of shrewd market sense.

I confess that when the B.C. court handed down its judgment, it occasioned me a certain amount of innocent glee – especially when rude and libellous T-shirts bearing slogans on the subject of telephone calls began to sprout in B.C. like the ferns in Stanley Park. But, on due consideration, I think the court did the right thing, though not for the technical reasons the court gave.

Accept that the Bennetts did nothing wrong and consider, instead, a parallel instance. You have a company, manufacturing, say, a new device to open garage doors. You are doing well with it, you take it public, and the shares sell sluggishly. You persuade your good friend Charlie to help you push them, and he buys a lot of stock, as well as persuading friends to buy stock, and that stock rises from $12 to $21. Suddenly, you get notice that you are going to be sued for patent infringement; what's more, the chances are pretty good that you will lose the patent-infringement suit. When news of this leaks out, the stock is going to take a nose-dive. You own 500,000 shares, representing $6 million at today's price – probably $250,000 at next week's price.

Two questions:

1. Do you unload your own stock while the unloading is good?
2. Do you call Charlie?

The answers, unless you are crazy, are Yes and Yes, but stock-market regulation works on the theory that you will say, "Well, goshdarnit, anyway" and hang onto your stock while it dwindles down the drain. You would be taking advantage, you see, of insider information, if you didn't tell everyone of this "material fact" affecting the value of your holdings – and the holdings of everybody else – at the earliest possible time. You and Charlie would be involved in an illegal conspiracy if you phoned him and the two of you, working through different brokers and, if possible, different exchanges, dumped your stock.

The insider-trading rules are voluminous and complex, but the nub of them is simple: you mustn't take advantage of information you have that other shareholders don't have to make a killing at the expense of less-well-informed investors. Sarita Purdy, in *The Investor's Handbook*, put this more formally. An insider is "Any senior company officer, director or major shareholder who has access to information about the company's affairs that is not yet available to the public." Insider trading is "The buying or selling of shares by insiders of a company based on confidential information." These legal definitions contain a couple of huge holes: What constitutes a "major shareholder"? And, how do you know whether a given trade was based on "confidential information"?

Since, as we have seen over and over again in these pages, the best way to win on the stock market is to act on access to information not available to the general public and to buy or sell shares just as fast as you can get your hands on confidential information, a certain difficulty arises. It is dealt with, in the main, by simply ignoring the fact that so much of the trading activity is driven by insider information and by pretending that it is not. Every now and then, someone has to be charged, to keep up appearances, but this is normally done through the internal regulatory process of the exchanges, which, as we know, are not vengeful gods. Instead, when the cases are shifted into criminal court, they are very likely to get thrown out. The standard of proof in a criminal charge is very high indeed, and given that almost everyone who can be called as a witness in these cases is involved in the business, it is hard to see how the problems of insider trading can be cured by hauling out the handcuffs. What is needed, as I will argue in Chapter Fifteen, is a fundamental shift in the markets themselves.

When the B.C. court acquitted the Bennett brothers, the Ontario criminal case was dropped, but the OSC tried to summon the brothers before a hearing panel. It turned out that the commission had no jurisdiction in the case. However, the trades in Doman stock were handled on a computer system that handles the TSE stocks. It is now being argued in Ottawa that a federal jurisdiction could be created to regulate a computer that operates in more than one province, and it is with this in mind that a claim for the need of a national security regulator has been launched.

I don't know whether it will succeed – Quebec, for one, is adamantly opposed to giving up jurisdiction over securities – but I do know that TSE officials think a federal regulator would be no bad thing. Frankly, they are fed up with trying to do the job themselves; it costs too much and it doesn't seem to have much effect. So the governors of the TSE have come out publicly for one national organization to take over the chores now shared among the exchanges and the Investment Dealers Association. The IDA would rather take on the national job itself, but, since it is the chief lobby group for the brokerage industry, it might be easier to sell the public a new agency, fashioned on the lines of the SEC.

The alternative is to forget the whole thing. Bud Jorgensen, the *Globe and Mail*'s beat man for the exchanges, asks, "Do we still need a regulatory system based on the retail trade, the market that serves small investors?" The answer, he suggests, is no.

This is part of the argument articulated by Saul S. Cohen, a partner in a New York law firm specializing in securities regulation. In the Spring 1991 issue of the Investment Dealers of Canada's *IDA Report* Cohen says, bluntly, "Securities regulation in the United States is dead, though the funeral notices may not appear for some time."

All the layers of regulation, he argues – state, federal, and self-regulatory bodies like the exchanges and dealers' associations – cost almost one billion dollars annually in the United States, or about ten thousand dollars for every stockbroker in the country.

(This is a little disingenuous, since much of the money goes to regulate the issuers of stock, not the salesmen, but let it pass.) And what does this lead to? Discontent, folks, discontent and dismay on every side: "Yet despite all these regulatory efforts, customers seem to be dissatisfied."

You and I, faced with such a scenario, might think of two possible solutions. One, maybe the crooks could stop stiffing the customers so much. Or, two, maybe a billion dollars a year is not enough, or is not spent in the right way, to produce clean markets. Maybe if we didn't let the bad guys sell their stocks at a profit to cover their fines, a different message would go out to the industry.

However, the solution, at least in Cohen's mind, is to relax the regulations. The small investor is disappearing, Cohen argues; he or she is putting his or her money into well-managed mutual funds, run by experts who understand the market and can look after themselves. Ergo, we don't need regulators any more; get rid of the bums.

He concludes by pointing out a poignant parallel: "To consider the fate of securities regulation, think of East Germany; a formidable authoritarian apparatus, existing for decades, that was obliterated in months when its subjects simply walked away."

I love the notion of the SEC as "a formidable authoritarian apparatus" – tell it to Ivan Boesky – and the rest of the regulatory gang forming some sort of Berlin Wall, but I have some problems with this argument. They begin with a complaint that echoes eerily what the wisest minds on Wall Street were saying in early 1929. Nor am I sure that you can really solve the problems raised by the fact that so many rules are broken so often by simply wiping out the rules.

Cohen's solution is to deregulate. This notion, which is shared by a number of professors of economics in this country, strikes me as a marvellously American one. In large U.S. cities where crime is rampant, the police simply refuse to enter certain districts or, as in Boston, post notices to tell the public that, if they want to go into this area after dark, they are on their own. Saves on bullets. This is deregulation with a vengeance.

Finally, I have less faith than Cohen in the brilliance of the people who manage large portfolios. If stocks are being manipulated, or trades based on insider trading are going down, it doesn't matter how smart you are, you're going to get burned, unless you are the one doing the dirty stuff.

I can see a scenario in which, for example, the entire investment fund of some large pension group came to be looted by the cupidity or stupidity of its trustees, or simply got blind-sided by the scams of others, as in the savings and loans debacle in the United States. There, the Reagan administration scrapped overnight the regulations confining the activities of savings and loans associations (known as S & Ls, or "thrifts," which became a wonderfully ironical nickname) mainly to residential mortgages and limiting the interest they could pay to depositors. At the same time, the budgets of watchdog agencies were hammered down, so there was no one to check whether the money that came in from depositors was going into solid assets or, as turned out to be the case far too often, into the pockets of the promoters. To complete the circle, the federal-deposit-insurance coverage on individual accounts was raised from $60,000 to $100,000. Now the S & Ls could go out and offer high interest rates to suck in deposits, and then do just about what they wished with the money. They went into an orgy of expansion; many of them were looted, while others were simply gambled away on real-estate ventures that would not have withstood real scrutiny for five minutes.

When the structure began to totter, and it appeared that regulatory measures might be reinstated with some vigour, the S & L lobbyists went to work on the politicians, and muzzled the regulators. Charles Keating, one of the thrift operators who was eventually charged, was asked by a congressional committee whether the $1.3 million he had advanced to five U.S. senators to intervene on his behalf may have induced them to vote his way. He replied, "I want to say in the most forceful way I can: I certainly hope so." When the inevitable collapse came, the taxpayer was roped in to pick up the pieces. The S & L disaster came about in large part because of a desire to save money on what was seen to be excessive regulation. In the end, it will cost American taxpayers somewhere in the neighbourhood of $600 billion. You can buy a lot of regulation for $600 billion.

What do we make of this? Michael Bliss, the Canadian historian, business author, and centrefold for the *Globe and Mail*'s *Report on Business* magazine, has the answer: "Intelligent regulatory decontrol could have prevented most of the mess." Yazzur. It appears likely, Bliss argues, that "Only about a fifth of the losses, perhaps fewer, can be blamed on thievery or obviously unacceptable business practice." In that case, it's clear, at least to Bliss, that the regulations should have been lifted entirely. It is certainly true that if we remove manslaughter from the Criminal Code, the reported murder rate will decline, but it doesn't strike me as an ideal solution. The argument is not spelled out in the article Bliss wrote for *Report on Business*; perhaps what he means is that the deposit insurance is what sucked in the investors, and if so, he has a point. What he and the rest of the deregulating gang seem to be saying, though, is that the regulations cost too much and don't work, so they should be scrapped. Issue everyone a gat and a sack, and let them go to it.

I think the argument that the way to make the bad guys into good guys is to remove the rules that define them as bad guys is somewhat shaky, but I think Cohen's prediction that securities regulation will be cut back is probably correct. And if the Americans do it, we will. The TSE wants out of the game, and if the federal government wants in, it will not get in without a great deal of bickering and compromise, and the likely result will be something even less effective than the regulation we have today. Well, then, maybe we can count on a vigilant press to keep things honest.

Oh, dear.

CHAPTER TWELVE

Honeyed Words

The Media and the Markets

The writers about the Street are Outside, and Wall Street tells them more or less what it wants. Wall Street is well paid, and the writers aren't, and when the writers learn enough they get offered jobs in Wall Street and off they go, perhaps satisfying their creative urge by working on a black comedy on the weekends. Then they are Inside and don't write about Wall Street any more.
– Adam Smith, *The Money Game,* 1968.

$

When I was a financial feature-writer for the late Toronto *Telegram,* the financial editor sent me over to Brantford, Ontario, to write a story about what a boost the takeover of a Canadian tractor factory by an American tractor company was giving that city. I was to show that the flow of U.S. dollars meant more jobs, better opportunities, and long-term growth, as well as an immediate increase in business for all kinds of merchants. There was none of the garbage you see in the journalism on television about investigating to see if the effects were indeed wonderful. The *Telegram*'s policy was that foreign investment was good, and my job was to illustrate this point, not question it. I drove over to Brantford and rounded up the usual suspects – mayor, Chamber of Commerce officials, local shop-keepers – who would confirm what my boss wanted confirmed. Then, foolishly, I went to talk to some of the people who actually worked in the factory.

That was when I learned about a small problem. It involved a number of pensioners, men and women who had worked as long as forty years in the plant before retiring on their well-earned pensions. Their pensions had disappeared in the takeover. The original company said it wasn't going to keep up payments, because it didn't own the factory any more; the American company said it wasn't responsible, because, dammit, these people never worked for it. So, the pension cheques just stopped coming.

I went to interview the new plant manager, and he confirmed that this was indeed the case. A few hundred people were out of luck, and wasn't it a darn shame? Somewhat excited, I dashed back to the hotel and telephoned my boss in Toronto to tell him that I had a "real story."

He didn't even ask me what it was. He made sure that I had all the material I needed for the upbeat feature about the glories of foreign finance (the Saturday financial pages had already been made up around hand-out pictures from the U.S. firm), and turned me over to the City Desk. I dictated the story to the City Desk about the crummy deal being handed to the pensioners, and then got myself transferred back to Financial, where I unrolled the story about the benefits of a foreign takeover. The first story ran as the main headline that afternoon, and led to an uproar in the provincial legislature; the law was later changed to make sure the pensions would be paid. The second story ran the next day in the financial pages. It wasn't until I was driving back home to Toronto that this performance struck me as a bit odd.

Now I realize, of course, that there was nothing odd about it. The business pages of a newspaper belong to business, even in good newspapers. So does the business segment of a television news broadcast, a fact stamped on our consciousness every day when the news reader leans into the microphone and says something like, "And now, here is 'The Arthur Vail Report,' brought to you by Canada's business airline, Air Canada," or (on my local station) "This is Business Brief, presented by Dominion Securities."

This doesn't even bother us, although we might react to, "And now, Bang Technologies, Designed To Kill, proudly presents today's war news," or even, "Here is today's round-up of natural disasters, sponsored by Sure Fire Insurance, We Pay Till It Hurts."

The most important business-news sources in the nation, the *Globe and Mail*'s *Report on Business* and the *Financial Post,* put the names of companies in bold-face type, so they will stand out, and carry an index of the names of companies mentioned in that day's reports. Some, but not all, company presidents get the bold-face treatment, too. The business pages do this even on the rare occasions when something critical is about to be divulged. I look forward to the day when I will read in my daily paper that "Seven of the rascals who run **So Long Finance** were hauled off to the hoosegow today, led by **'Fast Fingers' Gerlach**, the company president."

It is the thesis of the newspaper and television executives who make up these policies that a business community sufficiently cosseted will respond by buying ads – and so, by golly, it does. It is a corollary of this thesis that reporters who persist in knocking when they should be boosting ought to find some other line of work.

One of the more intriguing coincidences in this line came to light when, in October 1991, reporter Cecil Foster wrote a story for the *Financial Post* in which he quoted unnamed sources within Canadian Airlines International. These sources claimed that the company president, Kevin Jenkins, had been telling employees that unless Canadian Airlines could win major concessions from both its workers and the federal goverment, the company would be dead within a year. The airline was in a battle with its unions at the time. The story ran as the main headline on page one, and drew an immediate response from Canadian Airlines, which told the newspaper that it was going to pull all its ads, and that it would stop distributing the newspaper to airline passengers.

Within two days, the executive editor of the newspaper had been fired. Then the *Post* ran a make-up story, also on page one, in which Jenkins denied most of the bad news in the Foster article. Not long after that, Cecil Foster, the reporter, was taken off the transportation beat. Bud Jorgensen, who reported all this in the *Post's* rival, the ROB, was told that Stephen Petherbridge, the executive editor, was not fired "to appease Canadian Airlines," and that Cecil Foster was being reassigned "by mutual agreement."

It could even be true; hey, funny things happen all the time. But you have to admit that any *Post* employee in the future who finds himself or herself working on a story that the senior executives of a major advertiser are likely to find distressing is going to do a certain amount of soul-searching before sitting down to type out the bad news.

This sort of thing can make life a little complicated for journalists, especially if they find themselves writing for a special section. This is where the newspaper gets up a whole package of laudatory articles about a given subject, shoves them all together, and sells ads to the relevant industry. Sometimes the industry itself provides the copy, in which case you will probably see a little tag somewhere on the page that says "Advertising Supplement," although the material in all other respects looks exactly like the rest of the newspaper. The *Globe and Mail* runs so many of these babies that it has to carry periodical advertisements to let the ad agencies know when the next one is coming up, so they can get in on it. The one thing you can be sure of in all of these sections is that nothing embarrassing will ever be divulged. Once the section has been put to bed, all the journalists who worked on it go out and hoist a beer to the glories of objective journalism, or take in a speech by a tycoon, slamming the negative nabobs of the press.

In magazines, life can be even more wearing, as I discovered when I was the editor of *Today* magazine. The policy there was to have every manuscript submitted to the advertising department, and someone in advertising would mark, with one of those yellow highlighter pens, any words or phrases that were likely to offend an advertiser. Some of our stories looked as if they were suffering from terminal jaundice. The marked copy would then be sent to the publisher, who would send it to me, and I would throw it out. This may explain why *Today* magazine is no longer with us. One of the words that offended was "cancer." Cigarette advertisers, whose advertising alone kept the magazine's head (barely) above water, didn't like the word "cancer," even if not accompanied by the word "tobacco." Indeed, it was the policy of the ad folks, when they couldn't get the nasty word out by yellow-lining it, to phone up the ad agencies handling cigarettes and ask them if they wanted their ads pulled from the issue that had the C-word in it. They always did. I tried to meet this on one occasion by running a cover featuring the fifty-two articles found in every Canadian household that can cause cancer. I figured we would get over the whole hump at once. That nearly wore out all the *Today* yellow highlighter pens, and by the time all the ad agencies had been called, we had an issue almost innocent of advertising. And of revenue. It made us all wonder deeply whether we ever wanted to deal with the C-subject again. I had learned, as every journalist learns, sooner or later, that it is not love that makes the world go 'round, but advertising, and that what advertisers want from business journalism is more respect and less lip. By and large, they get it.

Nowhere is this more nakedly evident than in business coverage that touches on the delicate subject of stock sales, where the instincts of our many fine journalists to print the facts, and the instincts of our business community to embellish them, come into conflict daily. All too often, the embellishers win, and it is sometimes literally impossible to tell where the dividing line comes between shilling and telling.

I was intrigued to discover that the TSE sells the cover story in its magazine, the *Toronto Stock Exchange Review*. I did wonder for a while why every company that got a mention on the cover seemed to be such a terrific place to invest – "Strike Energy Inc. is a company poised for fast track growth" – but then I found the little notice, in tiny type on the masthead page: "The *Review* receives a fee from featured companies." There is another note to indicate that "no endorsement or promotion" is intended or implied by the exchange, but one is entitled to ask, Then what the hell is it doing on your cover?

This is called "providing a friendly environment for your product" in the talks ad salesmen give when flogging the newspaper, magazine, or television spot. It includes raising the utterly banal to the level of revealed wisdom, as when the *Financial Post*'s magazine quoted Donald Barkwell of Poco Petroleums Ltd. saying, "Don't do silly things. Use lots of common sense. Make good decisions." This profound stuff was put in headline type and boxed, so *Financial Post* readers wouldn't miss it. In the same issue, we learn, also in large type, that "Prenor's mission is to provide quality products and personal service." And you thought it was to turn a buck.

In the business sections, government – any government – is always wrong, always spends too much, always regulates too much, always interferes with the hard-headed boys and girls who just want to get on with the job. ("Scrappy and tenacious" Margaret Witter of **Royal Oak Resources Ltd.** is the subject of an open-mouthed *Globe* profile in which it is pointed out that, two weeks after taking over the company, she fired 100 out of 800 employees. "We had to stop the bleeding," she said.)

Business, in contrast to bloated, evil government, is lean and mean (except when Ross Johnson is calling for "about half an inch of 50s" or Michael Milken is laying on hookers for investors) and just as goldarn competitive as it can be – which means, by and large, that it buys up the competition and screws down the wages, to applause all around. This is called "meeting global competition." It used to be called "restraint of trade."

In short, journalists suck up to business, always have, always will, and when they cease to do so, they are often out of work. In consequence, the coverage of business news, including stock-market news, is not marked by the same rigour we expect of other journalism. At the *Telegram*, when I wrote a story the financial editor thought might offend one of his pals on Bay Street, he would simply spike it (literally; in those days, the editor had a spike on his desk, where the offending copy would be sacrificed on the altar of prudence). I would then rush a copy of the offending story upstairs to the managing editor, Arnold Agnew, who would, quite often, print it on the features pages. When the complaints came in to my boss, I could hear him explaining, "But it didn't appear in *our* section!" He also arranged for an ad salesman to be present when I was briefed on stock-market stories, and the ad salesman would tell me which brokerage houses I was to visit in my never-ending search for information and quotes – viz., those that advertised in the paper. I objected to this practice, so my boss very considerately changed it. The ad salesman would tell *him* where I was to go, and he would tell me.

Lord knows it is better than it used to be. When Jay Gould wanted a friendly voice in journalism, he simply bought the *New York World* and directed it himself to smite his foes and support his stocks. Through that newspaper's membership in Associated Press, he was even able to get the wire service to carry out his propaganda purposes, and no one thought the worse of him for it. We are not so crude today; today our financial barons don't have to buy the press to get friendly coverage – they buy it to make money, and the friendly coverage comes naturally.

In mid-1991, there was a tense political battle between the province of Ontario and Kimberly-Clark Corporation, a huge and aggressive international paper company, because Kimberly-Clark wanted to shut down one of its large plants in northern Ontario. This was going to mean the end of hundreds of jobs, so the province offered to step in and take on some of the assets. However, Kimberly-Clark asked for more money than the province wanted to pay, so the company threatened to pull out, anyway, and so it went. In the midst of this furor, the *Globe and Mail* ran one of its "Newsmaker" profiles of the chairman of the paper company, which began this way:

> Picture most executives in the North American paper industry as members of a well-trained dog team, running smoothly in the harness, starting and stopping and turning together when the terrain changes or the economic whip snaps. Then picture Darwin Smith, chairman and chief executive officer of **Kimberly-Clark Corp.**, as a lone wolf. He moves more or less with the pack, but at his own speed. He keeps an eye on what the trained dogs are doing, but also keeps his distance. He may swoop down on their food, but he will not lie with them. He chooses his own path.

Sheer poetry. There's another thousand words of this stuff, the nub of which is that Ontario Premier Bob Rae doesn't stand a chance against Darwin Smith, although we pause to note along the way that "Mr. Smith, it turns out, is also gracious and helpful, soft-spoken and personable, conscientious, hard-working and a little eccentric." We already knew he wasn't a son-of-a-bitch.

You can't, at least I hope you can't, purchase this kind of coverage; it has to be sincere.

So, one problem with journalists trying to cover the stock markets is that their lords and masters are made comfortable by chummy reporting, and uncomfortable by rude reporting. Then there is the fact that the reporters themselves are overawed by the movers and shakers, in exactly the same way that sports reporters so often become the adoring fans of the athletes they are paid to cover.

How else can we explain the gushing stories that surrounded people like Ivan Boesky and Michael Milken right up to the moment when the walls of their sand castles begin to shift and crumble? We have already seen how the gang of thugs who ran Wedtech Corporation received nothing but rave reviews right up until the cops closed in. When I was writing about Unity Bank, I read the financial files on Richard Higgins, the resident president – and crook – and found nothing but the highest praise for him, including one gushing story that wanted us to know that, despite all his success, the son-of-a-gun drove his own car, and didn't swank around with a chauffeur like some other bank presidents we could name.

Early in 1970, when Bernie Cornfeld was busy looting the till, the *Institutional Investor* invited him to address a conference it had arranged in New York. He did address it, too; he told the guys that the SEC commissioners were a bunch of bums. George W. Goodman, a.k.a. Adam Smith, the editor of the *Institutional Investor* and Bernie's host, also wrote for Bernie's IOS magazine, on the side. Incidentally, in October 1970, when the wheels were coming off IOS and the Fund of Funds had suspended redemptions on three-fifths of the assets in the fund – effectively wiping them out – the *Institutional Investor* ran a piece saying that IOS had "fared remarkably well." The *Washington Post,* on its way to the top of journalism's heap through its investigation of the Watergate scandal, invited Bernie as its unofficial guest of honour to its annual cocktail party the night before the *Institutional Investor*'s soirée. And so it went. *Business Week* described Bernie as "King of Europe's Cash," and *Time* said that he was "part Peter Pan, part Midas."

The potential investor who looks to the reporters to keep the markets honest ought to know that, as in most journalistic beats, the reporter eventually becomes too close to the subject; the assumptions shared by the business community become the assumptions of the journalist covering it. If you want to test this for yourself, read one or more of the agony columns in your favourite newspaper, the ones where the journalist answers the queries of (usually) outraged investors.

On September 21, 1991, Ellen Roseman, an experienced and conscientious journalist, used her "Your Money" column in the *Globe and Mail* to meet the concerns of a man named Wayne Wells, from St. John's, Newfoundland. Wells had invested $57,600 in mutual funds over the past four years; this had somehow shrunk down to $51,000 and, "He wonders if he would have been better off leaving the money in the bank."

Not a hard one to answer.

Yes.

If Wells had put his $57,600 into five-year Guaranteed Investment Certificates at 11 per cent, which he could easily have done in 1987, then on September 21, 1991, it would have been worth $97,060, which is better than $51,100.

But this is not the answer Ellen Roseman brings forth. "The first thing to remember," she writes, "is that, over long periods, stocks usually outperform other assets." She knows this to be true because ScotiaMcLeod Inc., the stockbroker, told her so.

> The total return on TSE 300 stocks for the 30 years from December, 1960, to December, 1990, averaged 10.22 per cent a year, according to ScotiaMcLeod Inc. Stocks outperformed residential mortgages (9.07 per cent), 90-day treasury bills (8.12 per cent) and long-term bonds (7.88 per cent.)

This must bring great comfort to Wells. If he holds on for another twenty-six years, by gum, the TSE 300 will do better than Treasury bills. This does not mean that his mutual fund will do better than Treasury bills; it might or, on the other hand, it might not. But he will have the pleasure of knowing that, on average, stocks are going to go up again. Wells, by the way, plans to retire in the year 2000, so there is a problem with catching up in time, but heck, nobody ever said investing was easy.

Thirty years ago, banks and trust companies were very different – and much worse – alternatives to the stock market than they are today. Thirty years from now, they will be different again. But Ellen Roseman wants him to hang in there. His losses, she says, "Are not as bad as he thinks." And why? Because he owns more units in the mutual fund now than he did before and, "These extra units give him a better chance to recoup his investment when the Canadian stock market eventually recovers." Or, alternatively, lose more when it dives again, although Roseman does not feel constrained to make this part of the argument clear.

The column finishes with one of those go-get-'em-guys flourishes. "'When markets are low, think opportunity, not despair,' says Peter Griffin of Gryphis Financial Consultants Inc. in Vancouver.

"'I can't think of a single good reason to invest in or hold equity funds at this time – and that's the single best reason to do so.'"

I hope you're making notes. What we are learning here is that common sense tells us that Wayne Wells has lost quite a lot of money by clinging to mutual funds, and that the outlook is worse now than it was before. Therefore, he should buy more. We call it contraryism. There are other words for it, but contraryism will do.

The truth is that most of the gushy reporting that masquerades as street smarts is based on sheer, dumb ignorance. (Ellen Roseman, of course, doesn't fall into this category, but many do.) All the guys on the street say Bernie Cornfeld is a smart cookie, so it is easier to go along than to kick against the trend. We don't know anyway. We can't read balance sheets worth spit, we don't understand the inner workings of corporations that operate under layers of secrecy, we haven't the foggiest notion what is really at stake in the average stock prospectus, so we call up somebody we trust and write down what he or she says, and then we come up with a wonderful metaphor – Peter Pan and Midas sound pretty good – to get it across to the reader.

When the company or the deal begins to go sour, someone will call us – in most cases – and there will be a series of off-the-record interviews. Then, and only then, when the people who actually do know what is going on begin to spill the beans, will contrary stories begin to leak out.

That is why you can expect to read mainly reassuring things about the company whose stock you are about to buy, or have just bought, and then to read an item informing you that the president of the firm is helping the police with their inquiries, and the treasurer is believed to be travelling abroad, for his health. Then expect to read a piece telling you that the insiders knew there was something rotten going on all along.

The reporter, you must understand, cannot admit his or her awful ignorance. He cannot admit it to you, to the boss, or even to himself. If you don't believe me, read *Trading Secrets: Seduction and Scandal at the Wall Street Journal,* by R. Foster Winans.

Winans is the reporter who made a deal with stockbroker Peter Brant to give advance knowledge to Brant about items that would appear in what was then the world's most influential stock-market column, "Heard on the Street," in the *Wall Street Journal.* The column's coverage moved stock prices; Brant acted on this and paid Winans to tell him what was going to appear in the column. Early access to the column, we are told, was like knowing "which horse would win the fifth race at Pimlico tomorrow."

The book is a fascinating account, even if somewhat self-serving. It turns out that one of the reasons Winans was so easily bent was that the *Journal* paid him so poorly. (I am only a crook up to the $40,000-per-annum level.) But the part that riveted my attention was not the ease with which Winans could be bought – I know a score of journalists who take free airline tickets and write friendly travel stories – but his appalling ignorance.

At the time he became co-writer of the most important financial column on the surface of the globe, he had six years' experience in journalism, much of it on a small newspaper in Trenton, New Jersey, covering "mostly local news, a few statewide developments, and an occasional national story." He had been at the *Journal* less than a year, although he had spent a couple of years feeding material onto the wire for the Dow Jones News Service, which required, he says, "mainly secretarial skills." When he took over on the "Heard on the Street" column, he made four serious errors of fact within a few months, which nearly got him fired. But didn't. He also dabbled in the stock market, disastrously, although it was strictly against *Journal* policy to do so. To cover himself, he opened a brokerage account in the name of his lover and roommate. Not that it did him much good; the only substantial profit he made on a stock speculation was on one he bought, then boosted in the column.

He was simply overwhelmed by the complexity of the markets, and fed stuff into the column mostly on the basis of tips from insiders he trusted. This is my interpretation; he appears utterly unaware of how ignorant he was, although he does get across one key paragraph about financial markets:

> Wall Street, after all, is about secrets – especially trading secrets. Like a high-stakes game of poker, the good players feint and bluff and never show their cards, even when they lose. When money talks, Mark Twain wrote, the truth is silent. Knowledge can be converted on Wall Street into money. The value of knowledge is inversely diminished by the number of people who have access to it. In other words, the only reason to invest in the market is because you think you know something others don't.

There is another way to put this, seen from a working journalist's perspective: the financial writer is entirely dependent on sources who know what he can never know. He can be used to plant the most outrageous tripe about a stock, and the great thing is that, if the market swallows it, the tripe becomes the truth and the stock a winner. And, just as Adam Smith notes in the quote at the top of this chapter, by the time a journalist finally gets to be informed enough to begin to get a glimmer of what is actually going on, without being led by the hand, he or she is ripe to be hired away at twice or three times the current salary, to work on the other side of the street.

A daily journalist has about six hours in which to prepare a story that will tell you whether it is a good idea to plunk your money down on the fortunes of any given company; that is why metaphors so often take the place of information. The same difficulties attend the reporting of any complicated subject, but there is this difference: it is the reporting of the events on stock exchanges that makes them central to the economy. Rumour becomes reality and has an effect in the real world out of all proportion to the effect of stock movements. Euphoria overtakes the land when the market rises, even when the number of people living below the poverty line is rising sharply at the same time, because the comfortable are comforted. On the other hand, gloom settles across the entire globe when the market totters, even though what happens is mostly the exchange of a series of digits in the innards of a computer. This despair – more often than the euphoria – becomes translated into political and economic decisions that can devastate the real world. Because shoals of suckers have been inveigled into paying too much for dubious stock, when someone actually discovers that the "underlying values" are not there, the whole edifice comes tumbling down. It is the speculative, not the investment, aspect of the stock exchange that does so much harm, and it is precisely this aspect that is fuelled by the pliant press – which is, we ought never to forget, very much a part of the process it describes with such awestruck zeal. The media carry stories about their own stocks, too, with never a knock.

If chumminess and ignorance were not enough to hamper business journalism, there is always terror, especially in Canada.

As a teacher of journalism, I always told my students, "Try not to libel a lawyer or a rich man. It doesn't cost a lawyer much to sue you, and a rich man will hammer you into the ground." That always brought a giggle, as if I had made a joke. No joke. Even if you win, you lose, when your work attracts a libel writ.

In 1969, I wrote a piece for *Maclean's* magazine about John Shaheen and Shaheen Natural Resources, which was then building a refinery at Come-by-Chance, Newfoundland. I wrote that it was a lousy deal for Newfoundland and Canada, because it was so structured that, if it worked, Shaheen would wind up with an asset worth $165 million, paid for by the taxpayers of Canada, and if it didn't, he would simply turn on his heel and walk away without a backward glance. Shaheen sued both *Maclean's* and me for $40 million, but, as soon as the real legal scrapping started, he backed right off. Victory. Nope. *Maclean's* didn't touch the subject for another seven years, until, surprise, surprise, the project went belly-up, and Shaheen walked away without a backward glance. We weren't beaten, just intimidated.

"Libel chill" is very real; it is the aspect that persuades the individual journalist and his editors – or, in broadcasting, his producers – that what the world needs most right now is not another story that will keep us all tied up in knots for six years and bring down the wrath of the bosses upstairs, but a cheery little story, cheap to do, on that dashing little mining stock the boss heard about at a cocktail party over the weekend. I have had one libel suit or another – sometimes two or three – hanging over my head since 1965, and frankly, I am fed up with them, which is why I am going to give up financial writing entirely, once I get another book out of my system, and cover travel instead.

Sunsets seldom sue.

Financial journalism, I repeat, is better, tougher, more informed than it was when I was chasing rainbows for the Toronto *Telegram,* but it is still not much of a shield for investors or the public against the vagaries and vicissitudes of the stock markets.

Well, then, what is? I am so glad you asked.

PART III

The Way Ahead

I believe in stock exchanges. I do not believe you should kill them. I do believe you should regulate them.

– Thomas G. Corcoran, lawyer and aide to FDR, 1933.

CHAPTER THIRTEEN

Five Market Myths.
And Some Realities

To spekilate in Wall Street when you are no longer an insider is like buying cows by candlelight.
– Daniel Drew, 1877.

$

We now know enough of the way in which the stock markets operate to be able to compare propaganda with reality, and to make up our own minds. We have been guided for decades by a series of assumptions, myths, revealed truths – call them what you will – about the efficiency of the market as a way of allocating capital and assessing the true value of various companies by passing judgement on their shares. There may be a problem, now and again, with some of the rogues who get loose in the place and make it harder for honest traders to turn an honest buck, but in the end, whatever its drawbacks, the market does what it must in the best way possible. That is the story we have been told.

We have also been assured that the "little guy" can make money in the markets; can, indeed, do better than the experts, just by applying his own native wit to his own portfolio. It all sounds very plausible, and it all has the effect of persuading us to swim with the sharks.

Most of what we are told is false, most of what we believe is nonsense, and before we can go on to consider what sort of arrangements might work better, we need to get rid of some of these prevailing myths.

Myth No. 1: The Market Is Efficient. This is a particular use of the word "efficiency"; it refers to the way the market allocates capital and judges the worth of companies. "Don't argue with the market," is the way it's usually put. Why not? The market is an ass. The market will tell you on Monday that a share in Old Fossil Mining is worth $70 and a week from Thursday that it's worth about fifty cents. The market rushes to extremes and responds to rumours. Time was when we could count on the stocks known as "blue chips" – named for the highest-value poker chips, which should be a tip-off – to withstand these flights of fancy, but no longer. Now everything tends to surge back and forth. A gang of rogues is caught paying off the losses of some fellow rogues in Japan, and the shares of hundreds of companies in Canada and the United States keel over in a faint. We come up to what Wall Street, that superstitious thing, calls a "triple witching hour," the last trading hour on the third Friday of March, June, September, and December, when options and futures contracts on stock indexes come due concurrently, and the markets go bananas, with massive trades. There is no sense in it. They used to burn witches; now they give them MBAs and corner offices and call them financial analysts.

The argument about market efficiency is a circular one. Because the market is so hysterical, we know that Tokyo's bad news will be reflected in New York, so we dump all our stocks. Then we can say, "See, that's the market's efficiency for you; look at how quickly it went bananas."

Anticipated hysteria is not the same thing as efficiency. In theory, the back-and-forth selling of stocks will establish their true value. So many people bidding against each other, up and down, will, by their actions, shade the price ever and ever closer to the exact worth of the stocks. Unless, perchance, all the back-and-forth is caused simply by gamblers jumping into and out of the shares with no idea on earth what they ought to be worth a week from now, only a guess as to what can be squeezed from them today. In this sense, we have done two fundamental things to destroy the efficiency of the markets. One is to make gambling, rather than investment, the focus of the exchanges and the Over the Counter action; the other is to reward the crooks. Insider trading may be illegal, but, by gum, it pays. Indeed, it may be the only kind of trading that really pays. As C. David Chase puts it: "On Wall Street you don't have a chance of becoming Street wise. The same thing keeps happening again and again because Wall Street is an insider's game."

When the overwhelming percentage of activity in this bizarre game consists of shovelling stocks and bonds and other financial instruments into and out of portfolios, the result is not efficiency, but waste. When we are persuaded to buy TIPs and S&P 500s and all the other "derivative products," we are not helping to raise capital for deserving entrepreneurs, we are giving the arm on the slot-machine another jerk, and diverting capital and energy from where it is needed to where it is not needed. In his autobiography, *The Max Ward Story,* Max Ward, a real entrepreneur, makes an interesting point:

> I once talked to Jim McDonagh, a mining man who was on the board of de Havilland, who told me that if he managed to get twenty-five cents out of every dollar raised in stock sales actually invested in the property, he considered that he had done well. I was shocked. I thought that when you bought mining stocks, they took your money and put it to work in the ground; but most of it went on promotion, legal fees, advertising, overhead and heaven knows what all.

It would be cheaper, and thus more efficient, to borrow money at 50 per cent than to spend a dollar to get a quarter, but hey, it isn't our money, it comes from the rubes on the street, so why worry?

"Liquidity" is the market's god; liquidity means that you can sell your shares in a hurry, and you certainly can. You can shift them from Halifax to Hong Kong in a nano-second on a computer system that is a marvel to behold. So what? That may benefit speculation, but it does nothing for real investment. Louis Lowenstein puts it this way: the ability to sell on short notice means something to a trader who wants to dump his stock again "within a few minutes or days," but has no value whatever in an "investment decision." Yet, he goes on, the shares in a company that is traded rapidly may double in price – and thus, the value of the company may double – simply because of the rapidity of the trades. Action in the market drives the price up.

This isn't efficiency, it's craziness, and it doesn't even fulfil the technical definition of market efficiency, which is that stocks are fairly priced at all times in accordance with their long-term expectations. They aren't. Those who continue, in the teeth of all the evidence, to maintain that the market shows its rigorous efficiency by setting prices accurately have to explain whether, in that case, the figures were too high by one trillion dollars before the "corrections" of October 19, 1987, or too low by one trillion dollars twenty-four hours later, and how, in either case, they could be called accurate. Either the market had overvalued the shares of these corporations by a colossal sum, or it was now undervaluing them by the same colossal sum, or – my version – the value placed on the shares, and therefore the companies, on the stock markets has almost no relationship to the long-term value of the assets.

In short, we are not dealing here with an efficient pricing mechanism. As Louis Lowenstein reminds us, the more shares are bought and sold,

> the more certain it becomes that people will think of themselves as owning not a part of a business but as

owning some intangible financial instruments, and the more likely that the price of the shares will bear little relationship to the 'Main Street' values.

If the Bonsecours market couldn't do a better job of establishing prices than the stock markets, it would be out of business.

We have spent the last three decades making it easier and easier to gamble, not to invest, and we are spending billions of dollars to tie the entire world into one gigantic, electronic poker game. No such effort has gone into cleaning up the markets or making them efficient in the real sense, such as delivering capital where it is needed and allocating it according to its proper productive use.

With all the lectures we get from our tycoons about productivity, we hear nothing about the waste of capital implied in slopping shares back and forth a dozen times a day for no gain, or about the waste involved in pouring millions of dollars into dud mines and cockamamie stock ventures which will never turn on a light, drive a drill, or indeed do anything but lift a number of wallets. Putting $64 billion in trades through the TSE in a year while raising $1.1 billion in new-equity financing is the opposite of efficient. In 1990, the value of stocks, warrants, and rights traded on North American exchanges came to $1.8 trillion – and that does not include another, almost equal, sum in Over-the-Counter trades and perhaps as much again on futures, options, and index trades that add nothing, save velocity, to the market. If one dime in $100 of this actually resulted in new investment in equity, it would be astonishing.

We have the whole affair backwards; we spend the overwhelming proportion of our time, money, and energy on liquidity and 1 per cent or less of it in doing what the markets are supposed to do.

Myth No. 2: The Market Is Well-Regulated. "Providing a market in which all participants are treated fairly is an important aspect of the Exchange's commitment to investor protection," according to the TSE's official literature. And *Barron's* finance-and-investment handbook lists twenty-three pages of regulatory agencies and market overseers. But the fact remains that, virtually every time a public company is taken over, in Canada or the United States, advance trading betrays the fact that insiders are cashing in. The two chapters of this book dealing with brokers and with regulators are chock-a-block with arguments that there has never been a time when "all participants are treated fairly" on the stock markets – and there never will be such a time.

This is not merely a matter of the mechanics of the markets, but of its attitude. The professionals admire winners, and have no namby-pamby reservations about how the deed is done. When Michael Milken drew a ten-year prison sentence, Harvard Law Professor Alan Dershowitz protested that it was ". . . too harsh. This is a man who built a legitimate business by almost entirely lawful means. The percentage of admitted criminal conduct was minuscule."

Ladies and gentlemen of the jury, except for the fourteen periods of less than ten minutes each when my client was standing in front of a bank teller with a drawn revolver, he has behaved as a model citizen. W. S. Gilbert put the same argument forward in discussing the unhappy lot of a policeman. He noted that when the enterprising burglar's not a-burgling, when the cutthroat isn't occupied in crime, he loves to hear the little brook a-gurgling, and listen to the merry village chime – touching on which, Michael Milken, after he was caught, became active in community work.

Another who was offended by Milken's sentence was Brian Greenspun, publisher of the *Las Vegas Sun,* who wrote: "It's a darn shame that a man with his talent and ability will be spending ten years in prison, when people with less talent and ability are on the loose making economic policy." Fear not, Milken will be out, in all likelihood, without serving more than 30 per cent of his sentence. He is currently doing time in a federal institution in Pleasanton, California, and is eligible for parole in March 1993. (He went in on March 3, 1991.) When he gets out, he can lend his talents to economists, and we can have a new policy of borrowing on worthless assets and paying 20 per cent for the privilege, like his clients at

Drexel Burnham. That should fix the economy, especially if we all drive around in limos to save cab fare.

According to James B. Stewart, in *Den of Thieves,* "Milken has told some former colleagues that pleading guilty was a mistake and he no longer believes that he did anything wrong." Milken isn't crazy, he is just reflecting the values that he picked up along the way.

The heros of the market are people who make indecent amounts of money shuffling paper back and forth faster than the eye can follow. They are the folks who used to operate on street corners, with one pea and three shells. Now they use a bank of computers, and are called arbitrageurs. Those are the honest ones; there are other names for the dishonest ones. They will never be regulated, in any meaningful sense, as long as we keep making it more profitable to cheat than to play by the rules, and their victims will always be society as a whole.

Myth No. 3: The Shareholder Is King. Tell it to Ross Johnson of RJR Nabisco, who tried to make $100 million by selling his shareholders' assets to himself at bargain-basement prices and, when he was caught, had to settle for a pay-off of a measly $52 million. Tell it to Bernie Cornfeld, who saw shareholders as simply so many pockets to be emptied. Tell it to Sir Derrick Holden-Brown, who wouldn't even let his shareholders know exactly what happened to the $270 million of their money that went walkabout from the coffers of Allied Lyons in foreign-exchange dealings. Tell it to the shareholders of Canadian Tire, who suddenly discovered that the non-voting shares they owned were worth about 10 per cent of the value of the voting shares held by a small group of friends and relatives of the Billes family because, when a takeover bid came for the company, only the voting shares were needed to assert control.

Companies are run by managements, who nominate their own boards which make decisions for the rubber-stamping of the shareholders – a group that comes in for ritual stroking once a year, around the time of the annual meeting, and is ignored for the rest. In the United States, where realism rules, some state laws governing proxy voting (authorizing someone else, usually management, to vote your shares) do not even require the corporation to leave any space on the proxy ballot for a No vote. Only Yesses need apply. It was, for years, good enough for the Soviet Union, why not for the international corporation? When companies were mostly small and tightly held, the shareholder did, indeed, have a key role to play, but in a widely held, dispersed corporation, only a group that has put enough shares together to make trouble will have any effect whatever on company decisions.

Now and then, we see how company managements really feel about shareholders. In 1987, the International Paper Company proposed a poison-pill stock arrangement to fend off any would-be takeovers of the company. The College Retirement Equities Fund (CREF), one of the largest U.S. pension funds and a substantial holder of International Paper stocks, objected, on the grounds that, "So many companies have them [poison pills] that we can't register our disapproval by selling our stock and investing elsewhere." It's a key point: the only way the shareholder can attempt to control a company is by the threat to sell shares, and International Paper was cutting off that route; you couldn't very well sell your shares to an outsider if doing so would trigger the poison pill and make the shares worthless.

The CREF, which had never opposed a management resolution in thirty-five years of holding International Paper stocks, simply wanted the poison-pill resolution to be discussed and voted on at some point in the future. The company's chief executive officer, John A. George, told them to drop dead. He didn't want any shareholder vote "on a matter which the board has decided." He wrote to the heads of three hundred other companies, to ask them to instruct the managers of their own pension funds to back him. A proxy-soliciting firm that was interested in gathering proxies for the CREF suddenly lost interest, and the matter died. The company got its way.

The blunt fact is that most managements welcome the money

the shares bring to the Treasury, but resent bitterly the notion that shareholders should interfere in any way with the company's operation. Not that most shareholders care. They want a quick turnaround and a quick profit, not the bother of having to decide what the company ought to be doing, for which they are totally untrained and unequipped anyway.

The shareholder is not the king, but the bootblack, well content with thrown coins.

Myth No. 4: Anyone Can Make a Million. This is actually the title of Dr. Morton Shulman's highly successful book, which might have done less well with a sub-title that read: Provided you are as smart as me, as nervy as me, and have my financial resources behind you. If you want to know what chances you really have to make a killing in the market, look at what happens to the highly trained professionals who play there.

The *Financial Post* created a promotional gimmick called The Hunter Fund, run by a street-wise professional who would explain, once a month, in the pages of the paper, what moves he had made with a hypothetical investment pool of $100,000 and why. He was aiming at an impressive return with the fund, and was willing to take a few chances. Within a couple of years, the fund quietly disappeared from the newspaper; it had lost about 20 per cent of its original worth. However, a second and more conservative *Financial Post* venture, the Talisman Fund, is still going. Limping, but moving. Between September 28, 1987, and June 28, 1991, Talisman's value, with the dividends paid on the shares ploughed back in, had gone from $100,000 to $127,800, a yield of 8.32 per cent annually. The same money ploughed into Guaranteed Investment Certificates in a trust company would have gone to $142,209, a yield of 9.82 per cent.

Well, anyway, it did much better than the TSE 300, which, over the same period, *lost* 11.7 per cent, translating the hypothetical $100,000 into $88,300.

You cannot become a millionaire investing in GICs, but you won't drop 11.7 per cent of your nest-egg, either. The average annual compound rate of return for the TSE 300 to February 28, 1991, was *minus* 2.38 per cent, while the blue-chip Toronto 35 Index went up by 0.05 per cent. In both cases, these figures include all the dividends paid on stocks. Hard to get rich that way.

The "You Can Do It" books operate on the thesis that you, the potential millionaire, are smarter than everybody else, better informed than everybody else, and luckier than everybody else. You may be; in which case, why do you need a book? I can give you all the dope you need in four words: buy low, sell high. Oh, yes, and don't make any mistakes.

If really clever market managers, working with the best information available, can make only about 2 per cent per annum over the increase in the cost of living by working the markets, and if people throwing darts can outperform the experts at picking stocks, you know that the average investor is likely to take a bath. Indeed, the entire system is geared to bathing him. The money is made by insiders, it is made by large institutional investors, and it is made, occasionally, by people with more luck than brains. But the essence of the thing is that you are entering a poker game in which everybody else has more money than you and a couple of them are working with marked decks. *Bon chance.*

Anyone can make a million. Anyone can lose his shirt, socks, and underwear, too. The trick is to pull off the former while avoiding the latter, and not everyone can do that.

Myth No. 5: Stocks Are Best, in the Long Run. This is the most persistent and pernicious of the myths. Stocks may have come off in price recently, the argument goes, but just you wait. This is not advice to hang onto any particular stock, which does make some sense for the investor, provided he or she had picked a solid company; rather, it is advice to have faith in the market to rise on the dead ashes of its former self to higher things. Or, as *Barron's* handbook puts it: "For total return over the long term, no publicly traded investment alternative offers more potential under normal conditions than common stock."

Two points need to be made concerning this argument. The first is that it is an argument about average increases in worth – and averages can be tricky. For instance, Conrad Black and I, on average, did well last year; our average take-home pay was in seven figures. When stock markets are rising quickly, most investors make money. When they are falling, most investors lose money, but your competition for the gains is better placed, better financed, and better informed than you are, so the market's average gain may leave you in the position of the pyjama-clad gent who discovers too late what an average daily mean temperature above freezing means at midnight in October.

The second point is that the claim is simply not true. It is made in print so often that it appears that it must be true, but it is something we can test for ourselves. I am going to give you this book's one and only table. I lifted a good deal of it from tables produced in the ROB's *Report on Mutual Funds* of July 18, 1991. It shows how various investments have done over various periods of time in their rate of return. The first column shows the investment vehicle, the second the rate of return over one year, the third over five years, and the fourth over ten years. I have ranked them from the highest rate of return, over ten years, to the lowest.

Rate of Return (%)

Investment	1 year	5 years	10 years
GIC – trust company, 5-year	11.75	9.82	12.6
Canada Savings Bond	11.24	9.59	12.2
Bank 5-year term deposit	11.0	7.83	11.52
90-day Treasury bills	12.31	10.7	11.51
S&P 500 Index	3.67	8.15	10.96
Dividend mutual funds	5.84	5.96	10.68
Balanced mutual funds	7.63	6.0	10.32
Bank savings account	7.58	6.75	8.02
Real-estate equity funds	4.58	9.42	7.10
TSE 300	1.87	5.92	7.84
Canadian equity funds	1.99	3.98	7.55

What the table suggests is that, over the past ten years, the best rate of return by a considerable margin was earned by five-year Guaranteed Investment Certificates, deposited with a trust company. Without risk. Without games. Without having to worry about whether the company president ran off with the treasury. The worst long-term investments were the average T S E stock and the average mutual fund based on Canadian equities. You did better to stick your money in a bank account than to fiddle with stocks, and you took no risks whatever. The *Globe* carried quite a different-looking version; where I have used average mutual-fund performances, the *Globe* used "Best-performing equity fund," etc. (that is, I took all the fund results, not just the top ones), which gives a much brighter picture, and does lead to the conclusion, or pious hope, that stock-market investments can do better than interest-bearing securities. The best-performing Canadian equity fund had a rate of return of 13.62 per cent, and the best-performing balanced fund, 13.91 per cent. All you have to do now is guess which will be the best-performing over the next ten years. The worst-performing Canadian equity fund and the worst-performing balanced fund – surely as useful as a guide, except to the *Globe's* ad department – lost money in both these cases. The comparison an investor needs is not to what one outstanding firm was able to accomplish for its small group of investors, but to what he or she is likely to encounter, with his or her own investments. Under that heading, stock-market returns come second-last and last. (The *Financial Post* magazine doesn't take any chances on the reader working out what the bum funds did; it carries only the best in its regular round-ups. This is like the sports pages giving us only the names of the teams that won.)

The way to make the stock markets look good is to do what Bernie Cornfeld and his gang did, and that is to take the numbers back until you find a really bad period, and march off the gains from then. The usual trick is to make the stock market look better by going back to 1929, when many of the other financial instruments now available weren't even on the scene.

In sum, stock-market investments wouldn't be the best bet for the average investor, even if you could make the average return on them. And, with the advantages your competitors have over you in money and time and expertise, you are unlikely to do as well as the average. If you want to give it a whirl anyway, be my guest; you may indeed be one of the clever and successful ones, but you are far more likely to wind up as shark bait.

The fact that so many people are being taken to the cleaners is of more than academic interest, as we discover when we examine the markets as they really exist. Currently, more than six million Canadians own stocks, according to an extensive survey conducted by the Toronto Stock Exchange in late 1989. They represent 23 per cent of the population, up from 13 per cent in 1983. It is unclear why this large jump took place; my guess is the influx comes mainly from the investments of the pension funds, who are now huge market-players, and from the proliferation of mutual funds. In addition, self-directed Registered Retirement Savings Plans, in which stocks can be accumulated free of the depredations of Revenue Canada, account for some more of the increase. I would not be surprised to learn that quite a few people who jumped in with their RRSPs will jump out again, in their skivvies, as the market melts their assets. The 1989 survey done for the TSE indicated that three out of every four of the indirect investors – that is, those who don't own shares in IBM, or whatever, but instead have units in a mutual fund – own these as part of a self-directed RRSP. (A great many of these, I suspect, have bought mutual funds to sock away in their RRSPs under the delusion that, because they bought the units from a trust company, they must be covered by the Canadian Deposit Insurance Corporation, up to a level of $60,000, if the trust company goes belly up. Not so; mutual funds are naked of CDIC protection. When this becomes more widely known, we may see a retreat from this practice.)

We spent decades being told what a timid and slothful people we Canadians were, because we lagged behind Americans in our addiction to the markets. However, in the United States, according to the most recent annual report of the New York Stock Exchange, "47 million Americans own stocks, directly or indirectly." That would put the American stock-holding population at just about 20 per cent, a little lower than our own, or, given the margin of error in these surveys, possibly the same as our own. In any event, we need no longer hold our heads down in shame; we are just as big suckers as the Americans when the roulette wheel begins its mesmerizing whirl.

The proportion of people who actually plunk down their dollars on stocks is less important than the fact that almost every citizen of every nation is affected by the stock markets. That is because, I repeat, those markets have such a disproportionate influence on the general economy. It is no longer the case that, when Wall Street totters, the world's financial system begins to unravel. However, it is still the case that reports of a disaster on the markets cause the same sort of panic and crisis, or very nearly so, that occurred when the exchanges really were the driving engines of capitalism. We can bring on a depression, or turn a recession into a depression, through the psychological and propaganda effects of a stock-market crisis.

Our entire economy is held in thrall to the gambling fever that has overtaken the markets, and which becomes more pronounced the more new instruments are invented to gamble with, and more and smarter software programs are fed into computers to drive the action. After the stock crash of 1987, the authorities installed what they called "circuit breakers" to control the craziness. Computers had been programmed to take advantage of differences between exchanges, and differences between the price of a basket of stocks on the exchange and the exchange's own stock index, by buying in one place and selling in the other, simultaneously. You can't make much on each transaction through this index arbitrage, but if you execute enough trades with large enough amounts, you can make a few million along the way. The trouble is that all these computers chasing each other cause the markets to swing around like an old rubber boot. The folks in charge of the exchanges had been denying since October 1987, when the market shed a trillion dollars in the most historical hiccup in history, that institutional program trading was at fault. Just the same, you know, just to be on the safe side, they installed these circuit breakers: rules that halted trading in stock indices when the going got too wild. You and I, being market illiterates, might say, Why not just stop index arbitrage, if it screws up the system and doesn't contribute a thing to the market's main function? That would show how ignorant we are. They have invented these incredible computers with fancy and expensive software, and they have to be used. The fact that they wreak havoc is a side issue. We just put out a press release saying the havoc was wreaked by something else, and no harm done.

Only about half the shares bought and sold in Canada move through the exchanges in five Canadian cities (Toronto, Montreal, Winnipeg, Calgary, and Vancouver); the rest are traded "Over the Counter", or OTC, which is to say that they are bought directly from securities dealers. When you think about it, the amount of money actually raised on the exchanges themselves is not very significant.

In 1990, for example, the total Quoted Market Value of the 1,212 corporations listed on the on the TSE came to an impressive $703.3 billion. However, the total amount of New Equity Financing raised on the TSE that year came to $2.3 billion. Another way to look at this is to say that, for every dollar of value in the companies on the exchange, about one-third of a cent was raised to finance new issues.

Stock sales that year came to $64 billion, so perhaps that makes a fairer comparison. For every dollar that flowed through the exchange in 1990, three-and-a-half cents was invested in new equity. Most of the rest just travelled around the wheel. There were, in fact, more delistings – ninety-six – than new issues listed that year – fifty-two.

There is an old adage on the stock market, we are told by Ellen

Roseman of the *Globe and Mail*, to the effect that "An investment is a speculation gone wrong."

It wasn't until I began to go over these figures that I understood what the old adage meant. It meant that you buy stocks as a gamble, sell them as soon as possible, and do it again. It is only if you have guessed wrong that you hold onto the damn things and hope for better times. We call this "investing in Canada's future."

Some of our companies are also listed on American exchanges, and Canadians also buy stocks on American and other foreign exchanges. All God's chillun got stocks. The Chinese opened an exchange in Shanghai in 1987, Yugoslavia opened one in 1989, and Hungary has just re-opened its *bourse* (which is what these things are called in Europe, in memory of the Hôtel des Bourses, in Bruges, near which currency dealers and commodity brokers used to meet during the seventeenth century). The *World Directory of Stock Exchanges*, available for $230 (U.S.), lists ninety-eight stock exchanges in fifty-two nations, although the largest, by far, are in Tokyo, New York, London, Zurich, Frankfurt, Paris, and, yep, Toronto, which usually ranks fourth or fifth among stock exchanges in the world, measured by stock-trading activity. This position is somewhat misleading, since there is a large gap between the sales on the TSE and on the two world leaders, Tokyo and New York. In 1990, 61 billion shares were sold on the thirteen North American exchanges, but almost two-thirds of these – 39.6 billion – moved through the New York Stock Exchange. Toronto's share was 5.6 billion, second on the list for volume, third for dollar value. By dollar value, the NYSE's $1,537 billion in sales represented 85 per cent of the total, the TSE's $64 billion represented 3.4 per cent. The TSE towers, in turn, over other Canadian exchanges in exactly the same way that New York towers over the TSE. In 1990, Toronto moved 76.1 per cent of the total value of all the shares sold on exchanges in this country; Montreal, our second-largest exchange, 18.3 per cent. Winnipeg, the smallest

North American exchange, moved a mere 197,000 stocks in 1990, worth $436,000. (The figures are from the *TSE Review,* April 1991.)

Chicken feed.

In fact, the U.S. Over-the-Counter market, which is called NASDAQ (for National Association of Securities Dealers' Automated Quotations), sold about $510 billion, or six times the TSE total, in stocks that didn't even move through an exchange, but were sold Over the Counter.

Thus, as in so many things, Canadians are much less important to the world markets than the world markets are to us.

As the securities business is taken over more and more by computers, it becomes easier to shunt between and among the various exchanges, and it is now the case that the casino never closes. Among them, with extended hours, the stock exchanges in New York, London, and Tokyo cover the market around the clock. In fact, at the moment, very few trades are made in the time slot between 5:00 p.m. and 10:00 p.m. Eastern Standard Time, although there is nothing to stop you from calling up one of the brokerage houses that carries ads for its twenty-four-hour service, and plunging in by moonlight in Sydney, Australia. Today, the most active round-the-clock financial market is in currency trading – betting the dollar against the pound, or the yen against all other comers – but there is a strong move afoot, which ought to be resisted, to create an international, interconnected global stock market, through which ordinary punters will be able to stare desolation in the face at all hours, simply by making a telephone call.

In the real world, then, stock exchanges affect us because many of us own stocks, and the rest of us feel the impacts on the economy of the stock-players. In the real world, the exchanges play a key role in providing secondary markets for the buying and selling of stocks, but only a minor role in raising capital for worthy entrepreneurs.

There are all kinds of regulations governing the markets, but they don't seem, in the real world, to do much to curb the crooks who represent a small proportion of the market operators, and a somewhat larger proportion of the successful market-players.

Peter Lynch, one of the Wall Street gurus, suggests that amateur investors ought to be able to outperform the market in general. That's the myth. In fact, one of the few detailed studies of how an individual market works for small investors is contained in *Fleecing the Lamb,* by David Cruise and Alison Griffiths. They note: "Vancouver Stock Exchange investors lose some of their money 84 per cent of the time and all of it 40 per cent of the time."

Whoever is making money on the VSE, it isn't the amateur investor.

We will not get far until we learn to separate the myths from the reality, but to help us out, I have constructed an investor's guide, in the next chapter.

CHAPTER FOURTEEN

An Investment Guide for Widows and Orphans. And Me.

The fact remains, so long as investors are persuaded to accept the teachings, preachings and shamming rationalizations of the wire services, the master hypnotists of the financial page, and radio and television newscasts, the devouring genius of the Stock Exchange will continue to devour them.

– Richard Ney, *The Wall Street Gang,* 1974.

$

Rule 1: An absolutely foolproof way to avoid losing money on stocks, bonds, options, futures, and commodities.

Don't buy any.

Rule 2: The greater the promised return, the greater the risk.

Rule 3: Exceptions to Rule 2.

There are no exceptions to Rule 2.

Rule 4: Buy any book entitled *Wealth Without Worry, How To Make Millions Without Risking a Dime, My Never-fail Stock-Market Guide,* or, the latest best-seller, *How To Get Rich Without Risk.*

Read it for entertainment only.

Rule 5: Never make up more than four rules at once.

Hey, but wait a minute, you are saying, where do we get to the part about what I should do with my money? Keeping it polite, of course. Very well then, bearing in mind that some genius in the publisher's marketing department may be able to fasten on this short chapter and stick a line on the cover that says, "Includes Sure-Fire Guide on How To Invest in the 1990s!" here we go.

I have no idea what you should do with your money. I don't know you, or how much money you have, or what you want to do with it. I can tell you what I would do with my money if I had enough to make the exercise worth while.

I would invest most of it in Guaranteed Investment Certificates, either within a Registered Retirement Savings Plan, if I had enough off-setting eligible income, or outside of one, in a trust company. The RRSP is the greatest rip-off the middle class has ever given itself, a truly scandalous method of transferring wealth from the comparatively poor to the comparatively comfortable through the income-tax system. The more you can put in, the bigger the tax break. And the best way to invest in RRSPs is through a fixed-return investment, not a self-directed plan. If you have to read as many financial advice columns as I do, you would become familiar with the shoals of letters from pensioners who decided they were too clever to have to pay some trust company to handle their RRSPs and wound up with nothing to comfort them in their old age but a broker's smile. Remember, GICs do not carry any risk in Canada. You can place them in various institutions in lumps of $60,000 or less and have them covered by federal deposit insurance. I would use a trust company, not a bank, because trust companies pay more and, since the money is insured, there is no appreciably greater risk.

Granted, this is flying in the face of the sage advice of Ira Gluskin, one of Canada's better-known gurus. In the preface to *Bulls and Bears: Winning in the Stock Market in Good Times and Bad,* he refers to GICs as "fixed-income instruments," and says they will be left behind by "canny stock-market investing," according to "study after study." He doesn't cite any of the studies, but I'm sure he wouldn't make a thing like that up. All I can say is that the study I did in the last chapter, which is pretty simple and straightforward, points the other way. I also note the use of the word "canny." If the investments aren't canny, all bets are off. And how do we know if they're canny? If they do better than fixed-interest investments. Like many of the arguments designed to show us how smart we would be to jump into the markets, this one has a somewhat circular shape. So, *pace* Ira Gluskin, my doubloons go into GICs.

I would put some money – I am making myself richer for this part – into Treasury bills. T-bills. This isn't so easy to do, because banks don't like to sell them to individuals, and only a preferred list of underwriters can buy them from the government, at auction. Banks will charge a fee, about 1 per cent, and do a lot of groaning, but a good customer can persuade the customer-service department of a large bank to arrange the purchase of T-bills in lots of $10,000 or more. (The minimum Treasury bill is $1,000.) A broker can sell them to you; his company can buy them in blocks from the banks. He or she will charge you a fee, without calling it a fee, by quoting a lower rate of return than his company paid the bank, which is perfectly reasonable. He won't be happy to sell you these securities, any more than the bank was, but he will do so if he thinks he is going to sell you some stocks as a result. He isn't. Not to me, anyway.

Treasury bills are valued backwards, like many bonds. That is, the banks bid on Thursday afternoons by offering less than $1,000 for a $1,000 T-bill. The bills themselves – which, I remind you, are called bills rather than bonds, because they are of such short duration – are sold in blocks of $1 million, with the Bank of Canada acting as the government's agent. The auction is electronic, and a computer works out how much of each batch of bills goes to each of the bidding banks, according to their bids. If a bank bid, for example, $96.513 for every hundred dollars worth of 91-day bills (which, for their own reasons, is the way the Bank of Canada calculates these matters), it would be offering an annual rate of 14.58 per cent. The auction is slightly phoney, in that the Bank of Canada tells the banks what bids it is likely to accept, and steps into the market itself if necessary. The average bid on 91-day T-bills determines the Bank Rate; that is, the Bank Rate is set each week one-quarter point, or .25 per cent, above the average amounts that the banks bid for these bills.

You don't really need to know all this; I just think it's interesting, and it shows that, barring catastrophe dreadful to contemplate, your money is as safe as houses – safer, in fact. Houses fall down; the Bank of Canada will not. What you need to know is that, if you have money, as we saw in the last chapter, you really can't find a risk-free way to do better with it, over the long run, than to put it into GICs and T-bills.

I would then buy some Canada Savings Bonds because, once more, they are almost without risk, and they have done well in recent years. All the instruments I have bought so far lack liquidity; that is, I can't cash them in at once. The CSB, I can, and that is why the return is slightly lower.

That's all.

If I were foolish enough to want to gamble with my money, I would take, say, $10,000 and chuck it into the equities market, buying stocks. I would write it off, and then, if I did happen to strike it rich, I would consider it to be found money. That is the proper way to gamble, with someone else's cash. And to make it clear, I have no objection to gambling, called by its own name. I won't buy lottery tickets, because I consider them to be a tax on the stupid, but I know many people who do buy them, and who get more than their money's worth in pleasure by deciding, each week, what they would do with the $10 million, or whatever, if they won, before learning that they didn't win, and throwing the stub in the trash. My objection is to making gambling into the principal activity of the markets and then trying to con us into believing it is not gambling, but investment, and therefore good for us – if not an actual patriotic duty. So, I won't gamble, because I can't afford to, but if you want to, go ahead.

Buy some bank stocks – they are always undervalued, but they pay steady dividends – and an industrial stock or two, and one of the high-tech stocks, because it might take off. Or, do what the pros down at the *Wall Street Journal* do, and let a dart pick your stocks for you.

The argument for gambling is that you can't keep much ahead of inflation with the fixed-interest investments I have chosen. You can't keep ahead of inflation by walking around in a barrel while your broker counts the change, either, so you have to choose. Real estate is a good long-term hedge against inflation. Unless it isn't. You can never get to be really rich on my sissy scenario, but I don't want to be rich. I just don't care to be poor. In the financial-planning game, we call this "Setting your goals." My goal is no barrels.

But if I did leap into the markets, I would use a discount broker to do the buying, unless I really knew a full-service broker personally and well. I have come across too many instances of broker ignorance to think that the higher average rates full-service brokers charge are worth the advice they have to proffer ("buy!"). I have been flirting for some time with ScotiaMcLeod's discount brokerage, because the man who sends me bits of material in the mail never bugs me. I dropped a number of others who bugged me. I am not going to buy anything from this gent, so it is quite wrong of me to lead him on, but I can attest that there is at least one discount broker that has some retail salespeople who are content to let the customer make the move.

I won't buy mutual funds, because I don't see why I should pay someone else to take wild guesses on my behalf, but if I did, I would buy one of the balanced funds with a good long-term record. This would take some investigation on my part, because the vast majority of mutual funds haven't been on the scene long enough to have a long-term record, and many of those that have such a record have done very badly. I might, if I chose to go this route, put some money into one of the sounder ethical funds, like Vancouver's Ethical Growth Fund. Even if I didn't make much, I could feel morally superior.

I won't buy stock indexes or futures or options, out of sheer prejudice against the damn things and what they do to the markets, but if I really wanted to gamble, I would. No crap game in the world can match the risks of options or commodity futures; they are the Bungey Jumps of finance. I would buy pork bellies, just to be able to throw it into the conversation. Got a good bunch of pork bellies down in Chicago, today. Anybody care for a slice?

I might also, getting carried away, buy gold bullion (makes a terrific doorstop) or gold stocks, which are a good hedge against inflation, because, as the dollar goes up and becomes worth less, gold increases in value.

I would certainly, as in Rule 4 above, buy some of the "How To" books, for amusement and reassurance. It is nice to know, for example, that the "major depression" predicted by 1983 in Douglas R. Casey's No. 1 best-seller, *Crisis Investing*, is still ahead of us. It will be accompanied, Casey said, by wage and price controls, foreign-exchange and travel restrictions, hyper-inflation, and massive unemployment, "with rationing, black markets, searches, seizures and confiscation sure to follow." Also, "Riots, protests, and crime in the streets (all of a violent, convulsive nature.)" It would be a bit of an anticlimax to have riots, protests, and crime in the streets of a passive nature.

But, not all is lost, brothers and sisters – there will be, for the upright and believing, good news. "The creation of a whole new class of millionaires who have prepared for the depression," viz., by buying Casey's book. They will sock all their cash into gold and the stocks of gold mines, especially South African gold mines, and then whip the proceeds over to a Swiss bank account.

The crisis didn't arrive on time, but one can only hope Casey will not become discouraged by the delay. Bound to have a winner one day. And, in the meantime, he did rather well out of the book.

And of course, I would buy some extra copies of this book and hold onto them. Bound to increase in value, over the years. Just ask your broker.

CHAPTER FIFTEEN

If I Were King of the Forest

Proposals for Reform

All markets are manipulated, by the way.
— Thomas R. Keyes and David Miller, *The Global Investor*, 1990.

$

The thesis of this book has been that the stock markets are badly out of whack, for two reasons. The first is that speculation has overwhelmed investment; the second is that the way the markets are currently run tends to reward cheaters and punish honest people. The result is that the markets are expensive, unwieldy, technical marvels that perform extremely well in sustaining the elixir, liquidity, and very badly in doing what they are supposed to do, which is to supply an honest venue for the buying and selling of financial instruments. We can ignore, I think, their claim that they help to build the economy by, as the TSE's promotional literature puts it, "providing a link between people with savings to invest and companies that need money to grow." Stock markets are so expensive, as a place to raise capital, that there are a dozen better ways for worthy entrepreneurs to find cash. Bank loans, bonds, debentures, tapping the till of a venture capital company,

291

or using the firm's own earnings to finance growth are all much more efficient ways for worthy entrepreneurs to raise funds than floating a public issue. It is the unworthy entrepreneurs who ben-efit most in the stock markets, because they have discovered that these markets allow them to use other people's money for their ventures, at little risk to themselves, while scooping off most of the cash on the way through. It doesn't matter that half the money is blown away on promoting the stock, because it's all being provided by the suckers over yonder.

The Japanese firms that we are always being asked to admire raise capital from their own cash flows or through loans from banks with which they are affiliated, and they see their stock mar-kets almost entirely as places to gamble.

If we look at our own stock markets clearly, we can see that they have only one legitimate function, and that is to provide a second-ary market for the buying and selling of shares that have already been created.

And they perform this function very badly, from the public's point of view. They have wondrous computers, and woeful regulators.

The future, frankly, looks worse than the past. With the global-ization of finance, more and more transactions will take place within the innards of computers and beyond the reach of any sort of regulation. The futility of trying to keep any serious check on the players will become apparent, and we will cut costs by forget-ting about it. The recent multiplication of disclosure laws has not really made much difference. There was a great deal more infor-mation available to the small investor – and mountains more available to the sophisticated investor – in 1987, than there was in 1929, but that did not prevent a trillion dollars in value vanishing almost overnight. Since 1987, squadrons of scholars, mostly in the pay of the securities industry, have been put to work to prove that that crash was not, repeat not, caused by program trading and the wild gambles of arbitrage experts armed with computers. That's nice. Unfortunately, it means that nobody knows what the hell happened. We can recreate, thanks to the silent witness of the recording tapes, every detail of the market's moves, but it means nothing. We see the little option fall, but we have no idea who pushed it out of the nest.

The massive technology and the massive stupidity of the markets have grown up side by side, and not by accident. It is important to those who run the exchanges, the stockbrokers who live on their liquidity, to be able to track and record millions of transactions, to speed up the pace of trading, to let the casino run all night, lest any more business escape to the Over the Counter market or, gasp, in unregistered trades. It is equally important not to ponder the net result too deeply, not to wonder whether there isn't a better way to do things. The exchanges, poor lambs, are nearly frantic with worry as it is; as the trades move increasingly onto the computers, commissions get harder and harder to collect. Somebody out there somewhere, dammit, just sold shares to somebody else without giving us our cut. What we need, then, are bigger and faster and more sophisticated – and more expensive, did I mention more expensive? – computers to capture the business again. And a wider variety of products.

Within a few years – and I hope I turn out to be no better a prophet than Douglas Casey – we will have all the markets interlinked by computer, running twenty-four hours a day, and database in a tax haven offshore. The main computer will be capable of keeping up with any number of transactions at once, instead of taking three seconds to complete a deal between Toronto and Tokyo, as at present. Mutual funds, bonds, and every variety of index known to the mind of man will be traded. Inevitably, some smart cookie is going to work out a way to turn football and baseball and basketball scores into a market instrument. Why not? This would be very little more remote from productive industry than some of the stock-index products that are sold today. More and more of our energy and talents will go to playing the markets, more and more of our brightest young lawyers and accountants and mathematicians will be absorbed by the industry.

In the name of competitiveness – five syllables that mean, "The Americans are doing it, and even if it's a crappy idea, we must imitate the Americans" – market regulation will be eased formally, not just by escaping through the computers. There will still be the show trials, from time to time, of a few of the market heroes who turned out to be crooks, but paying fines for overstepping the bounds will be, even more than today, just another licensing fee for the operators. In the most notorious of modern cases, Michael Milken pleaded guilty to six counts, and ninety-two others were dropped. Following this logic, if you rob ninety-eight banks, you should only have to face the music on the first six. Milken's particular genius, wrote Benjamin J. Stein, a Los Angeles lawyer, in *Barron's,* lay in corrupting others:

> Michael Milken's ability to take academics who had never even thought of being bribed or co-opted, pass them a few shekels and get them to produce learned documents about how safe his junk bonds were without regard to truth is undoubted. So is his gift for paying journalists lavish speaking fees and getting them to sit up and bark for him.

Considering the way Milken was treated, it takes no deep thought to realize that the pattern will be repeated, and will lead, before long, to another market crash, probably worse than the one in 1987, and a huge investigation that will discover that the damage was done by parties unknown in ways unfathomable, and is no way traceable to the fact that the markets have become a crazy place. The survivors will return to the gaming tables and begin again.

My personal reaction to this straightforward description of events-to-be is to stay the hell away from the markets. Don't play in the traffic, and don't mess with the manipulators. The honest workmen who remain will operate at an ever-increasing disadvantage, and the small investor will be stamped out by institutional investors acting for pension funds and other cash-rich bodies. He has already been discounted by the smart cookies. The money now provided by these bit players will be invested indirectly on their behalf, instead, through their pension funds and mutual funds, so that entire groups of people may be vacuumed – as they were in the Principal Group collapse in Alberta, and in the savings and loan debacle we looked at in Chapter Eleven – on a more or less regular basis.

Which means that my personal retreat from the mess won't do much good, in the end. We cannot escape the consequences of what is happening on the markets, because we will pay for it, in the misallocation of capital, in the effects on the general economy of recurring financial crises, and in the tax burdens we will bear to salvage something from the wreckage, whether we own any stocks or not. Surely the ultimate irony of the markets is the way they soak the taxpayer on behalf of the gambler and call the result "efficient."

Martin Mayer argues that, "Of all the reasons that can be adduced for the virtual disappearance of productivity growth in the American economy, the misallocation of capital from the domination of our markets by institutional investors is, I think, the most convincing." The difficulty with this argument is that it attempts to prove a negative. We don't know what would have happened if investment money went less into the hot stocks favoured by institutional investors and more into productive growth. That does not invalidate the argument; it is easy to see that there is a tremendous pool of funds in the markets that doesn't do anything but rush from stock to stock, and it is equally easy to see that worthy firms are left short of capital. We can't measure this allocation accurately, any more than we can calculate the number of gallons in a flood. But we can see that somebody is getting soaked.

We spend more and more of our resources trying to make money make money, instead of using it to produce goods and services. Think, for just a moment, of what we could do if we spent some of the trillions that whirl around the world's exchanges annually on some of the jobs that really need doing, from cleaning up pollution to improving our schools and health services. Let us have just some of the $600 billion that will go glimmering on the savings and loans debacle; it will do to start.

If I were king of the forest, if I could truly re-order the markets, they would look quite different:

There would be a National Securities Commission in Canada, whose chairman would report to the minister of finance in Ottawa. Political interference, you cry. Well, of course. There is another phrase for political interference; it's called the vote.

The fees the stockbroker-dealers now pay themselves to run the exchanges would be paid to an independent body, whose board would report to the securities chairman, and which could never have a majority of stockbrokers (the VSE's Board has fifteen members; thirteen stockbrokers).

Stock trades would require twenty-four hours to take effect, and every stock would be subject to a day limit, as commodities are now. As soon as a stock moved more than, say, 10 per cent in one session, trading would be suspended.

Brokers and investment dealers would be pried apart again, and given back their old distinctions, so that investment dealers would be principals, and brokers would be agents only; no dealing in their own accounts. The only exception would be for the purposes of market-making (maintaining firm bid and offer prices in a given security), as now, but the difference would be that it would be up to an outside regulator, not the stock exchange, to draw the lines.

The banks would be sent packing from the brokerage business just as quickly as it could be arranged.

If the same firm owned an investment dealer and a brokerage, the broker would be required to inform any potential purchaser if the stocks or bonds he or she was considering were in a deal underwritten by the firm.

Non-voting shares would not be eligible for trading on any

registered stock exchange. Like all the steps above, this would simply restore us to the position we were in a few years ago.

At least 20 per cent of the board of directors of publicly traded companies would, by law, be nominated by individual shareholders, and their names would be carried on a proxy statement sent to all shareholders, and voted separately from the management slate. Management could have all its directors, but there would be at least some guaranteed independents.

There would be . . . but this is foolishness, this is dreaming; the financial community, the same people who contribute so handsomely to election campaigns, would never permit anything like a real reform of the markets.

Let me then content myself with one reform proposal only, which is simple, effective, and not my own.

Bring back the transfer tax. Every time you buy or sell a share, you should pay a tax. Why not? It is a good, isn't it?

A dozen experts, from Louis Lowenstein and Martin Mayer in the United States to Eric Kierans in Canada, have put forward this suggestion; surely it ought to be considered.

West Germany had a transfer tax of 1 per cent until it was dropped in 1990, in the name of competitiveness. New York State had a tax of five cents a share, which was dropped for the same reason. Competitiveness, you will recall, is the argument that says that we all have to work for less than the peons in Mexico or the factory hands in South Korea. Only in this way can we get rich. Well, somebody can get rich. But there must be some argument on the other side, on behalf of the elemental proposition that we ought to make our policy match what it is we want the stock markets to do.

What we want the markets to do is what we always wanted: to set reasonably accurate prices, provide a reasonably honest forum of exchange, and give entrepreneurs a reasonably efficient way to raise capital for business ventures. We can do all this if we can just make the damn things slow down. John Maynard Keynes thought this was the key fifty-five years ago, and John Maynard Keynes was right. In *The General Theory of Employment*, he noted, "It is usually agreed that casinos should, in the public interest, be inaccessible and expensive. And perhaps the same is true of Stock Exchanges." His solution?

> The introduction of a substantial Government transfer tax on all transactions might prove the most serviceable reform available, with a view to mitigating the predominance of speculation over enterprise in the United States.

Virtually every serious academic, not in the pay of the securities industry, who has looked at the markets, has said the same thing, one way or another. By reducing the liquidity only the speculator will be harmed, not the true investor.

And most of them have come up with the same way to do this. A tax. Past taxes on stock transactions have been aimed at making money for the government, not at controlling the craziness. New York state's tax was a money-raiser, and so was a tax proposed by House Speaker Jim Wright in 1988 in the United States. He wanted a federal levy of .05 per cent on every stock trade. A better tax, in my view, is one to curb "the predominance of speculation over enterprise."

Warren Edward Buffett, a former investment salesman, security analyst, and corporate executive from Omaha, has put forward what seems to me the ideal instrument, which he calls a "non-tax tax." He put this forward before he was put into the post of Chairman of Salomon Brothers, when that brokerage firm got caught cheating in mid-1991, and a wholesale clean-out of the top echelons seemed to be indicated. He hasn't said much on the subject since, so perhaps he has changed his mind, or merely decided to keep his mouth shut. Nevertheless, his non-tax tax is just as good an idea as it was when he propounded it in a 1988 speech. It is a tax only in that the taxing mechanism is used to accomplish the policy goal.

Buffett's non-tax tax would be a 100-per-cent levy on all gains from the sale of stocks or derivative securities – options, and their ilk – which are held for less than one year. Suppose you buy the shares of Locket, Socket, and Trunk for $35 a share; you hold them for three months, and sell for $38. The three bucks goes into a special fund, from which, if I were king, the money would come to provide market regulation. You hold the stocks for a year and a day, and sell them for $40. You keep the profit. You are not penalized for wanting your money back; the market's blessed liquidity is not banished, merely reduced. The main task of the tax is to signal that stocks are not the proper vehicle for short-term speculation.

This is not a radical change, although it would have dramatic effects. Under U.S. law, investors who take more than 10 per cent of a target company are required to declare their holdings, and required to keep the stocks for a period of six months. All the Buffett proposal does is to extend the hold period to a year, apply it more broadly, to all investors rather than just those who cross some percentage threshhold, and use the tax mechanism as an enforcement tool.

Back in 1903, Sereno S. Platt (how could you deny a man with a name like that?), in a study called *The Work of Wall Street*, made the key distinction. He said,

> When a security is bought and paid for in full, put away in a place of safe keeping and held for the income it produces – that is called an *investment*. . . . [when] it is bought on margin and held for sale as soon as the price advances – that is *speculation*.

He noted that, even then, the "great bulk of the dealings in stocks are speculative."

Well, we are not killing speculation with our tax, Buffett and I and the rest of us, we are simply stretching it out; we are making the investor speculate on a longer term, on the grounds that we will all be better off that way – with the exception, of course, of insiders and others for whom the bets are not so much a speculation, anyway, as the cashing in of a sure thing.

All the trades in stock-index futures and options would disappear overnight. And a good thing, too. In the words of Louis Lowenstein, "These synthetic products are at best a parasite and at worst a cancer on the stream of useful activity." Goodbye, TIPs and Nikkei puts, and good riddance.

Mutual funds would not be much changed, except that they, too, would work to a longer time-frame. Most mutual funds are managed for the long term, anyway; all this tax would do would be to cut down the back-and-forth trading that creates those invisible management fees, making mutuals a slightly better investment vehicle.

The people who would really be knocked on the head are the greenmailers. There could be no profit for them, because even if they did manage to browbeat the management of a company whose stock they had purchased into buying it back at a higher price, the gain would go elsewhere. Genuine takeovers, where a new group tries for control of a company in the honest belief that it is badly run, or could be better run, would not be disturbed. All the invaders have to do is hold their stock for a year, surely a minimal period in which to make the needed changes, to realize a real gain.

Junk-bond operations would be affected severely, if indirectly, since the junk-bond operation depends, in the end, on being able to sell the stocks of the target company, as a key part of its assets, to finance the bonds.

This non-tax tax would not apply to the commodity markets or to bonds, but bonds, except of the junk variety, are today a legitimate investment vehicle, held for the long term. As for the commodity markets, there is really nothing much a Canadian can do about them. Our own commodity markets run very much better than those in Chicago and New York, where the huge trades are made. I would leave them alone, as unreformable, and let all those who want the opportunity to roll the dice do so there.

I am aware of the difficulty of getting this tax implemented; brokers' eyes bulge when I mention it. (I have yet to run into a broker who has heard of such a thing, or indeed has read anything significant about proposals to reform the stock market. Most brokers believe, with Richard Whitney, that their institution is perfect; all it needs is to be made bigger.) It may be argued that there is no hope of establishing the Buffett tax, when we can't even get the market-players to pay the GST.

I have never been able to see any reason in the exemption of stock trades from the Goods and Services Tax. Why should you have to pay GST on the purchase of a book, but not on the shares of Moonlight Flit Finance? The official explanation I got from one of the nameless in Ottawa was that, "It was seen that to apply the GST to stock sales would interfere with the free, competitive market."

So it would. The GST interferes with the free, competitive market in books, too, and clothing, and almost anything else you can think of, but that doesn't hinder its application. When I raised this with a broker I ran into down at the TSE, he gave it to me straight.

"But 90 per cent of the shares would jump over the border," he said.

I said, "So?", and we just stared at each other for a minute, before he turned on his heel in a marked manner and walked away, without even trying to sell me any shares. I think he detected a lack of perfect understanding between us. I don't believe for a minute that 90 per cent of the companies now listed on the TSE would fly across the border if sales in Canada attracted a 7 per cent GST – the reasons for listing in Canada, for most companies, are well worth putting up with some nuisance. Just the same, there is no doubt that trying to collect the GST on stock transfers would bring down lightning bolts from every publicly traded corporation in the country, and to try to slip a 100-per-cent non-tax tax into law would produce, among other things, apoplexy in the boardrooms, and the drying up of political contributions for any political party foolish enough to suggest it.

I do not put this modest proposal forward here, then, with the hope that this modest, clear, eminently sensible idea will be adopted. Certainly not unless and until the Americans adopt it.

I therefore raise the argument simply to keep it in discussion, to point out its worthy antecedents, and to hope that someday, after the next crash, or the one after that, someone somewhere in power will begin to look around, and ask himself or herself, if there isn't, just maybe, a better way to do things.

Until that happens, I am going to stay out of the markets.

Glossary of Terms

all-or-none order: An order to buy or sell securities only if all those required can be obtained at the offered price.

Amex: The American Stock Exchange in New York.

arbitrage: Buying and selling securities, currencies, or commodities at the same time in two or more markets, to take advantage of differences in prices. If ABC mining is selling at $10 a share in Toronto, and at $10.05 in New York, the arbitrageur can buy and sell large blocks in the two places simultaneously, and pocket the difference. Obviously, this only works with large trades; otherwise, the cost of the transaction will gobble up the profit. The theoretical justification for arbitrage is that it promotes efficiency by making prices more uniform. In fact, it mainly promotes volatility, as huge sums of money fly from market to market.

asked price: The price at which a stock is offered for sale.

assets: Anything owned by a corporation or an individual having commercial or exchange value .

authorized shares: The shares of any class a firm may create under the terms of its articles of incorporation. Not all the shares authorized will usually be issued, that is, be sold out of the company treasury.

back-end loading: In a mutual fund, a charge levied on the investor when the money is withdrawn.

bear: Anyone who thinks the market in a stock, or all stocks, is going to fall, and speculates accordingly.

bid: The highest price a potential purchaser is willing to pay for a given stock. Together, the *bid* and *ask* prices constitute a *quotation,* and the difference between them is called the *spread.*

303

block trading: Buying or selling a large quantity of the same stock. Usually, a sale over 10,000 shares constitutes a block trade.

board lot: The number of shares of a given stock generally sold as a unit. It may vary from 100 to more than 1,000, depending on how many shares are normally traded in the stock.

boiler-room: A telephone operation to sell stocks, usually by relays of salesmen using high-pressure tactics and claims that will not stand up to scrutiny. In the early days, telephone exchanges were often set up in the boiler-rooms of legitimate investment houses for this activity; thus, the name.

bond: A security representing debt in the issuing corporation. Bonds bear interest, and the principal is repaid at the time specified on the security, although it may be redeemed later. *Bondholders* do not have any corporate ownership privileges, such as the stockholder's right to vote his or her shares.

book value: The value at which an asset is carried on a balance sheet. It may differ considerably from *market value,* the price at which the same asset may be sold publicly. Corporations normally carry their real estate at the value at which they purchased it, but its market value may be much higher.

bottom: The support level for any security.

bought deal: A transaction in which newly issued shares are bought at the same time they are issued, by the investment house organizing large buyers in advance, so the public has no opportunity to buy. Bought deals are common in Canada, but usually forbidden in the United States.

bridge financing: A loan or loans made to tide over the purchaser of a corporation during the takeover period. Bridge financing usually ensures that the takeover artist has very little real money involved, and it is usually repaid out of the assets of the firm that is taken over.

bucket shop: A stock-selling organization that accepts orders, but doesn't execute them at once. If the market behaves as the customer expects, so he stands to make money, the order is simply thrown out. If the market behaves contrary to the customer's expectation and he loses money, the bucket shop will confirm the order, and keep any profit made on the sale. Bucket shops are illegal, but

common. Why would anyone patronize such a place? Ask
P. T. Barnum.

bull: Anyone who thinks the market is going to boom, and invests
accordingly.

call option: The opposite of a *put*. The right to buy a given quantity of
shares of a stock or stock index at a set price within a pre-set
deadline. The buyer pays a premium for this right, and can either
sell the shares in due course, or sell the call beforehand.

cash sale: In commodity markets, *cash* or *spot* sales represent
immediate transactions, as opposed to future sales.

Chartist: Someone who believes trading patterns recur, and can
therefore be anticipated. Chartists are in the same position as those
who try to anticipate where someone is going by tracking the
footprints of where he has been. They are highly regarded
nonetheless.

Chinese Wall: The division which is said to exist inside an investment
house to keep one branch of the operation from knowing what is
happening in another, because that would lead to charges of
conflict of interest. Thus, the Mergers and Acquisitions group is
not supposed to know that the Corporate Finance Group has just
learned that a company that M & A is trying to acquire for a client
is strapped for funds. Most Chinese Walls appear to be constructed
of porous material.

churning: Buying and selling shares for a customer over and over, to
create commissions on the sales. In its highest form, *churn 'em and
burn 'em*, the process continues until the customer has no money
left. Then he is advised to close the account. *Churning* is illegal, but
common.

circuit breaker: A technical device to halt *program trading* when
fluctuations in prices become extreme.

closed-end fund: A mutual fund with a limited number of shares
outstanding. In an *open-end* fund, the operators keep issuing
shares as long as anyone will buy them.

collateral trust bond: A corporate-debt security backed by other
securities, which are usually in the hands of a neutral party, such as
a bank or trust company.

common stock: The units representing the ownership of a corporation.

Usually, but not always, the common stock carries voting rights, and anyone who controls anything over 50 per cent of the company's common stock can make decisions binding on the corporation. When the company declares a *dividend* out of its profits, the dividend is divided in proportion to the number of shares of stock owned. In recent years, a new class of stock, which has no voting rights, but still represents shares in the ownership, has come into vogue. It is sometimes known as *b* stock. This separates the responsibility of the stockholder entirely from the activities of the corporation.

convertible bond: A debt instrument of the corporation, like any other bonds, but with the ability to be converted into common shares of the corporation within a specified time at the rate shown on the bond. The great advantage, for the holder, is that, if the company's shares go up in value, he or she can convert the bonds to shares and gain a profit on that increase in value. If there is no such increase, the bond will still pay the agreed interest rate and return of principal in due course.

crossed trades: Trades of existing securities, offset against each other without coming onto the exchange. Other investors are deprived of any opportunity to participate in the trade. This practice is outlawed on most U.S. exchanges, but is common in Canada.

curb market: The market outside the regular exchanges. In the United States, the American Stock Exchange was referred to as the "Curb Exchange" until 1921, when it began to regularize and register stocks sold under its auspices.

current yield: The annual interest on a bond, divided by its market price.

day order: An order to buy or sell a stock or other security that must be fulfilled by close of trading at the specified price, or cancelled.

day-trader: Someone who normally buys and sells the same stocks within a trading day.

debenture: A debt security backed by the integrity and name of the borrowing corporation, rather than any specific asset, such as a *mortgage bond.*

deposit insurance: In Canada, accounts and eligible Guaranteed

Investment Certificates held within banks and trust companies are insured by the Canada Deposit Insurance Corporation, up to $60,000 per account. In the United States the figure is $100,000. The advantage of the system is that it prevents runs on financial institutions, since the government promises to make good the deposit. The disadvantage is that it removes the incentive for the investor to keep track of the activities of the institution. A badly run bank is every bit as safe, from the investor's point of view, as one that is prudently managed, right up to the moment when the investor has $60,001 in the till.

discount broker: A stockbroker who provides only minimal services, executing buy and sell orders for securities, for a commission that is usually, but not always, lower than that charged by a *full-service broker.*

dividend: The distribution of earnings from a corporate treasury. Dividends are paid to the owner of the stock at the time the dividend is declared, and in proportion to the stock owned. The owner of 100 shares of a stock on which a twenty-five-cent dividend has been declared will get 100 x .25, or $25.00. The owner of 1,000 shares will get $250.00. Dividends are usually paid quarterly, and may be paid in money, stock, or scrip. Dividends are not the same as *earnings,* since the corporation will usually distribute only a portion of its earnings as dividends, keeping the rest for expansion or other purposes. Some corporations will pay dividends even where there are no earnings, in order to keep the price of the stock up.

Dow Jones average : A market index made up of sixty-five stocks traded on the New York Stock Exchange. Actually, it isn't an average, since the various stocks are weighted according to their groupings in industrial, transport, and public-utility stocks. It isn't even a particularly good index, since it leaves out so many sectors – such as finance – and includes so few stocks. It is, nonetheless, faithfully reported every day, and stock-players buy and sell accordingly. All part of the rich pageant of stock-market hokum.

earnings: A bit tricky, this one. The difference between what a company takes in and what it spends provides the earnings, except that, due to the miracle of modern accounting, a company may be showing earnings when it is just about to fall over a cliff. Nonetheless, a company's profit, if any, is usually expressed as *earnings per share,* annually, which is the net income divided by the number of shares outstanding. If it is a loss, it is usually shown in brackets.

effective yield: This is a fiction, but one that makes mutual funds look better than they are. *Effective yield* is the average daily yield of the fund over a period of seven days, pro-rated to cover a period of one year, and assuming that all the returns will remain the same over the year, and that everything within the fund that might be distributed to the owners is instead reinvested and compounded. A mutual fund can show an effective yield of over 10 per cent when, in fact, its shares are worth less at the end of the year than they were at the beginning.

Elliott Wave: A theory propounded by an American economist that stock prices can be predicted by applying the mathematical patterns of a series of numbers worked out by an Italian who lived in the thirteenth century. I am not making this up.

equity: The ownership interest possessed by the shareholders in a corporation, as expressed in the common and preferred stocks. The key distinction is between *equity,* expressing ownership, and bonds, debentures, or mortgages, expressing debt.

ethical fund: A mutual fund guided by some set of consistent principles, such as concern for the environment, or a refusal to buy any shares of corporations that trade with South Africa.

first-mortgage bonds: Debt instruments backed by a mortgage on real estate.

floor ticket: A summary of the information concerning a sale on the floor of a stock exchange.

front-end loading: Sales charges applied to an investment, especially a mutual fund, when it is first purchased. This practice means that an investor in a mutual fund who puts in $1,000 may in fact earn a return on only $900, since $100 has already been deducted as a front-end load.

full-service broker: A stockbroker who supplies analysis and advice as well as buying and selling securities for the customer. Charges are usually, but not always, higher than those of a *discount broker*.

fundamentalist : Someone who buys shares in a company on the basis of an analysis of its performance as a business, rather than its stock-market performance. Louis Lowenstein writes that a fundamentalist "buys shares of a company as if he were buying the whole company."

futures contract: An agreement to buy or sell a specified quantity of shares, or a commodity, at a named future date and at a named price. The contract obligates the buyer to buy and the seller to sell, unless the contract has itself been sold, the contracted amount of whatever is covered by the *settlement date*. This is unlike an *options contract,* where the buyer may choose to exercise the option or not by the named date.

going long: Buying shares to hold them until the price rises.

going short: Selling a security or futures contract you don't actually own, in anticipation of a drop in price. You borrow the securities, usually shares, and buy them back later, when the price has dropped, so that you replace the shares you have sold for, say, $10 each with shares you will buy in the future for $5. Your profit is the difference. Of course, if the price goes up to $15, you have to pay $15 for shares you have already disposed of for $10.

good through date: An order, as above, but only to be filled if it can be exercised by a specified date.

good till cancelled: An order to a broker to buy a given stock at a given price, not within a specified period of time, but whenever the stocks become available, until you cancel the order.

greenmail: Buying shares in a company with the sole purpose of having the management buy them back from you at a profit, to keep you from becoming a nuisance.

head-and-shoulder formation: One of the many shapes stock-market prices are seen to follow, in the eyes of the faithful. In theory, once you have detected a head and shoulder in the making, you can predict what will happen to the price of the stock by where it is presently in the formation. To repeat, I am not making this up.

hedging: A strategy used to offset market risk. You might, for example, hedge on a stock price by going long and short on the same stock. *Puts* and *calls* are used as hedges. A perfect hedge is said to be one where the possibility of future gain or loss is entirely eliminated. In poker, we call this "coppering your bet."

holding company: A corporation formed to hold the shares of other corporations.

incorporation: The formal act of creating a company, through articles of incorporation, which set out its purpose, authorized shares, and other details.

index: The statistical composite that measures changes in an economy or market. The CPI is an index of consumer prices; the TSE 35 is an index of thirty-five stocks on the Toronto exchange, while the TSE 300 is calculated from 300 stocks. The indices are all weighted; thus the TSE 300 is calculated by taking something called the "Aggregate Float Quoted Market Value," which is in turn made up by a calculation of the price that day of all outstanding shares minus shares in control blocks, dividing this value by the trade-weighted average quoted market value for all the original stocks that were in the index in 1975, and multiplying the result by 1,000. Don't try it, you'll only get a headache. The indices are important only because they tend to show the market trends as they go up and down from day to day.

index arbitrage: Buying and selling securities derived from the indices of various markets in two or more exchanges at the same time, to profit from differences in the price.

initial public offering (IPO): The first offering of a corporate stock to the public.

insider: The term usually refers to directors and major shareholders, but includes anyone with access to key information inside a corporation before it is announced. In theory, and law, it is wrong and bad to take advantage of insider information to, for example, buy shares in the firm because you know an outsider has offered to purchase those same shares for more than they are worth today. In fact, insider information is the basis for most of the profits that are made on the market.

issued shares: The shares from the corporation's store of *authorized shares* that have actually been issued to the market.

joint-stock company: A corporation with unlimited liability for the shareholders, because each owner of shares is legally liable for all its debts. Joint-stock companies still exist, but are no longer common.

junk bond: Technically, this is a bond with a credit rating of BB or lower with standard bond-rating companies. By and large, the phrase refers to high-risk, high-yield bonds, often issued to fund takeover bids.

leverage: In the stock markets, this refers to the practice of enhancing the possible returns without increasing your investment. Buying stocks on margin or buying rights or warrants are examples of leverage.

leveraged buy-out (LBO): The takeover of a company, often by its own management, by the use of funds borrowed against the security of the assets of the company itself.

limit order: An order to your broker to buy or sell a specific stock at a specific price or better.

limited liability: The rule that limits the interest of the shareholder to the amount he or she has invested in a corporation, in the event of its failure. The contrast is with the *joint-stock* company, where any debtor could come after any shareholder for the entire amount of a debt.

liquidity: The ability to buy and sell securities, i.e., convert them into liquid cash, quickly, and without significant loss.

margin: The amount a customer deposits with a broker to buy securities. The rest is borrowed from the broker. In Canada, the margin is usually 50 per cent of the value of the shares, while commodities can be purchased on 10-per-cent margins.

market maker: The trader assigned the responsibility by the exchange for maintaining an orderly market in a given stock, if necessary by buying and selling from his or her own inventory to ensure that a transaction can be completed.

market order: An order to buy or sell a security immediately at the current market price. If you place a *limit order* with your broker to buy Dig Deep Mines at $30 a share and the price at the time the order hits the floor of the exchange is $32, it will not be filled. If it is a *market order*, it will be.

minimum guaranteed fill (MGF): To ensure that small investors can have their wants seen to, the TSE provides that small quantities of stocks will be provided by the *market maker* in that particular stock, if they are not otherwise available.

money markets: The market for short-term debt securities, such as T-bills, certificates of deposit, and commercial paper.

MSE: Montreal Stock Exchange.

mutual fund: A fund operated by an investment company by selling units or shares of the fund itself to investors, and using the money thus collected to buy stocks, bonds, commodities, money-market securities, or other instruments. The funds are managed by professionals, and a management fee is charged.

naked option: An option for which the buyer or seller has no shares or other securities to fulfil the contract. Very, very risky.

NASDAQ: National Association of Securities Dealers' Automated Quotations system. The computerized system that provides price quotations for securities traded *Over the Counter* in the United States.

net worth: The amount by which a company's assets exceed liabilities.

net asset value per share (NAVPS): This is the market value of a share or unit in a mutual fund. It is calculated by taking the market value of all the assets of the fund, subtracting liabilities, and dividing by the total number of shares or units outstanding. Since the fund's liabilities include all the costs of its management, a mutual fund may show itself as having a return of 10 per cent per annum, when the NAVPS shows it to have lost money.

NYSE: New York Stock Exchange, also known as the "Big Board."

open outcry: Shouting out the prices on the floor of the exchange.

open-end fund: A mutual fund in which there is no limit on the number of shares or units that may be created and sold. The contrast is with a *closed-end* fund.

option: The right to buy or sell securities or commodities within a given time at a given price. If the option is not exercised, it expires, and the holder loses the money he put up for the option. The contrast is with a *futures contract,* in which the holder is obliged to complete the transaction. Options allow market-players to gamble extensively, since they only risk a small portion of the actual money required to complete the purchase.

Over the Counter (OTC): A security sold outside the confines of an organized exchange. About half of all stocks sold in Canada today are sold OTC.

P/E: Price/earnings ratio. The price of the stock is compared to the earnings as shown in company documents. A stock selling for $10 in a company whose earnings were $1 per share, would have a P/E of 10/1, but the second figure is left out; the P/E is expressed merely as 10.

par value: A value equal to the face value of a security. A $500 bond selling at par would sell for $500; at $600, it would be selling at a premium; at $400, it would be selling at a discount.

partial fill: You have ordered 1,000 shares of Dig Deep Mines at $10, but the broker is only able to obtain 900 at that price. You have a *partial fill*.

poison pill: A tactic by a company that is the object, or suspected object, of a takeover bid, to make itself less attractive. The target company may, for example, buy another company and load itself with debt, or pass a resolution to issue a whole new shoal of shares if any outsider gets more than a certain percentage of its stock. Another trick is to issue warrants that would allow current shareholders to buy shares at a deep discount in the event of a takeover. Also known as *shark repellent*.

Ponzi scheme: Carlo Ponzi was a fraud artist who invented an investment scheme based on the notion of pyramid letters. The participants were paid "earnings" out of the contributions of new investors, but finally the pyramid collapsed when there were no new investors to be found.

portfolio: The combined holdings of an investor in stocks, bonds, commodities, or other paper assets.

preferred stock: The class of stock of any corporation that has preference over common stock in the payment of dividends and, in the case of bankruptcy, in the division of assets. Preferred stock usually, but not always, pays dividends at a specified rate, even if there are no earnings. Most preferred stocks are cumulative; if dividends called for are not paid for any reason, they must be paid up before common stocks can receive dividends, and continue to accumulate until paid.

primary market: The market for new issues of securities, as opposed to the *secondary market,* where securities which have already been issued are traded. If the proceeds of the sale go to the issuer, usually a corporation, the market is primary.

program trading: The computerized trading of securities or indices, usually by institutions or arbitrage specialists.

prospectus: The formal written offer to sell a security, which must be filed with the exchange in the case of registered stocks. The prospectus contains a good deal of information, usually written in language designed to conceal more than it reveals.

proxy: A written power of attorney given to someone else, usually a representative of management, to vote your shares.

put: An option that carries the right to sell a specific number of shares at a given price by a given date. The put-option buyer pays a premium. This is the other side of a *call.*

pyramiding: Using financial leverage; in particular, by using the unrealized profits from one deal as collateral to buy other securities or commodities on credit.

quotation: The highest bid and lowest offer currently available on a security or commodity. If an investor is told the current quote – same thing – on Dismal Outlook Resources is 55 to 60, this means that the best bid for that stock is currently $55 a share, while the lowest price a seller has offered to sell it for is $60.

random walker: Someone who believes that past prices are of no use whatever in trying to determine the future behaviour of a security. Synonym: realist.

resistance level: The level at which, allegedly, a price ceiling is established for any given security. If Dismal Outlook generally sells between $55 and $60 a share, $55 is its *support level,* and $60 the *resistance level.* This is until, of course, it begins selling at some other level, when the term must be redefined. The theory is that Dismal Outlook will be a safe buy at $55. Don't count on it.

right: Properly, a *subscription right.* This is the privilege granted by a corporation to its existing shareholders to buy shares of a new stock issue before it is offered to the public. The right generally expires in three or four weeks, and can be traded like any other financial instrument. Unlike a *warrant,* which it otherwise resembles, the *right* is usually priced below the current market price for the stock.

rump: The shares left in the underwriter's hands if a new issue is under-subscribed. Do not pursue this metaphor.

secondary market: Stock exchanges and Over the Counter markets where securities are traded after their original issue in the *primary market.*

settlement price: The price at which a new issue is struck on *settlement day,* when the funds for the subscription are turned over to the issuing corporation by the investment house.

share: Same as stock, the unit of equity ownership in a corporation.

shareholders' equity: Same as *equity,* the ownership interest represented by all common and preferred shares in a corporation.

shark repellent: Another name for *poison pill.* The process of releasing *shark repellent* is sometimes known as "protecting the Crown jewels," which are the most desirable assets within a corporation.

split stock: Shares which have been divided to bring the price down and promote distribution and sales. If a $100 stock is split three-for-one, the owner of each share will receive, instead, three new shares worth $33.33 each.

spot sale: Same as *cash sale,* the immediate sale of a commodity, as opposed to a *future.*

spread: In stocks and bonds, the difference between *bid* and *ask* prices.

strike price: The price at which a stock or commodity represented by a *put* or *call* option can be purchased, in the case of a *call,* or sold, in the case of a *put.* Sometimes called the *exercise price.*

support level: See *resistance level.*

T-bill: Treasury bill. Short-term government securities auctioned by the Bank of Canada every Thursday afternoon to provide ready cash for government operations. They are resold to the general public, or kept by the purchasing banks for the interest they bear.

TIPS: Toronto 35 Index participation units, an investment vehicle that allows the holder to gamble on thirty-five stocks at once. Dividends paid by the participating stocks are divided among the TIPs holders.

Toronto 35 Index: An index based on thirty-five key stocks in most major industrial groups (though no stocks representing real estate or construction are included) on the Toronto Stock Exchange.

TSE: Toronto Stock Exchange.

TSE Composite Index: An index of 300 stocks traded on the TSE, covering the fourteen major groups of stocks on the exchange, weighted and compared to a base date in 1975.

VSE: Vancouver Stock Exchange. Not our tidiest.

warrant: Properly, a *subscription warrant*. The same as a *right,* but with a longer shelf-life. Warrants usually allow the holder to buy a set amount of stock at a given price, which is usually higher than the price at the time the warrant was issued, for a period of years.

wash-trading: Buying and selling the same stock back and forth between co-conspirators, to create the illusion of a demand for it.

watered stock: Shares representing an inflated value for the underlying assets of a corporation. If a company owning $10 million in assets and with a net worth of $1 million, manages to unload $50 million worth of shares on the market, that stock is well and truly watered. The phrase arose from the practice of depriving cattle of water for a few days, and then allowing them to drink their fill before selling them, according to weight.

yield: In general, the return on invested capital. In particular, with bonds, the rate of return on a bond, arrived at by calculating annual interest payments, the purchase price, the redemption value of the bond, and the time remaining to maturity. Also known as *maturity yield.* In stocks, the *yield* is the return paid out in dividends as a proportion of the price of the stock. A stock selling for $100 which pays annual dividends of $10 has a *yield* of 10 per cent.

Bibliography

Adams, James Ring, *The Big Fix: Inside the* S&L *Scandal,* New York, John Wiley, 1991.

Allen, Frederick Lewis, *Only Yesterday,* New York, Bantam, 1946.

_____, *The Great Pierpont Morgan,* New York, Harper, 1957.

Anderson, Hugh, *Bulls & Bears: Winning in the Stock Market in Good Times and Bad,* Toronto, Penguin, 1990.

Auletta, Ken, *Greed and Glory on Wall Street: The Fall of the House of Lehman,* Boston, G. K. Hall, 1987.

Barron's, *Finance and Investment Handbook,* Second Edition, New York, 1987.

Baumol, William J., *The Stock Market and Economic Efficiency,* New York, Fordham University Press, 1965.

Berle, Adolf A., and Means, Gardiner, C., *The Modern Corporation and Private Property,* New York, Harcourt Brace, 1967.

Braudel, Fernand, *Civilization and Capitalism, 15th-18th Century,* especially, *Volume III, The Perspective of the World,* London, Collins, 1984.

Bruck, Connie, *The Predators' Ball,* New York, Penguin, 1989.

Brutus, (pseudonym), *Confessions of a Stockbroker,* New York, Little, Brown, 1972.

Burrough, Bryan and Helyar, John, *Barbarians at the Gate: The Fall of RJR Nabisco,* New York, Harper & Row, 1990.

Canadian Securities Institute, *How To Invest in Canadian Securities,* Toronto, 1988.

Carrière, Charles, *L'Espace commercial marsellais,* quoted in Braudel, *Civilization and Capitalism.*

Casey, Douglas R., *Crisis Investing,* New York, Stratford,1980.

Chanell, Ralph, *How to Make Big Money in Low-Priced Stocks in the Coming Bull Market,* New York, Morrow, 1981.

Chase, C. David, *Mugged on Wall Street,* New York, Simon & Schuster, 1987.

Cobleigh, Ira, and Dorfman, Bruce K., *The Dowbeaters: How To Buy Stocks That Go Up,* New York, Macmillan, 1984.

Cruise, David, and Griffiths, Alison, *Fleecing the Lamb: The Inside Story of the Vancouver Stock Exchange,* Vancouver, Douglas & McIntyre, 1987.

Dalton, John M., *How the Stock Market Works,* New York, New York Institute of Finance, 1988.

Engel, Louis, and Boyd, Brendan, *How to Buy Stocks,* Toronto, Bantam, 1982.

Erdman, Paul, *Paul Erdman's Money Book,* New York, Random House, 1984.

Farbicand, Burton P., *Beating the Street: How to Make More Money in the Stock Market,* New York, D. McKay, 1969.

Fetherling, Doug, *Gold Diggers of 1929: Canada and the Great Stock Market Crash,* Toronto, Macmillan, 1979.

Flynn, John, *God's Gold: The Story of Rockefeller and His Times,* Westport, Greenwood Press, 1971.

Forbes, Robert E., and Johnston, David L., *Canadian Companies and the Stock Exchange,* Don Mills, CCH Canadian, 1980.

Friedman, Milton, and Schwartz, Anna Jacobson, *The Great Contraction, 1929-1933,* Princeton, Princeton University Press, 1965.

Galbraith, John Kenneth, *The Great Crash 1929,* London, Penguin, 1961.

Givens, Charles, *Wealth Without Risk for Canadians,* Toronto, Stoddart, 1991.

Graham, Benjamin, and Dodd, David L., *Security Analysis,* New York, McGraw-Hill, 1934.

Graham, Benjamin, *The Intelligent Investor,* New York, Harper & Row, revised edition 1973.

Graham, Howard, *Citizen and Soldier, The Memoirs of Lieutenant-General Howard Graham,* Toronto, McClelland & Stewart, 1987.

Griesing, David, and Morse, Laurie, *Brokers, Bagmen and Moles: Fraud and Corruption in the Chicago Futures Markets,* Chicago, Wiley, 1991.

Holbrook, Stewart H., *The Age of the Moguls,* New York, Doubleday, 1953.

Hoover, Herbert, *Public Papers,* U.S. Government Printing Office, 1974.

International Investor, *The Way It Was: An Oral History of Finance,* New York, Morrow, 1988.

Josephson, Matthew, *The Robber Barons: The Great American Capitalists, 1861-1901,* New York, Harcourt Brace, 1934.

Keyes, Thomas R., and Miller, David, *The Global Investor,* Longman Financial (no city shown), 1990.

Keynes, John Maynard, *A Treatise on Probability,* Edinburgh, R. and R. Clark, 1921.

_____, *The General Theory of Employment, Interest and Money,* New York, Cambridge University Press, 1936.

_____, *Essays in Persuasion,* New York, W. W. Norton, 1963.

_____, *The Collective Writings of John Maynard Keynes,* edited by Donald Moggeridge, New York, Macmillan, 1983.

Kierans, Eric, and Stewart, Walter, *Wrong End of the Rainbow,* Toronto, Collins, 1988.

Lane, Wheaton J., *Commodore Vanderbilt: An Epic of the Steam Age,* New York, Knopf, 1942.

Lapham, Lewis, *Money and Class in America: Notes and Observations on the Civil Religion of Our Time,* New York, Weidenfeld & Nicolson, 1988.

Leeb, Stephen, *Getting in on the Ground Floor,* New York, Putnam, 1985.

Levine, Allan, *The Exchange: 100 Years of Trading Grain in Winnipeg,* Winnipeg, Peguis, 1987.

Lewis, Michael, *Liar's Poker: Rising Through the Wreckage on Wall Street,* New York, W. W. Norton, 1989.

Lopez, Claude-Anne, and Herbert, Eugenia W., *The Private Franklin,* New York, W. W. Norton, 1975.

Lowenstein, Louis, *What's Wrong with Wall Street,* New York, Addison-Wesley, 1988.

Lynch, Peter, *One Up on Wall Street*, New York, Simon & Schuster, 1989.

Mayer, Martin, *The Markets*, Toronto, Macmillan, 1988.

McQueen, Rod, *Blind Trust: Inside the Sinclair Stevens Affair*, Toronto, Macmillan, 1987.

Meyers, Gustavus, *A History of Canadian Wealth*, Toronto, J. Lewis & Samuel, 1972.

_____, *History of the Great American Fortunes*, New York, Modern Library, 1964.

Miller, Nathan, *The Founding Finaglers*, New York, D. McKay, 1976.

Mitchell, Samuel, *How to Make Big Money in the Stock Market and Avoid Losses*, New York, F. Fell, 1968.

Mongo, Raymond, *Cosmic Profit: How to Make Money Without Doing Time*, Boston, Little, Brown, 1980.

Nagan, Peter, *Fail-Safe Investing: How to Make Money with Less than $10,000!*, New York, Putnam, 1981.

Naylor, Tom, *The History of Canadian Business, 1867-1914*, Toronto, Lorimer, 1975.

Ney, Richard, *The Wall Street Gang*, New York, Praeger, 1974.

_____, *Making It in the Market*, New York, McGraw-Hill, 1975.

Nielsen, Erik, *The House Is Not a Home*, Toronto, Macmillan, 1989.

O'Connor, Richard, *The Oil Barons*, Boston, Little, Brown, 1971.

O'Donnell, John R., *Trumped! The Inside Story of the Real Donald Trump*, New York, Pocket Star Books, 1991.

Olive, David, *Just Rewards: The Case for Ethical Reform in Business*, Markham, Penguin, 1988.

O'Shea, James, *The Daisy Chain: The Tale of Big Bad Don Dixon and the Looting of a Texas S&L*, New York, Simon & Schuster, 1991.

Pape, Gordon, *Gordon Pape's 1991 Guide to Mutual Funds*, Scarborough, Prentice-Hall, 1990.

Phillips, Susan M., and Zecher, J. Richard, *The SEC and the Public Interest*, Cambridge, MIT Press, 1981.

Pratt, Sereno S., *The Work of Wall Street*, New York, Appleton, 1903.

Raw, Charles, Hodgson, Godfrey, and Page, Bruce, *Do You Sincerely Want to be Rich? Bernard Cornfeld and IOS, An International Swindle*, London, Andre Deutsch, 1971.

Ripley, William Z., *Main Street and Wall Street*, Boston, Little Brown, 1927.

Ross, Alexander, *The Traders: Inside Canada's Stock Markets,* Toronto, Totem, 1985.

Rothchild, John, *Going for Broke: How Robert Campeau Bankrupted the Retail Industry, Jolted the Junk Bond Market, and Brought the Booming Eighties to a Crashing Halt,* New York, Simon & Schuster, 1991.

Safarian, A. E., *The Canadian Economy in the Great Depression,* Toronto, McClelland & Stewart, 1970.

Samuelson, Paul A. and Scott, Anthony, *Economics,* Toronto, McGraw-Hill, 1975.

Schlesinger, Arthur, *The Age of Roosevelt,* especially *Vol. II, The Coming of the New Deal,* Boston, Houghton Mifflin, 1958.

Shulman, Morton, *Anyone Can Make a Million,* McGraw-Hill Ryerson, 1972.

Smith, Adam (pseudonym), *The Money Game,* New York, Random House, 1968.

Smith, Courtney, *How to Make Money in Stock Index Futures,* New York, McGraw-Hill, 1989.

Sobel, Robert, *The Big Board: A History of the New York Stock Market,* New York, Free Press, 1965.

Sternberg, William, and Harrison, Matthew C., *Feeding Frenzy: The Inside Story of Wedtech,* New York, H. Holt, 1990.

Stewart, James B., *Den of Thieves,* New York, Simon & Schuster, 1991.

Stewart, T. H., *How Charts Can Make You Money,* Cambridge, Woodland-Faulkner, 1986.

Stewart, Walter, *Hard to Swallow,* Toronto, Macmillan, 1974.

_____, *But Not In Canada,* Toronto, Macmillan, 1976.

_____, *Towers of Gold, Feet of Clay: The Canadian Banks,* Toronto, Collins, 1982.

Tan, Dominic, *How to Make Money in Blue Chip Stocks,* Surrey, B.C., Hancock House, 1984.

Tobias, Andrew, *The Only Investment Guide You'll Ever Need,* Boston, Hall, 1978.

_____, *The Only Other Investment Guide You'll Ever Need,* New York, Simon & Schuster, 1987.

Tugwell, Rexford G., *Roosevelt's Revolution: The First Year,* New York, Macmillan, 1977.

U.S. Congress, House Committee on Energy & Commerce, 99th Congress, *Corporate Takeovers: Public Policy Implications for the Economy and Corporate Governance,* Washington, 1986.

U.S. Securities and Exchange Commission, *The October 1987 Market Break,* Washington, 1988.

Wall Street Journal Guide to Understanding Money and Markets, New York, Access Press, 1990.

Ward, Max, *The Max Ward Story,* Toronto, McClelland & Stewart, 1991.

Warfield, Gerald, *How to Buy Foreign Stocks and Bonds,* New York, Harper & Row, 1985.

Warren, Ted, *How to Make the Stock Market Make Money for You,* Los Angeles, Sherbourne Press, 1966.

White, Bouck, *The Book of Daniel Drew,* New York, Doubleday, 1910.

Winans, R. Foster, *Trading Secrets,* New York, St. Martin's Press, 1986.

Index